What Your Colleagues Are Say

In this astounding book, Dougherty and Venenciano skillfully illustrate tasks that develop students' reasoning, problem-solving, and communication skills. They thoughtfully include guiding and reflective questions along with suggestions for differentiation and extensions of each task. The wide range of topics makes this perfect for any algebra course!

Laura Ashley Young
High School Mathematics Teacher
Honolulu, Hawaii

Bring the love of learning mathematics back into your classroom by implementing effective mathematical practices, building numeracy skills in your students, and providing rich algebra tasks that are engaging. Dougherty and Venenciano have done some great work to support educators that will enhance students' learning and grit.

Katie Majeres
Best Practice Math Coach, Northwest AEA of Iowa
Le Mars, IA

Dougherty and Venenciano provoke us to reframe our thinking from "can my students get the correct answer for this task?" to "how can I use this task to help further my students' understanding of the mathematics?" The authors provide a vision, tools, and practical advice for strategically using engaging tasks to enhance students' understanding of mathematical ideas and processes.

Dewey Gottlieb
Educational Specialist, Hawaii Department of Education
Director, NCTM Board
Honolulu, HI

This is a treasure trove of amazing tasks and supporting materials! Framing the tasks in an overview of research-grounded practices promotes fidelity and provides access for all students. Tasks presented in Part 2 spell out the mathematical topics, content and practice alignments, watch-fors, anticipated solutions, prompts, and post-task notes that allow them to be efficiently integrated.

Jessica Ivy
Associate Professor, Bellarmine University
Louisville, KY

It's important to implement rich tasks that support students' math proficiency, drawing from their strengths and assets. It can be difficult locating or creating math tasks that are both rich and asset-based. I am excited to use tasks from this book in my work at the university with preservice teachers, in professional development with in-service teachers, and working with grades 6–12 students.

Jonathan D. Bostic
Professor of Mathematics Education, Bowling Green State University
Bowling Green, Ohio

Classroom-Ready Rich Algebra Tasks is a must-have resource for all algebra teachers. Dougherty and Venenciano outline how to implement these tasks in your classroom and give numerous examples that could be used today. After more than a decade of teaching algebra and supporting algebra teachers, this is a resource I wish I had when I started.

Nick Davies
K–12 Administrator
Vancouver, WA

Classroom-Ready Rich Algebra Tasks, Grades 6–12
The Book at a Glance

Each task calls out the Mathematics Focus, Mathematics Standards, Mathematical Practices, and important Vocabulary highlighted in the task.

Task 4.3
Change Exchange

TASK

Change Exchange

1. Suppose 30 pennies are lined up on a table. Using a supply of nickels, dimes, quarters, and half-dollars, follow these instructions in the order given.

   a. Replace every second coin with a nickel.

   b. Replace every third coin with a dime.

   c. Replace every fourth coin with a quarter.

   d. Replace every fifth coin with a half-dollar.

2. How much money is on the table after all the exchanges have been made?

3. What patterns did you notice?

4. What exchanges were made if the amount on the table after all exchanges totaled $4.48?

TASK PREPARATION CONSIDERATIONS

• How will I model the introduction of the task?

• Will some or all students need to continue modeling the action to see the patterns?

• What materials will I provide them to do the modeling?

SCAFFOLDING OR DIFFERENTIATING THE TASK

• As a class, have student volunteers take turns to model each step of the original problem.

• Suggest that students model the problem with manipulatives such as chips or cubes.

• Have students use different colors to represent the coins and create a legend to help them remember which one is which.

• Make sure that students know how to count coins.

Mathematics Focus

• Students look for patterns as a strategy for solving nonroutine problems. Students persevere in problem solving through a nonlinear iterative process.

Mathematics Content Standard(s)

• The focus of this task is to introduce students to problem solving through sequencing and patterns based on familiar mathematics content as a way to activate prior learning.

Mathematical Practice(s)

• Make sense of problems and persevere in solving them.

• Reason abstractly and quantitatively.

• Attend to precision.

• Look for and express regularity in repeated reasoning.

Materials

• 1 Change Exchange task per student

• 30 chips or other counters per pair (optional)

Each task includes a short description of the mathematical idea that will be tackled as well as extensive preparation and differentiation notes.

Each task includes a list of the necessary materials needed to complete it.

Each task is labeled with the Task Type(s).

Task Type

	Conceptual
	Procedural
	Problem-Solving Application
X	Problem-Solving Critical Thinking

X	Reversibility
X	Flexibility
X	Generalization

WATCH-FORS!

- Students may not be sure how to count to the ordinal position.

- Students may lose track of the coins they are swapping.

- Students may not be organized in their exchanges.

EXTEND THE TASK

Have students predict what would happen if a sixth coin exchange were added. Then have them test their prediction.

LAUNCH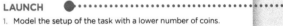

1. Model the setup of the task with a lower number of coins.

   » Use a similar set of directions and demonstrate the exchange process.

2. Arrange students in pairs.

3. Distribute the Change Exchange task and chips/counters as needed.

4. Allow 10–15 minutes for students to work. Students may want to use chips or draw diagrams to model the actions in the task. Encourage students to devise ways to keep track of all their exchanges.

FACILITATE

1. Monitor the groups. If a group is having difficulty with the problem, consider these questions:

   a. Did you try using a different color or representation for each coin type?

   b. On problem 2, can you find a combination of coins that will give you that amount?

2. Have students share their strategies and solutions. Discuss as needed.

   a. What patterns did you notice as you solved the problem?

   b. How did you keep track of your exchanges?

EXPECTED SOLUTIONS

1. $5.38

2. Start with 30 pennies. Replace every second coin with a half-dollar. Replace every third coin with a nickel. Replace every fourth coin with a dime. Replace every fifth coin with a quarter.

Extensive facilitation notes support educators in guiding the implementation of the task-lesson.

All activity sheets and online resources provided in the Materials section of each task are available for download or viewing on the companion website.

CLOSE AND GENERALIZATIONS

1. Highlight the mathematical patterns students identified and have students share why those patterns make sense.

2. Have students discuss effective ways for keeping track of the exchanges.

3. Ask students to compare this task to Seeing Squares and The Symmetric Staircase. How are the problems alike? How are they different?

4. Have students identify connections in their solution strategies and highlight the mathematical practices that they are developing.

TASK 4.3: CHANGE EXCHANGE

 Available to download at **resources.corwin.com/classroomreadymath/algebra**

POST-TASK NOTES: REFLECTIONS AND NEXT STEPS

• Did students use any of the solution strategies from the previous tasks to get started with this one?

• Was modeling a simpler problem in the launch sufficient for students to understand the task?

• Were the manipulatives students used the best choice for the task?

• What strategies did students use when they were "stuck"?

Additional room for writing follows each task to allow for personalization as you plan the use of the lesson for your classroom.

Classroom-Ready
RICH ALGEBRA TASKS

GRADES
6–12

Classroom-Ready

RICH ALGEBRA TASKS

GRADES 6-12

Engaging Students in Doing Math

Barbara J. **DOUGHERTY** • Linda C. **VENENCIANO**

FOREWORD BY **KEVIN DYKEMA**

CORWIN **Mathematics**

For information:

Corwin
A SAGE Company
2455 Teller Road
Thousand Oaks, California 91320
(800) 233-9936
www.corwin.com

SAGE Publications Ltd.
1 Oliver's Yard
55 City Road
London, EC1Y 1SP
United Kingdom

SAGE Publications India Pvt. Ltd.
Unit No 323-333, Third Floor, F-Block
International Trade Tower Nehru Place
New Delhi - 110 019
India

SAGE Publications Asia-Pacific Pte. Ltd.
18 Cross Street #10–10/11/12
China Square Central
Singapore 048423

President: Mike Soules
Vice President and Editorial Director:
    Monica Eckman
Associate Director and
    Publisher, STEM: Erin Null
Content Development Editor: Jessica Vidal
Senior Editorial Assistant: Nyle De Leon
Production Editor: Tori Mirsadjadi
Copy Editor: Melinda Masson
Typesetter: Integra
Proofreader: Dennis Webb
Indexer: Integra
Cover Designer: Scott Van Atta
Marketing Manager: Margaret O'Connor

Printed in the United States of America.

Library of Congress Cataloging-in-Publication Data

Names: Dougherty, Barbara J., author. | Venenciano, Linda, author.
Title: Classroom-ready rich algebra tasks, grades 6-12 : engaging students in doing math / Barbara J. Dougherty, Linda Venenciano.
Description: Thousand Oaks, California : Corwin, [2023] | Includes bibliographical references and index. | Audience: Grades 10-12
Identifiers: LCCN 2022049322 | ISBN 9781071889268 (paperback) | ISBN 9781071909201 (epub) | ISBN 9781071909195 (epub) | ISBN 9781071909188(pdf)
Subjects: LCSH: Algebra--Study and teaching (Middle school) | Algebra--Study and teaching (Secondary) | Algebra--Study and teaching (Middle school)--Activity programs. | Algebra--Study and teaching (Secondary)--Activity programs.
Classification: LCC QA159 .D68 2023 | DDC 512.0071/2--dc23/eng20230112
LC record available at https://lccn.loc.gov/2022049322

This book is printed on acid-free paper.

23 24 25 26 27 10 9 8 7 6 5 4 3 2 1

Contents

Visit the companion website at
resources.corwin.com/classroomreadymath/algebra
for downloadable resources.

Foreword

Think back to when you learned algebra. Or perhaps it's better phrased as think back to when you were taught algebra. If your experience was anything like mine, you sat passively and listened to the teacher give step-by-step explanations of how to manipulate symbols. Perhaps you had guided note packets, and you diligently filled in the missing pieces. I recall primarily doing the even-numbered practice problems, as the odd-numbered problems had the answers in the back of the book. Rarely were there any application problems, and they were always at the end of the set of exercises. I received very good grades, but did I truly learn algebra?

Fast-forward then to when you started teaching. I know I finally learned the algebraic concepts when I started teaching them. It was only then that I finally moved from algebra-through-memorization to algebra-through-understanding. I finally started to see some connections and applications. Why should this wait until adulthood? Shouldn't we want our students to experience this? I believe we are doing our students a disservice if our classrooms today look and feel the same way as when we were students.

We've heard for many years that we need to be implementing rich tasks into the mathematics classroom. Doing so actively engages our students in their learning. We know we need to help our students think more deeply about the content, rather than just memorize procedures, but what does that look like in practice? Rarely are we provided concrete examples of what our instruction should look like . . . until now! *Classroom-Ready Rich Algebra Tasks* does just this. It is chock-full of concrete examples of rich tasks that can be easily implemented into the algebra classroom.

Classroom-Ready Rich Algebra Tasks provides the necessary support to implement these rich tasks into the classroom. Dougherty and Venenciano use research-backed guidance around student-centered learning for mathematics and put it into action by supplying the structures necessary to utilize rich thinking tasks. They help educators pay attention to preparation, how to support students during the task, and how to facilitate whole-class discussion, among other things. The framework they provide is consistent throughout all the tasks, making them very user-friendly.

Using rich tasks to build solid student understanding may be a different way of teaching than many have used in the past. It does require some different tools for an educator more accustomed to providing students with step-by-step procedures. One such tool is the ability to anticipate potential student errors and misconceptions. Anticipating allows for planning our responses so that we rescue and support student thinking rather than rescue answer-getting. This is a vital skill for teachers to develop, and one that can take some time. Dougherty and Venenciano provide this support for each one of the tasks.

Furthermore, equity is at the forefront of each of these rich tasks. They should be used not just with students who are currently excelling but rather with each and every student, and the tasks provide clear ways to meet all students where they are. For example, the scaffolding and differentiating ideas support students who need additional help as they productively struggle with learning the concepts or practicing skills. Similarly, for students who need some additional challenge or who finish tasks more quickly than others, the authors supply extensions to further student thinking and deepen student understanding.

I encourage you to work collaboratively with your peers to implement these tasks. This collaboration will allow you to have the support needed and provides a place to share your successes as well as your struggles as you expand the way you teach. Having that peer support is so powerful in implementing change in your instructional practices. Ultimately, these efforts will increase their learning as students become more engaged in thinking deeply about the mathematical content through these wonderful tasks and see themselves as capable of truly learning mathematics.

Kevin Dykema
President, National Council of Teachers of Mathematics, 2022–2024
Eighth-Grade Mathematics Teacher, Mattawan, MI

Preface

We are very excited to share with you this book of rich algebra tasks, which is as much about interesting mathematics for students to work with as it is about effective instruction. Having been classroom teachers and university faculty working with preservice and in-service teachers, we have firsthand understanding of the challenges and opportunities that go with classroom teaching. We know how hard you work to make your algebra lessons meaningful, challenging, and accessible to your students. We also know that your time is valuable and likely in short supply. We want to honor teachers' desire and need to infuse rich tasks into their teaching without spending hours searching for them online or in instructional resources outside of their core curriculum. We want to take that heavy lift off your shoulders.

In this book, we have paired each task with instructional notes to support the field-tested implementation and facilitation that we found to maximize both student learning and joy in teaching mathematics. This book is divided into two parts. Part 1 covers the background and important information about the meaning and value of rich algebra tasks, how the tasks in this book support and extend effective mathematics teaching practices, and important instructional guidance to add to your own teacher toolbox for implementing and facilitating these tasks. Part 2 includes the tasks themselves, organized by topic. At the beginning of Part 2 you will find a table that aligns each task to various standards, though be aware that even if a task is aligned with a lower grade-level standard than the one you are teaching, it may still provide opportunities for you to (1) connect the new content to prior knowledge, (2) provide a problem-solving experience, or (3) focus on a concept that may not be well developed. Many of the tasks include student materials that can be downloaded at **resources.corwin.com/classroomreadymath/algebra.**

You may be tempted to jump straight to a chapter with tasks and assign one or more. However, by doing so you may miss critical opportunities to lay the groundwork and set expectations for problem-solving behaviors and classroom interactions. We encourage you to read Part 1 of the book first, and we hope that the ideas and suggestions provide you with ways to continue developing and fine-tuning your instruction with your colleagues. With the foundation you create to structure teaching with rich algebra tasks, your students can develop complementary skills to be stronger learners of mathematics.

If you enjoy the approach and tasks in this book, please share the other books in this series with your elementary colleagues:

Classroom-Ready Rich Math Tasks, Grades K–1: Engaging Students in Doing Math

Classroom-Ready Rich Math Tasks, Grades 2–3: Engaging Students in Doing Math

Classroom-Ready Rich Math Tasks, Grades 4–5: Engaging Students in Doing Math

Acknowledgments

Our goal for this book is to provide tasks that can support conceptual as well as procedural understandings for middle and high school students. We designed these tasks based on what we have learned from classroom testing in multiple settings. In this book we showcase what we believe yields the strongest learning with engaging and highly productive learning experiences for your students.

The tasks included in this volume are certainly not exhaustive of all the great tasks that are available from a variety of resources. But we hope that they are a springboard for you to consider characteristics of tasks that construct student understanding and to then look for those same characteristics in other tasks. These characteristics can enhance other tasks as you revise and create your own.

As you implement these tasks, you may find that they can support a professional learning community or lesson study experience for you in your professional growth. We hope you enjoy doing the tasks as much as we have!

From Barb and Linda:

Thank you, Beth, Karen, and Skip. Your work has helped us organize and present our ideas in a way that we believe will appeal to secondary teachers. Our book format is built from your amazing work on the other books in this Rich Tasks series and beyond.

Thank you, Fay Zenigami! This endeavor would not be possible without the earlier iterations that have informed our work all along the way. We cherish your patience as we tinkered and trialed the tasks and instructional strategies. We also cherish (with aloha!) your tolerance and candor as we tossed around theories and experimented. Thank you for keeping us honest.

Thank you to our publisher, Erin Null, and the Corwin reviewers and staff. We started this endeavor with a collection of ideas that sounded great in our heads, and you have helped us articulate our thoughts and organize them in a cohesive manner that can reach a wide audience.

Thank you to our former and current students. You have been and continue to be our best teachers! A special shoutout to the students and teachers at the University Laboratory School where many ideas have germinated and advanced.

Thank you to our former colleagues at the Curriculum Research & Development Group at the University of Hawai'i. We have fond memories and value all that we learned by teaming with you.

From Barb:

A very special thank-you to all the teachers beyond our research group who have implemented earlier versions of the tasks and given us feedback. The tasks would not be as substantive as they are without your thoughtful comments.

Thank you, Linda, for engaging in this work with me. Your thoughtfulness and enthusiasm for mathematics education is amazing.

From Linda:

Thank you, Barb. I have thoroughly enjoyed your leadership and companionship on this journey. I continue to be amazed by your stamina. Your passion for mathematics education is contagious!

Thank you, Bill, Taylor, and Carly. Your love and support are at my core.

Publisher's Acknowledgments

Corwin gratefully acknowledges the contributions of the following reviewers:

Frederick Dillon
Consultant
Strongsville, OH

Ruth Harbin Miles
K–12 Mathematics Supervisor (Retired), Olathe (Kansas) Public Schools
Professional Learning Consultant and Adjunct, Mary Baldwin University
Madison, VA

John F. Mahoney
High School Mathematics Teacher (45 Years)
National Teachers Hall of Fame Inductee (2005)
Bethesda, MD

Michele Mailhot
Independent Mathematics Consultant
Oakland, ME

Ayanna Perry
Associate Director, Teaching Fellows Program, Knowles Teacher Initiative
Bow, MD

Brian Shay
Mathematics Teacher, Canyon Crest Academy
San Marcos, CA

Paul Spicer
Educator and Instructional Coach, Grades 6–12
Durham, NC

About the Authors

Barbara J. Dougherty is the past director of the Curriculum Research & Development Group and a professor in the College of Education at the University of Hawai'i at Mānoa. She is a former member of the board of directors of the National Council of Teachers of Mathematics and is the co-chair of the Mathematics/Special Education Workgroup, a partnership between the NCTM and the Council for Exceptional Children. She served on the author panel for the *What Works Clearinghouse Practice Guide* on assisting elementary school students who have difficulty learning mathematics for the U.S. Department of Education Institute of Education Sciences. She is the author or coauthor of approximately 22 book chapters, 29 articles, and 36 books, including M^{Power}: *A Pathway to Understanding Algebra*. Her research, funded by more than $11.5 million in grants, emphasizes supporting students who struggle in middle and high school, with a focus on algebra. She holds teaching certifications in middle and high school mathematics and K–12 special education.

Linda C. Venenciano is a professor in the School of Learning and Teaching at Pacific University, where she teaches and supports early childhood through high school preservice teachers in mathematics education. She is a former classroom teacher and has taught mathematics to students from first grade through undergraduate. She previously served as the interim director of the Curriculum Research & Development Group and as an associate professor of mathematics education at the University of Hawai'i at Mānoa. She is the author or coauthor of 21 peer-reviewed publications and 12 books. Linda is currently serving on the editorial board of *Investigations in Mathematics Learning* and has served as a program chair for the annual meeting of the Research Council on Mathematics Learning and as a guest editor for a special issue of *Educational Studies in Mathematics*.

Getting Started With Rich Algebra Tasks

The first three chapters of this book help to frame your reading and understanding of the tasks and how to implement and facilitate them. As teachers of secondary students, you are probably very familiar with the range of prior mathematics learning experiences your students have had prior to their first day with you. We also recognize the challenges and opportunities that come with teaching secondary students! In Chapter 1 we describe what we mean by *rich algebra tasks* and why they are valuable for classroom use. We share our thinking behind the design of the tasks and how you can use them to capitalize on students' assets and promote a class culture for students to take ownership in their learning. Chapter 2 continues with a brief discussion of effective mathematics teaching practices and the features of our rich algebra task layout. In Chapter 2 and continuing in Chapter 3, we describe several effective instructional tools for implementing and facilitating these tasks as well as for your own teacher's toolbox.

Rich Algebra Tasks

What Are They, Why Are They Valuable, and How Do I Plan for Implementation?

In this chapter, you will explore what characterizes a mathematical task as a *rich* mathematical task and why this distinction is valuable for the teaching and learning of algebra. By the end of this chapter, you will

- understand the need for and importance of rich algebra tasks;

- explore the design of rich algebra tasks that concurrently develop conceptual understanding, procedural fluency, and problem-solving skills; and

- explore types of tasks that prompt students to develop robust mathematics thinking and reasoning abilities.

When students begin their study of algebra, they will likely have had several years of mathematics instruction. The transition from a focus on arithmetic to one on algebra can be challenging for students. Students typically begin learning mathematics from a counting approach (Devlin, 2009). This approach leads them to expect operations to result in number answers, which is generally helpful in solving arithmetic problems. Unfortunately, this path has not sufficiently provided the foundation students need for the successful study of algebra (Blanton et al., 2015). In addition to understanding number and basic operations, students must be able to look for patterns, reason and generalize, and think relationally to be successful in solving algebraic problems. Students need opportunities to engage in algebra through tasks that are accessible, connect to what they have previously learned, and yet challenge them to promote their continued development.

What Is a Rich Algebra Task?

A *mathematical task* is a problem or set of problems that focuses students' attention on a particular mathematical idea and/or provides an opportunity to develop or use a particular mathematical habit of mind. Mathematical tasks are available to teachers from a multitude of sources. An internet search by mathematics topic or standard will yield seemingly thousands of activities. However, such quick search "gems" often are undefined or disconnected to standards and engage contexts or mathematics that do not meet students' needs.

Findings from the American Instructional Resources Survey reported in *The Rise of Standards-Aligned Instructional Materials for U.S. K–12 Mathematics and English Language Arts Instruction* (Kaufman et al., 2021) show that 47% of middle school teachers and 51% of high school teachers surveyed use curriculum materials they create themselves. Furthermore, results from this study show that the respondents (*n* = 2,306) regularly use Teachers Pay Teachers (48%), YouTube (37%), Kahoot! (33%), Khan Academy (32%), a search engine (28%), and other resources obtained through social media sites (22%) to find tasks or problems to supplement their curriculum. Although these materials may address identified needs at the moment, they may not sufficiently support the development of foundational and conceptual understandings, skills, and processes for later learning or provide a cohesive instructional sequence that leads to robust learning.

A *rich mathematics task* is part of a balanced approach to mathematics that includes conceptual understanding, procedural fluency, and application and offers every student the opportunity to engage in meaningful, rigorous mathematics. Similarly, Smith and Stein (2012) describe the qualities of a *good* task as having the potential to engage students in high-level thinking and as being designed to take into account students' developmental abilities, prior knowledge, and experiences, as well as the norms and expectations of the mathematics class.

> " A *rich mathematics task* is part of a balanced approach to mathematics that includes conceptual understanding, procedural fluency, and application and offers every student the opportunity to engage in meaningful, rigorous mathematics. "

Rich tasks

- require more time as they promote a more student-centered instructional approach,

- should be engaging to diverse groups of students,

- encourage students to use multiple solution approaches,

- draw on important topics in the school curriculum, and

- promote mathematics ideas that may be novel to the students.

These characteristics apply to the rich algebra tasks that you find here. In middle and high school courses, students' sophistication of thinking and independency has developed so that your facilitation of a task will engage students and promote a strong ownership in the learning process. With these rich algebra tasks, you will serve as the facilitator by encouraging students to go beyond getting a correct answer and by raising extension questions when students share their solutions. These tasks should provide opportunities to use multiple representations and engage in robust discourse while providing multiple entry points into the tasks. The design of the tasks should make mathematical structures more transparent and help students notice the underlying mathematical concepts and generalizations. These generalizations will further develop your students' ability to think flexibly with generalized ideas, such as being able to determine that $2x$ is not always greater than $x + 2$.

Rich algebra tasks are also designed to take into account students' prior experiences and possible misconceptions students may have, as well as their yearning for more advanced mathematics than what they had in the earlier grades. Students who may have previously been encouraged to fixate on memorizing and applying procedures may not have embraced the connections to concepts or the structure of the problems that help them solve related problems.

Even though students may have already experienced a topic, rich algebra tasks present a different perspective on the topic. For example, in seventh grade, students learn how to perform computations with integers. That does not preclude the use of rich algebra tasks related to integer computations in later grades because the design of the task will provide new ways for a student to think about the mathematics. Thus, rich algebra tasks can be used as (1) a review of a previously learned topic, (2) an introduction to a new topic, or (3) a problem-solving experience.

Why Are Rich Algebra Tasks Valuable?

Deep conceptual knowledge is integral for adaptive reasoning and expertise in mathematics. Students are often provided with opportunities to engage in rigorous mathematics tasks, but they fail to "notice or draw the relevant structural connections" (Richland et al., 2012, p. 198). This noticing of the structural connections constitutes the early stages of deep conceptual understanding, but this is where critical mathematics learning often breaks down.

When students are asked to think about mathematics as interconnected sets of relationships or as mathematical structures, students struggle (Richland et al., 2012). Very likely, this struggle is rooted in their previous learning. Middle school students often assume that the procedural rules they learned in their elementary grades will continue to apply to more challenging mathematics tasks (Karp et al., 2015). When asked to think about expressions and equations, students tend to focus on manipulating symbols and to expect algebraic procedures to serve the same objective as arithmetic procedures (Linchevski & Herscovics, 1996). For instance, in the expression $4 + 5x - 2x + 11$, the purpose for grouping like terms might be to simply identify a structure that represents the more general form of $a + bx$ rather than to arrive at a numerical solution (such as 18). Being able to make these types of connections is critical for students to succeed when they encounter higher levels of mathematics.

Algebra curricula (and teachers) sometimes presume students have the prerequisite skills and understandings to continue along a successful learning trajectory in mathematics. What is often overlooked is the support students need to meld together their knowledge and skills from arithmetic to algebraic habits of mind. Algebra is a more complex field, and although it may be the next course students take in their course sequence, students will be misled to view it as a mere transition from the mathematics of the earlier grades. Students need support in shifting their mindset and adjusting their approach to solving problems. In this book, we address this need to help learners develop conceptual understanding, which we define as the ability to see connections among mathematical operations, procedures, and representations that form the big ideas of algebra.

> **Students need support in shifting their mindset and adjusting their approach to solving problems.**

To design rich algebra tasks that mediate conceptual learning, we consider a set of processes, discussed by Krutetskii (1976), in successful mathematics students. He described these processes as reversibility, flexibility, and generalization (RFG). *Reversibility* is an ability to switch from a direct to a reverse train of thought. That is, students may work backward from the solution to a problem to create the problem. *Flexibility* has two meanings. It is an ability to consider multiple solution approaches to a problem, and it also refers to an ability to use a known solution path and apply that to solving a new problem. *Generalization* refers to two complementary processes, using generalized characteristics to find a specific case and making a general statement from specific cases.

These three processes were considered in the design of problems and have become a framework for teaching and learning essential topics (i.e., National Council of Teachers of Mathematics Putting Essential Understandings into Practice series, 2014–2019). The RFG framework has also served as a strategy for teaching students who struggle with learning mathematics (Dougherty et al., 2015). According to Dougherty et al. (2015), these types of tasks have been found to promote students' awareness of how the structure of problems or situations relates to appropriate algorithms. Since opportunities for developing RFG processes yield some success with students who have historically struggled with algebra, we believe they hold similar promise for all students in a general classroom context. An example of how a traditional task can be redesigned is presented in *The Math Pact, High School* (Dougherty et al., 2021).

Figure 1.1 RFG Examples

Simplify $3(2x + 1) - 4(1 - 2x)$

Reversibility Task	Flexibility Task	Generalization Task
What is an algebraic expression that simplifies to $14x - 1$?	Simplify: $3(2x + 1) - 4(1 - 2x)$ $3(2x + 1) + 4(1 - 2x)$ $3(2y + 1) - 4(1 - 2y)$ What do you notice?	What is an algebraic expression with four terms that simplifies to a monomial? A binomial? A trinomial? A polynomial with four terms? A polynomial with five terms?

Source: From *The Math Pact, High School* (Dougherty et al., 2021), Figure 6.3, p. 99.

The redesigns of the task in Figure 1.1 provide teachers with tools to engage students in thinking more deeply about the concepts. The reversibility task presents students with the simplified form and poses a question that has endless possible solutions that a student can generate. The teacher can then have the class check the algebraic expressions to verify that they indeed simplify to $14x - 1$. The flexibility task prompts students to look for what changes and what stays the same and to avoid simplifying each expression as if they were three separate exercises. After students have developed some skill and knowledge about algebraic expressions and simplifying, a generalization task can be fodder for a culminating discussion or to support the development of the big ideas, concepts, or algebraic generalization. These examples show how a straightforward task can be transformed to rich tasks that promote noticing mathematics connections and press students to develop a foundation that supports success in algebra and beyond.

Reflect

1. How do you address student access to mathematics learning? Ask yourself:

   a. How can this task be accessed by each of my students?

   b. Will this task fully engage each of my students in learning concepts?

   c. What are the entry points for my students?

2. What issues do you face as you plan for and implement algebra tasks designed for deep conceptual knowledge?

How Do I Plan to Implement a Rich Algebra Task?

Where science classes typically dedicate time for students to plan and conduct scientific experiments, these tasks are designed for students to plan and carry out algebra problem-solving tasks. These should not replace a curriculum but rather serve as a supplement to an algebra or prealgebra course. Teachers can use them as a replacement lesson or as an application of or extension to recently learned concepts and skills. Rich algebra tasks provide teachers with an alternative to a class routine in which students may have a more passive role in the learning—one where they are engaged in doing and talking about their mathematics.

The role of the teacher is central to student success. While mathematics textbooks, online resources, and a school district's mathematics curriculum may provide task-based lessons, it is unlikely that any prescribed curricula will meet the needs of all students at the level of depth and rigor that they need to become proficient in mathematics. The teacher ultimately makes planning and implementation decisions that impact how students experience and learn mathematics.

SELECTING THE TASK

First, let's use the questions in Figure 1.2 to consider the decision points around task selection.

Figure 1.2 Making Decisions About Task Selection

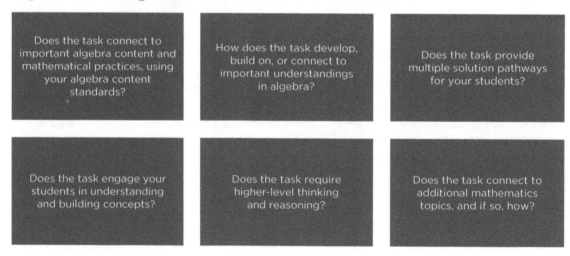

Next, consider how you would answer the questions in Figure 1.3 as you prepare to implement the task in your classroom.

Figure 1.3 Implementation

How will you position the task within a class session? How much time is needed for your students to engage in the task during the launch?	How and when will students use different representations (e.g., concrete, semi-concrete, abstract) as they engage in the task?	How and when will you make the mathematics visible by explicitly connecting students' representations and other examples of students' thinking on the task?
How will students share their solution strategies and the task's solution?	How and when will you build in feedback to students regarding their performance on the task?	How will you strategically use tasks to lead to important generalizations in algebra?

Summing Up

Rich algebra tasks have potential to support student understanding through experiences that are facilitated by the teacher. Rich algebra tasks build the bridge between the knowledge and skills students have in arithmetic and the demands and skills called on for successfully learning algebra. These tasks have been thoughtfully designed to provide teachers opportunities to surface big ideas that will engage students in uncovering the interesting mathematics of algebra.

Professional Learning/Discussion Questions

Read and discuss the following questions with colleagues in your department.

- In your own words, describe the benefits of engaging your students in algebra tasks designed to develop RFG processes.

- What is most important to consider as you select/create and implement an algebra task in your classroom?

- What concerns you about locating, creating, or adapting mathematics tasks?

- What concerns you about inserting rich algebra tasks in your curriculum?

- How will you make decisions on where to insert rich algebra tasks in your curriculum?

CHAPTER 2

Laying the Groundwork for Teaching With Rich Algebra Tasks

In Chapter 1, you gained familiarity with the underlying foundations of the design of rich algebra tasks and some important considerations for their use in your classroom. In this chapter, we look more specifically at the components of rich algebra tasks as you begin to consider how a task template can assist you in planning to implement the tasks. You will further explore their implementation in Chapter 3. In particular in this chapter, you will

- consider effective mathematics teaching practices;

- explore the mathematics content standards, Standards for Mathematical Practice, vocabulary, materials, and types of tasks as part of the task template; and

- understand how rich algebra tasks promote strengths-based teaching and learning to provide accessibility and equity, differentiation and scaffolding, and productive struggle.

Effective Mathematics Teaching Practices

To build student understanding, effective teaching practices must be aligned with the ways students optimally learn and with good tasks (Sullivan et al., 2012). The National Council of Teachers of Mathematics (NCTM, 2014b) publication *Principles to Actions* gives eight teaching practices that take into consideration the research on teaching and learning. These eight practices are foundational to supporting robust student learning, and the instructional approaches used with the rich algebra tasks incorporate several of these practices.

Figure 2.1 NCTM's Effective Mathematics Teaching Practices

Effective Mathematics Teaching Practices	
Establish mathematics goals to focus learning.	Effective teaching of mathematics establishes clear goals for the mathematics that students are learning, situates goals within learning progressions, and uses the goals to guide instructional decisions.
Implement tasks that promote reasoning and problem solving.	Effective teaching of mathematics engages students in solving and discussing tasks that promote mathematical reasoning and problem solving and allow multiple entry points and varied solution strategies.
Use and connect mathematical representations.	Effective teaching of mathematics engages students in making connections among mathematical representations to deepen understanding of mathematics concepts and procedures and as tools for problem solving.
Facilitate meaningful mathematical discourse.	Effective teaching of mathematics facilitates discourse among students to build shared understanding of mathematical ideas by analyzing and comparing student approaches and arguments.
Pose purposeful questions.	Effective teaching of mathematics uses purposeful questions to assess and advance students' reasoning and sense making about important mathematical ideas and relationships.
Build procedural fluency from conceptual understanding.	Effective teaching of mathematics builds fluency with procedures on a foundation of conceptual understanding so that students, over time, become skillful in using procedures flexibly as they solve contextual and mathematical problems.
Support productive struggle in learning mathematics.	Effective teaching of mathematics consistently provides students, individually and collectively, with opportunities and supports to engage in productive struggle as they grapple with mathematical ideas and relationships.
Elicit and use evidence of student thinking.	Effective teaching of mathematics uses evidence of student thinking to assess progress toward mathematical understanding and to adjust instruction continually in ways that support and extend learning.

Source: National Council of Teachers of Mathematics. (2014b). *Principles to Actions: Ensuring Mathematical Success for All*. Reston, VA: Author.

In the tasks in this book, you will see the opportunity for students to build their reasoning and problem-solving skills as they use and connect mathematical representations. Each task will include strategies for facilitating discourse so that students have opportunities to share, compare, and critique each other's thinking. Additionally, you will find questions to elicit and enhance student thinking by clarifying, extending, and generalizing the mathematical ideas. Finally, the tasks support productive struggle by providing multiple ways in which students can engage in each task.

The rich algebra tasks likewise provide implementation support and are presented in a template that can be used for planning other tasks (see Figure 2.2). In this chapter, we will discuss the template's components that are related to the planning stages, including

- mathematical focus (foci),

- content standards,

- mathematical practices,

Figure 2.2 Template for the Rich Algebra Tasks

Task Name
Mathematics Focus
Mathematics Content Standard(s)
Mathematical Practice(s)
Task
Vocabulary
Materials

Task Type:

	Conceptual
	Procedural
	Problem-Solving Application
	Problem-Solving Critical Thinking

	Reversibility
	Flexibility
	Generalization

Task Preparation Considerations
Scaffolding or Differentiating the Task
Watch-Fors
Extend the Task
Launch
Facilitate   **Expected Solutions**
Close and Generalizations
Post-Task Notes: Reflections and Next Steps

online resources 🖰 Available to download at **resources.corwin.com/classroomreadymath/algebra**

- vocabulary,

- materials,

- task type, and

- task preparation.

We will discuss the remaining elements of the template in Chapter 3.

Mathematics Focus, Content Standards, And Practices

Your state may be using the Common Core State Standards for Mathematics (CCSS-M) (National Governors Association Center for Best Practices & Council of Chief State School Officers, 2010), a state-adapted version of the CCSS-M, or standards that were developed within your state. Regardless of which of these your state uses, it is important to identify the larger mathematics goal that a task supports with the understanding that rich algebra tasks should be sequenced in such a way that students develop the larger understanding(s) expressed in the standard. The learning progression may vary based on your state, so the information given in the task will help you decide where to use it.

Each chapter of tasks begins with a description of the tasks as they relate to the mathematical content and complexity. The description provides a guide for you in selecting tasks that meet the needs of your students in a particular unit of study. However, keep in mind that the actual complexity level is relative to the prior experiences your students have had. Some tasks that appear to be complex in Grade 7, for example, may serve as a useful review of previously learned content for students in Grade 9 that you can then build upon.

MATHEMATICS FOCUS

The mathematics focus of each rich algebra task is specific to the individual task. This information, in conjunction with the continuum, will help you determine the placement in an instructional sequence so that student understanding is built in a cohesive, connected way. The focus is not written as a behavioral objective; it is written to indicate the mathematical learning that students should gain as they engage in the task.

MATHEMATICS CONTENT STANDARDS

The mathematics content standards are included in the task template so that you can see which standards the task will support. It is important to keep in mind that given the size and complexity of the standards, no single task will "teach" the standard; each standard has an instructional sequence that is needed for students to understand the content. Thus, the content standards that are referenced in the task are those most closely aligned with an instructional sequence that builds students' understanding in that grade level. However, tasks aligned with standards in earlier grade levels can be used as ways to review previously learned content in later grade levels.

> " It is important to keep in mind that given the size and complexity of the standards, no single task will "teach" the standard. "

MATHEMATICS PRACTICES

The Standards for Mathematical Practice (SMPs) are the basis for the mathematical practices given for each task. The SMPs are based on the NCTM's (2000) process standards and the mathematical proficiencies found in the National Research Council (NRC, 2001) publication *Adding It Up* (see Figure 2.3). Each task references the SMPs to ensure the expertise that students should develop as they do the task is clear.

Figure 2.3 NCTM Process Standards and NRC Mathematical Proficiencies

NCTM Process Standards	NRC Mathematical Proficiencies
1. Problem solving: Students use a repertoire of skills and strategies for solving a variety of problems and situations.	1. Conceptual understanding: Comprehension of mathematical concepts, operations, and relations.
2. Reasoning and proof: Students apply inductive and deductive reasoning skills to make, test, and evaluate statements to justify steps in mathematical procedures.	2. Procedural fluency: Skill in carrying out procedures flexibly, accurately, efficiently, and appropriately.
3. Communication: Students use mathematical language, including terminology and symbols, to express ideas precisely.	3. Strategic competence: Ability to formulate, represent, and solve mathematical problems.
4. Connection: Students relate concepts and procedures from different topics in mathematics to one another and make connections between topics in mathematics and other disciplines.	4. Adaptive reasoning: Capacity for logical thought, reflection, explanation, and justification.
5. Representation: Students use a variety of representations, including graphical, numerical, algebraic, verbal, and physical, to represent, describe, and generalize.	5. Productive disposition: Habitual inclination to see mathematics as sensible, useful, and worthwhile, coupled with a belief in diligence and one's own efficacy.

The SMPs embody these 10 processes and proficiencies to construct the ways in which students should engage in doing mathematics. The rich algebra tasks are designed to support students in developing their ability to communicate mathematically, articulate and justify their mathematical reasoning and process, analyze relationships, and recognize patterns that can lead to generalizations. The eight SMPs include the following:

1. Make sense of problems and persevere in solving them.

2. Reason abstractly and quantitatively.

3. Construct viable arguments and critique the reasoning of others.

4. Model with mathematics.

5. Use appropriate tools strategically.

6. Attend to precision.

7. Look for and make use of structure.

8. Look for and express regularity in repeated reasoning.

The designation of the associated SMPs in a task is based on these characteristics of each SMP, as shown in Figure 2.4, but keep in mind that the SMPs are practices that *students* demonstrate. The characteristics provide insights into the tasks' potential to have students develop and exhibit those practices.

Figure 2.4 Characteristics of Problems That Promote the SMPs

SMP	Characteristics of Problems
1. Make sense of problems and persevere in solving them.	• Do not have obvious solution pathways or lend themselves to algorithmic solutions. • May have multiple solutions or solution strategies.
2. Reason abstractly and quantitatively.	• Focus on relationships among quantities, including generalized quantities. • Promote the use of number and operation sense. • Can lead to generalizations about big ideas.
3. Construct viable arguments and critique the reasoning of others.	• Include justifying or explaining reasoning, as opposed to explaining or only showing steps to a solution.
4. Model with mathematics.	• Incorporate a contextual situation that requires a symbolic representation. • Use mathematics to capture a situation with potentially messy data.
5. Use appropriate tools strategically.	• Allow students to select their own tools. • Require tools to be used appropriately and strategically.
6. Attend to precision.	• Use mathematical vocabulary. • Require accurate measurement and computations with regard to any units.
7. Look for and make use of structure.	• Include mathematical relationships whose structure is key to the solution approach. • Prompt students to make generalizations based on their noticing of structural aspects.
8. Look for and express regularity in repeated reasoning.	• Ask students to develop generalizations based on recognition of patterns.

Vocabulary

Communicating effectively in a mathematics class requires students to use the appropriate vocabulary to convey a precise description of their thinking. The vocabulary provided in each task is meant to highlight the mathematical words that fit with the content of the task. The intent is not that the vocabulary be taught outside of the task to students but rather is to highlight particular mathematics as they arise in the lesson—that is, to teach the vocabulary within a context (Snow & Uccelli, 2009).

> "Consistent use of precise mathematics vocabulary creates shared understanding of what is being communicated so that discourse is enhanced and students' written explanations are easier to follow."

The mathematical language we use should be consistent from grade to grade and course to course (Bush et al., 2021; Dougherty et al., 2021). Consistent use of precise mathematics vocabulary creates shared understanding of what is being communicated so that discourse is enhanced and students' written explanations are easier to follow.

Within a particular curriculum or consistent with a Mathematics Whole School Agreement (Bush et al., 2021; Dougherty et al., 2021), there may be other vocabulary that you use. That mathematical language can be woven into the tasks in place of vocabulary that we offer.

Materials

Each rich algebra task includes a listing of the manipulatives or other materials that will be needed to support students' engagement in the task. The materials are presented as mathematical tools as part of a theme of students developing a tool kit of strategies to support their mathematical development. They are also related to representations that provide a means for students to experience mathematical relationships and processes in different ways.

When we talk about representations, we are referring to *concrete* (e.g., manipulative, hands-on, and physical materials), *semi-concrete* (e.g., graphs, pictures, and diagrams), and *abstract* (e.g., numbers, variables, and operation symbols) means to represent mathematical ideas, processes, and relationships. As students model the mathematics with concrete materials, you will notice that the task also includes a semi-concrete and abstract representation. The three are presented together in what Dougherty et al. (2021) call the CSA approach, which promotes students' development of a mental image or residue of their actions with the materials (Dougherty, 2008; Okazaki et al., 2006). The CSA approach allows students to see the relationship among the different representations so that they form connections (Dougherty et al., 2016; Moreno et al., 2011).

Task Type

The rich algebra tasks are created to focus on four different types of student understanding: (1) conceptual, (2) procedural, (3) problem-solving application, and (4) problem-solving critical thinking. Each type is described as follows.

Conceptual tasks focus on the mathematical underpinnings such as why an algorithm works the way it does or relationships that may not be evident in skill-based problems. One foundational idea in algebra involves the concept of variable and the ability of students to not only understand the different roles a variable can take, but also interpret generalized relationships. For example, students should be able to compare two expressions such as $3 + x$ and $x + 5$ and write an inequality ($3 + x < x + 5$) without substituting values for x. This would indicate that they are reasoning that if x is any number, adding 3 to the number would create a quantity less than the quantity that results when 5 is added to the same number.

Procedural tasks are designed to support students' acquisition of efficient methods or strategies including algorithms to solve skill-based problems. These tasks will not be practice activities; they will provide ways for students to compare and contrast solution methods that help them understand how the structure of a problem may be better solved by one method or algorithm over another. For example, if students are solving the system of equations $x + y = 15$ and $y = 2x - 3$, they may realize that substituting the expression $2x - 3$ is easier to use than other methods.

Problem-solving application tasks are those that require an application of a concept and/or procedure to solve a contextual problem. For example, students may be asked to compare and contrast two different travel packages to determine which one is the best bargain for the context of the trip. This may entail graphing or solving a system of equations to find a solution.

Problem-solving critical thinking tasks may include a nonroutine problem (a problem for which there is no known solution pathway) or a problem that asks students to identify patterns and to make conjectures or generalize their observations. Sometimes, the generalization may not be readily evident to the students, but through the questions provided in the task, you can focus students' attention to make the mathematics more transparent or visible. For example, students may be asked to find the height of a stack of paper that is the result of halving and stacking one sheet of paper 20 times. Finding the height of such a stack is an interesting problem, but the purpose of the task is to introduce students to exponential form.

Preparing to Implement the Task

Planning is key to an effective lesson. In the case of using rich algebra tasks, there are three considerations that you need to think through before you use the tasks in your classroom: (1) grouping structures and other aspects of implementing the task, (2) how you will debrief with the class on the task solutions and solution methods, and (3) models or representations you will use. You also need to consider the needs of your students to determine how you will adapt the launch and facilitation phases to support them in accessing the task to build the intended mathematical understandings.

GROUPING STRUCTURES

Grouping structures are the ways in which you have students work together to complete the task. Each task has a recommendation that was classroom tested, but the needs of your students may influence how you use the recommendation.

It is helpful to have students work in pairs or small groups of three or four so that they have opportunities not only to hear how others are thinking but to hear their own thinking as they share out in their pair or small group. Hearing their own thinking will help students determine the accuracy of their thoughts and allow them to monitor and self-correct. Additionally, working in a pair or small group gives students the confidence to share their ideas with the whole class, creating more participation and engagement.

We recommend that you use different grouping techniques and change the groups relatively frequently, such as every two weeks. This gives students an opportunity to learn a variety of discourse strategies to gain a respect for how diverse the thinking about mathematics might be. In the classroom tests of these tasks with middle and high school students, random grouping techniques were used. For example, students might draw a number from a stack of cards and then find three other students who have the same number to form a group of four. Or, a picture of a mathematician might be cut into four pieces and students draw one piece, then find the other three people who complete the picture to form a group.

FACILITATING THE TASK

The process you use to facilitate the discussion of a task once students have completed it is equally important as the way in which you group them to do the task. Some students may be hesitant to share their ideas with the whole class even though it is important to hear from all students in the class. You can help students gain their confidence to share more often. One strategy is to use *Think-Pair-Share* where students think independently first for about one minute, then share their ideas with their partner. You can then ask students to share what their pair decided, lifting the weight of what is shared from the individual to a pair perspective. The way in which you phrase the question can influence what and how students share. Asking what each pair (or group) decided or found is not as threatening as asking students to individually share their thoughts and solutions.

Another strategy is to have two students present ideas together from their group. If a student who has been randomly selected does not feel comfortable sharing, they can initially come to the front of the class with another student and participate by doing a small part of the presentation, even if it is only pointing to relevant sketches or other representations. As students recognize the accepting nature of your classroom environment, they will gain more confidence over the course of the year.

Five different presentation processes have been classroom tested with these tasks: (1) collaborative, (2) poster, (3) carousel, (4) expert group, and (5) sharing. Each is briefly described here.

Collaborative presentations are created by the pair or small group. Each student in the pair or group has the opportunity to provide input and ask questions to clarify what is going into the presentation, and thus any student can be selected to share the ideas. Students can be selected randomly from a group, which also provides an individual accountability and expectation that everyone in the pair or group participates in the solution process so that everyone understands.

For *poster presentations*, each group of four puts their solution process to an assigned part of the task on chart paper. The posters then are passed around to each group to compare the originating group's thinking to their solution process. Each group writes a comment similar to one of the following:

We agree and did the same process.	We had a different method, but we got the same answer.
What did you mean by _____?	We had another solution.

When the posters are returned to the originating group, they work together to resolve the questions and comments. You have an opportunity to further explore the solutions or questions and comments with the whole class.

The *carousel presentation* is very similar to the poster presentation except in the way in which groups review each other's posters. In the carousel presentation, each student in the group has a sticky note (one for every poster). Students put their initials on the notes and write an individual response to each group's poster.

Expert group presentations provide an opportunity for each student in a group of four to become an expert on one part of the task. After students complete the task, they should number off from 1 to 4. All of the 1s get in one group and share their thinking and process on one part of the task, 2s do the same on another part of the task, and so on. Then, students return to their original group and share their discussion, comparing the expert group discussion to their solution process and solution(s). You can also engage the class in a whole-group discussion where you further extend their thinking.

Sharing presentations are similar to collaborative presentations with one change. After groups have prepared their presentation, you will collect the presentation and give it to another group to review and revise. Then, the second group actually gives the presentation.

Each task has a suggestion on grouping and some facilitation techniques. However, you can add in these techniques to create some diversity in your instructional strategies so that students do not get bored with the same discourse routines. The techniques also provide accountability that all students will participate in the solution process and the expectation that, since they had the benefit of engaging in the discussion and asking questions to clarify, anyone from the group should be able to explain the process and justify the solution. When you decide to use a task, consider incorporating one of these techniques in your facilitation of the discussion of problem solutions.

MODELS OR REPRESENTATIONS USED IN THE TASK

An important part of planning the implementation of the task is to determine which representations or models are most helpful to students. When we refer to modeling with representations, we do not mean what *you show* students, but rather we are referring to the models and representations that students will use in the task to build their mathematical understandings and to demonstrate their thinking.

If your school or district has developed a Mathematics Whole-School Agreement (Dougherty et al., 2021), then you are aware of the CSA (concrete, semi-concrete, abstract) approach to using representation, introduced earlier in this chapter and shown in Figure 2.5. A CSA approach means that students model mathematical ideas using concrete materials (physical materials such as algebra tiles and pattern blocks) while at the same time representing their actions on the concrete materials with sketches, drawings, graphs, and so on (semi-concrete representations) and finally using mathematical symbols (variables, operation signs, and so on) as the abstract component. By doing all three of these representations at one time, students are more likely to make connections among them and thus deepen their understanding. (See Chapter 4 in *The Math Pact, High School* [Dougherty et al., 2021] for more information on representations.)

Figure 2.5 CSA Approach

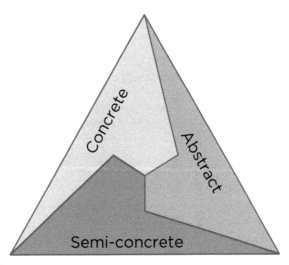

Source: Dougherty et al. (2021, p. 48).

You will notice in the rich algebra tasks that concrete materials are often used to help students "see" the mathematical relationships that aren't evident in only drawings or symbolic representations. They are most frequently used when a new idea is introduced or when a concept is complex. As students go through your instructional sequence, these materials may be used less frequently, but it is important that students who need to model longer than other students have access to the materials.

Other Considerations

As these tasks were developed, six considerations were taken into account to better support student learning: (1) classroom culture, (2) accessibility and equity, (3) scaffolds and differentiation, (4) productive struggle, (5) strengths-based feedback to students, and (6) effects noted from classroom tests. You will see evidence of each of these as you go through the tasks.

CLASSROOM CULTURE

To prepare your students for engaging in these algebra tasks and working effectively in groups and as a whole class, you must carefully cultivate the classroom culture in a way that is conducive to rich tasks. You will be asking students to collaborate, represent, think deeply, and explain in ways that they may not have experienced in earlier mathematics classes. They have to learn to trust other students when they share ideas so that each one feels like they are being listened to and respected.

> " Forming a classroom that embraces correct and incorrect ideas and encourages multiple solution approaches begins the first day students walk in the door. "

Forming a classroom that embraces correct and incorrect ideas and encourages multiple solution approaches begins the first day students walk in the door. We have found that students acclimate more quickly to a different classroom environment when you begin on day one with the same vision of what you would like your class to look like at the end of the year. Therefore, you want to consider what you want students to be doing on that last day of school such as quickly engaging in a task, effectively working together, explaining their thinking, searching for multiple solution approaches or solutions, and using multiple representations. Whatever your vision is for your students, you will want to select tasks that will embody the characteristics of your vision for the first one or two weeks of school.

Rather than a typical first-day assessment or review, consider using tasks such as the ones in Chapter 4; tasks that invite students to use their mathematical lens to investigate an uncomplicated question to a shared observation, such as those found at https://blog.mrmeyer.com/ (Meyer, n.d.); or noncurricular tasks that have students explore other interesting mathematics, such as those found at www.peterliljedahl.com/teachers/good-problem (Liljedahl, n.d.) or in *Building Thinking Classrooms in Mathematics* (Liljedahl, 2020). These tasks provide opportunities for students to engage in an interesting task that does not require fluency or automaticity as they work together to think creatively and then share their results with the class.

When students first arrive at class, have their groups of four set up so that they can quickly move into a task. Before they begin a task, however, ask students to brainstorm what it looks like and sounds like when you effectively collaborate in a group. Have students discuss in their groups and then share one or two main ideas as you record them on the document camera (see Figure 2.6).

Figure 2.6 Example of Student Brainstorming of Effective Group Work

3rd Period Algebra I
- Everyone contributes and talks
- People ask questions if they don't understand
- We respect each other
- It's ok to disagree but do it in a nice way
- Don't waste time
- Double check the math!
- stay focused.

Then, present the task to the students and remind them that they should consider the practices they recommended for effective group work as they solve the task. As they work to find a solution to the task, monitor the groups for effective and efficient discussions. Sometimes students have not had substantive experience working productively in groups. If this is the case, it is helpful to model what a mathematics discussion looks and sounds like so that students have an example to work from. You can model a small-group discussion with students or with a colleague or two. Your students can hear the academic language you use, listen to the way you question ideas to clarify, and see how you all equally share in the task solution process.

When they have completed the task, ask groups to share their solution method first, and then their solution. It is important to refrain as much as possible from interjecting or interrupting the group as they are explaining so that you can hear how they use mathematical language and the ways in which they think, as well as to demonstrate respect for the group's work. As you listen to their explanations, the strengths students bring to your class will be evident and provide a foundation on which to build. Before you ask any follow-up questions, pause for at least 20 to 30 seconds to let students have an opportunity to guide the discussion with their questions or alternative solution strategies. Then, be sure to ask questions like "Did anyone solve it a different way?" or "Did any group have a different solution?"

Changing a mathematics classroom's culture is not a fast process. It takes students time to change their expectations and patterns of behavior that were formed from their previous experiences to those that require them to be more active in the learning process. And, it's an acclimation process for you as you implement new ideas! Using nonroutine tasks that allow students to think creatively as they work with others for one to two weeks at the beginning of school provides a kick start to a productive classroom culture. After those first weeks, being consistent in your expectations including using rich algebra tasks will bring about a change. Within six weeks, you will see students engaging more and taking more ownership over the mathematical ideas.

ACCESSIBILITY AND EQUITY

NCTM issued a position paper in 2014 that describes ways to address access and equity across the grade levels:

> Practices that support access and equity require comprehensive understanding. These practices include, but are not limited to, holding high expectations, ensuring access to high-quality mathematics curriculum and instruction, allowing adequate time for students to learn, placing appropriate emphasis on differentiated processes that broaden students' productive engagement with mathematics, and making strategic use of human and material resources. When access and equity have been successfully addressed, student outcomes—including achievement on a range of mathematics assessments, disposition toward mathematics, and persistence in the mathematics pipeline—transcend, and cannot be predicted by students' racial, ethnic, linguistic, gender, and socioeconomic backgrounds. (NCTM, 2014a)

In their statement, it is important to note the need to provide students with high-quality curriculum—in this case, rich algebra tasks—that can be differentiated to meet the needs of your students. Students' engagement in the tasks leads to stronger learning.

Luria and colleagues (2017) noted that concept-based learning and open-ended problems were two ways to promote equitable access to mathematical learning. According to Hiebert and Grouws (2007), to build conceptual understanding involves

> discussing the mathematical meaning underlying procedures, asking questions about how different solution strategies are similar to and different from each other, considering the ways in which mathematical problems build on each other or are special (or general) cases of each other, attending to the relationships among mathematical ideas, and reminding students about the main point of the lesson and how this point fits within the current sequence of lessons and ideas. (p. 384)

The rich algebra tasks support these ideas through the design of the tasks by using multiple representations or creating multiple entry points or solution approaches. For example, some tasks have geometric representations that are aligned with more abstract patterns or ideas. The use of geometric representations in combination with tables and graphs can provide opportunities to understand more abstract ideas in a different way. Additionally, reversibility questions from the RFG (reversibility, flexibility, and generalization) framework described in Chapter 1 allow students to enter into a task at their level. For example, if students are asked to create an equation whose solution is $y = -3$, some students might give $3 + y = 0$ while others write $y^2 - 9 = 0$ and indicate that it has a solution of $y = -3$ and $y = 3$.

SCAFFOLDS OR DIFFERENTIATION

Scaffold and differentiation supports are provided in the rich algebra tasks to assist you in creating opportunities for students to engage. They are focused on maintaining an appropriate level of mathematics so as not to water down the algebra in which students engage and to create an equitable pathway for all students, including multilingual learners. Additionally, they incorporate principles from the Universal Design for Learning framework (CAST, 2018), which provides ways in which to revise or adapt tasks to reduce barriers that limit how students access a task.

One way to scaffold or differentiate a problem is to remind students of a simpler problem that they have already solved and focus on the structure of the problem or the mathematical relationships that are similar to the new task. The connections to other problems are key in helping students to see the mathematics and then be able to use those mathematical ideas to solve other more complex tasks. It is also possible to change the numbers in a task to make a simpler or more complex problem. For example, if the task uses negative rational numbers, they could be changed to positive rational numbers for some students or include irrational numbers for others. This doesn't mean that you shift the cognitive load and then stop there. Rather, these are strategies that increase access for some as a step in the direction to more complex problem solving, and to increase rigor for others who are ready for the challenge. This is what a truly differentiated heterogeneous classroom looks like.

You can also scaffold and differentiate a task by changing or adapting the representations that are used. Some students may better access the mathematics by using concrete materials or manipulatives while others may be ready for or prefer semi-concrete representations. This includes providing calculators so that students can focus on the mathematics in the task and not be hindered by computations.

The grouping structures discussed in this chapter and referenced in the tasks are also strategies to scaffold and differentiate tasks. Having students work in pairs and small groups builds confidence and provides the opportunity to affirm (or refute) their thinking as they talk through the solution and solution approach. It also provides them with opportunities to think critically and justify their thinking, which often leads to new thinking. As the groups or pairs share their solutions and solution methods, you can further differentiate by allowing students to choose which part of the task they discuss.

Another strategy is to pose questions that help students focus on important mathematical ideas in the task without being didactic and explicitly telling students how to solve the problem. Questions such as "How could you represent the relationship in this problem?" or "What patterns do you see that could help you?" are used so that students see a potential pathway to solving the problem.

As students share their solutions to a task, it is likely that they will share multiple solution approaches. This gives you the opportunity to have students compare and contrast the solution methods to identify relationships among the methods and the problem structure.

PRODUCTIVE STRUGGLE

Hiebert and Grouws (2007) describe struggle as when "students expend effort to make sense of mathematics, to figure out something that is not immediately apparent" (p. 387). This means that the sense-making activity has to be on the part of the student, and it is not something that teachers can tell students (Richland et al., 2012). Students need to be active participants in the mathematics lesson rather than watching the teacher or others solve problems.

The grouping structures and the design of the rich algebra tasks support students in persevering in solving the tasks. The grouping structures that are suggested for sharing their thinking and task solutions promote the expectation that all students can and should contribute to the group's presentation. When you use a random method to select a presenter, students recognize that everyone in the group needs to be confident and comfortable with the mathematics and solution approach described in their presentation.

The design of the rich algebra tasks themselves also contributes to productive struggle in that the tasks have multiple access points so that the diverse range of students can engage. The open-ended nature of the tasks provides an opportunity for novice as well as more expert learners to have input into the solution pathway. Additionally, the inclusion of multiple representations (concrete, semi-concrete, and abstract) supports students so that they feel successful and are more likely to persevere and remain engaged.

STRENGTHS-BASED FEEDBACK TO STUDENTS

The feedback you provide students as they solve a task and share their results contributes to students' success and their view of themselves as mathematics students and mathematicians. It is important to focus on a strengths-based approach when you provide feedback to students so that they can "build bridges to areas that need attention" (Kobett & Karp, 2020, p. 6). You can use the list of potential strengths that students may demonstrate, provided in Figure 2.7 (Kobett & Karp, 2020), for suggestions on language that you can include in your feedback.

CAST (2018) also provides recommendations for student feedback that complements a strengths-based approach. Their recommendations include

- encouraging perseverance;

- emphasizing effort, improvement, and achievement of a standard;

- being timely, specific, and frequent; and

- focusing on substantive and informative (rather than comparative and competitive) feedback.

It is important, however, to recognize that the feedback should focus on helping students readjust their thinking, not explicitly telling them it is correct (or incorrect). This gives students the opportunity to make sense of the mathematics and rethink their interpretation of or solution to the problem. This type of feedback requires you to consider a series of questions that will support students as they relook at the problem and its solution. Some general questions that may help students reevaluate their interpretation of the problem or their solution include the following:

- What are you trying to solve? What is the problem asking you to do?

- How did you decide what solution process to use?

- Have you solved a similar problem? If so, what solution approach did you use?

- Would a diagram be helpful? An equation? A number line? Could you model it with physical materials?

- How did you use the information in the problem in your solution process?

- What do you predict the solution will be? Does your answer seem reasonable? Is it close to your prediction?

- How convincing is your solution? Are you confident in your solution?

Specific questions related to the task can be raised as students are working (see the "Facilitating a Rich Algebra Task" section in Chapter 3 on cuing). The feedback students receive as they work on a task allows them to move forward in a productive manner, builds their confidence in attacking and solving problems, and encourages them to persevere through problems that they may at first have perceived as daunting. This boosts students' self-efficacy as it conveys that the teacher is interested in and supportive of their engagement in the mathematics.

Figure 2.7 Potential Student Strengths

Dispositional	Processes and Practices	Content
• Perseveres	• Creates varied representations (e.g., manipulatives, drawings, numberlines)	• Understands concepts
• Works well with other students	• Sketches mathematical ideas	• Understands and uses procedures
• Uses novel or creative approaches	• Links manipulatives to abstract concepts	• Uses number sense
• Compromises with others when working on strategies and solutions	• Explains strategies and ideas	• Identifies and understands patterns
• Knows when to ask for help	• Explains thinking	• Converts measurements
• Asks good questions	• Connects mathematical concepts and procedures	• Connects real-world problems
• Takes risks	• Listens to others' ideas	• Regularly estimates quantities
• Recognizes making mistakes is part of learning	• Uses and applies appropriate mathematical vocabulary	• Has algebra sense
• Can teach/mentor others	• Identifies and understands patterns	• Has graph sense
• Demonstrates a positive attitude towards mathematics	• Enjoys solving puzzles	• Has fraction sense
• Enjoys mathematics	• Enjoys finding another way to solve a problem	• Has spatial sense
• Sees mathematics as a way to understand the world	• Regularly seeks multiple ways to solve problems	• Has number sense
• Listens to others' ideas	• Uses reasoning	• Visualizes mathematics
• Works independently	• Uses manipulatives well	• Knows basic math facts
• Is curious about mathematical ideas	• Perseveres	• Understands and regularly uses mental math
		• Interprets information from a chart, table, or graph
		• Converts measurements

Dispositional	Processes and Practices	Content
• Enjoys finding another way to solve a problem • Creates mathematics problems • Brainstorms new approaches	• Works analytically • Knows when responses are reasonable • Thinks and works logically • Explains mathematical information • Identifies important and unimportant information • Justifies results • Translates data into different forms • Thinks flexibly • Organizes information • Uses novel or creative approaches • Appropriately sequences multiple steps or directions • Asks probing questions • Regularly seeks multiple ways to solve problems	• Remembers and uses previously learned mathematics ideas • Understands concepts • Identifies the correct operation • Regularly estimates quantities • Explains the meaning of procedures

Source: Kobett & Karp (2020).

CLASSROOM TESTED

The tasks in this book have been classroom tested by the authors and other collaborating teachers in middle and high school mathematics classes with heterogeneous classes. Across all teachers, there were some common effects on students. These include, but are not limited to,

- an increase in sustained engagement in the mathematics class discourse and activities,

- explanations of their thinking that became more robust as students gained experience with the tasks,

- more confidence in sharing before the whole class and within pairs or small groups,

- an expectation that learning mathematics requires active participation from all (i.e., not just the teacher),

- an expectation that problems can be solved in more than one way and that multiple solution methods are desirable,

- consistent and proficient use of mathematical vocabulary, and

- shared understanding that multiple representations are connected.

Summing Up

In this chapter, we have described the mathematics focus, standards, teaching practices, and dimensions of the rich algebra tasks. We have also included some of the key ideas that should be considered as you are planning to implement the tasks. In Chapter 3, we move to the implementation aspects of rich algebra tasks.

Professional Learning and Discussion Questions

Read and discuss the following questions with colleagues in your department.

- Which of the effective teaching practices are you most successful implementing? Which present challenges for you? What suggestions can you share for improvement?

- Which SMP do you think your students demonstrate well? Which do you find more challenging?

- What considerations will you make as you plan to implement these tasks?

- How will you decide when to use a conceptual task? A procedural task? A problem-solving application task? A problem-solving critical thinking task?

- What processes or tasks do you use to create a classroom environment or culture at the beginning of the academic year?

- How do you introduce students to your expectations for group work? For mathematical discussions?

- What strategies do you use to differentiate or scaffold tasks to make them accessible for your students?

- How do you support productive struggle in your class?

- What strategies do you use for students sharing their solutions and solution methods?

- What new insights do you have about the design of mathematics tasks? About grouping? About facilitating?

- What types of feedback do you provide students as they work on tasks? On their solutions?

 Available to download at **resources.corwin.com/classroomreadymath/algebra**

CHAPTER 3

Implementing Rich Algebra Task Lessons

Now that we have considered the important aspects of planning for the use of a rich algebra task, we turn our attention to the actual implementation of the lesson. In this chapter, we will describe the five critical components of implementation: launch, facilitation, close and generalizations, and reflection. By the end of the chapter, you will have considered

- ways to launch the task to create student interest and engagement;

- strategies to optimize grouping structures as part of the task solution-finding process and class discourse;

- techniques for closing a lesson to make the mathematical skills, processes, and generalizations more visible; and

- the importance of reflecting on the lesson and archiving your notes.

Before The Launch

> Expecting high student engagement means that you must take time yourself to actively engage in the mathematics *before* you introduce the task to students.

Once you have created a classroom environment that promotes student interaction and engagement, you are ready to consider which tasks you will use and how you will use them. One of the goals for implementing these tasks is to provide interesting learning experiences that cultivate student engagement. Expecting high student engagement means that you must take time yourself to actively engage in the mathematics *before* you introduce the task to students. We encourage you to solve the task before you look at the suggested strategies or the answer so that you can better understand how students might approach the task. Smith and Stein (2018) call this the anticipating stage of the five practices for orchestrating productive class discussions. Although the content may seem familiar to you, by taking time to do the task, you give yourself an opportunity to think about the mathematics concepts more deeply than you would if you just read through the suggested strategies in the tasks (or looked up the answer).

As you do the task, think about the solution strategies students could use or the multiple solutions they might generate so that you can plan how to conduct the discussion. You should also consider possible places where they may need some prompting questions or where you may want to minimize any barriers that might limit access to the task. You might even consider asking friends or colleagues to complete the task so that you can get a broader lens on the ways your students might approach the mathematics. Your knowledge of your students can also help you identify areas that may lead to misconceptions. Considering these aspects before you launch the task will optimize the learning experience for the students and increase the effectiveness of your instruction.

Additionally, before you use a rich algebra task, you can set the stage for students to be successful by considering the format of your class in general. Most classes start with a warm-up that gets students ready for what is to come in the lesson. Even though warm-ups take time from the main lesson, typically 5–8 minutes, they set the stage for learning by providing opportunities for students to (1) review a prerequisite mathematical skill or idea, (2) solve a critical thinking problem, or (3) engage in an intriguing opening to the lesson or the upcoming task. Furthermore, the more consistently you use warm-ups, the more students will adapt to a class culture of making every minute count.

REVIEWING A PREREQUISITE MATHEMATICAL SKILL OR IDEA

Reviewing a skill or idea that is integral to the lesson or task is one way in which students can connect ideas from previously learned topics to the new learning. This is a form of distributed practice (Nazari & Ebersbach, 2019) that may already be part of your instructional sequences. For example, if you are introducing a unit that has a task for the properties of exponents, you might want students to review how to compute the value of an exponential expression such as 2^4, 2^0, or 2^{-3}. In this warm-up, you would limit the number of problems to five, depending on the skill or idea, to allow time for students to respond and for any discussion that might follow.

SOLVING A CRITICAL THINKING PROBLEM

Another type of warm-up is to start with a problem that involves critical thinking. For example, if your lesson or task involves computations with positive and negative rational numbers, you might start with a Which One Doesn't Belong? task—for example:

$-\left\lvert\dfrac{1}{2}\right\rvert$	$-\dfrac{3}{6}$
$\left\lvert-\dfrac{4}{8}\right\rvert$	$-\dfrac{3}{2}$

ENGAGE IN AN INTRIGUING OPENING

Still another way to launch a task is to present a problem that initiates a curiosity about what is coming up in the lesson or task. For example, if you are using Seeing Squares in Chapter 4, you might use a related problem such as the equilateral triangle problem, in which students are shown a triangle divided into smaller triangles and asked to find the total number of triangles in the picture:

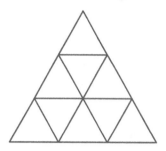

Notice that while this launching problem promotes critical thinking, it doesn't require as much thought as and has different patterns than you would find in the rich algebra task Seeing Squares.

Selecting the most effective task to construct robust student understanding requires consideration of several different criteria beyond the grade level and specific outcomes of a course you are teaching. These criteria may include the following.

1. **Instructional sequence.** Some tasks can serve as an introduction to a topic so that students interact with new ideas to connect with old learning and begin to build conceptual understanding. As the instructional sequence progresses, tasks can change to integrate more concepts and skills and thus be more complex than the introductory ones. Additionally, later tasks can include more procedural or skill aspects than earlier tasks when the foundation for the topic is being laid.

2. **Representations.** The types of representations used in your curriculum should include concrete (physical materials), semi-concrete (sketches, number lines), and abstract (symbols, numbers) representations. The type and consistency of the representations should be consistent and accessible by students as well as readily available for you to use. In some cases, the materials given in the task can be exchanged for similar materials that are more in line with your curriculum and students.

3. **Mathematical consistency.** The curriculum you use has a mathematics foundation that is used to build each mathematical idea. As you select a task from our book, it is important to consider how the mathematics in the task fits with the consistency of the mathematics in your curriculum. For example, one task may utilize a table format to show the equivalent equations and the property that justifies the transformations used in solving a linear equation. This may not fit with your curriculum, but it may provide an alternative way for you to think about the mathematics to supplement the approach your curriculum uses.

4. **Instructional shift.** The tasks give you and your students an opportunity to take a brief departure from your curriculum and engage in algebra tasks that may have a different flair from typical problems. Depending on how your curriculum is designed, instructing with a rich algebra task may mean your students explore more and you tell or show less. Be prepared to put on a facilitator's hat and provide supports for students who may need encouragement and guidance to effectively participate during these class sessions.

There is no one best way for selecting a task, which can feel both empowering and risky. Keeping notes on which tasks you use and when, and how effective you thought each task was for what you had intended, will help you in making future selection and implementation decisions.

Launching a Rich Algebra Task

The opening or launch of a rich algebra task is as important as the warm-up is for the entire lesson. It sets the tone for how students will engage in the task; provides a preview of what they will be doing in terms of content, process, and materials; and specifies the expectations for what students will be responsible for when they complete the task. Before you start students on the rich algebra task, it is helpful to give them time to read through the task so that you can clarify any vocabulary, directions, or other aspects of the task. If there are students in your class who need some support in reading, you can have students read the task aloud in a pair or small group.

Once you feel students understand the task and you have clarified any vocabulary or directions, you need to be sure that you set the parameters for the task so that the students are aware of your expectations. You will first want to direct them to work individually, in pairs, or in small groups, and announce how much time they have to complete the task. If it is early in the year and you are establishing the classroom routines, you may want to reiterate the norms that you are expecting for the grouping configuration. For example, you may want students to discuss the expectations of the task and brainstorm solution approaches before they start working.

Most of the rich algebra tasks in this book are structured to take about 20–40 minutes of a class period. This includes solving the task and sharing in some way with other groups or with the class as a whole. It is helpful to display a virtual or other type of timer so that students can monitor and make good use of their time on the task. This also helps to build independence and create a productive work experience.

Students should also be told what materials will be available for them to use or what is needed for the task. The materials may include manipulatives such as the two-color counters that are used to represent integers in the tasks in Chapter 5. If it is the first time that students are using two-color counters to model integers, for example, you should demonstrate how to model several integers, both positive and negative, before they start on the task. The task will be more accessible and their work will be more robust if students are familiar with the materials. In the launch of some tasks, we have suggested ways to demonstrate the manipulative being used, but you may want to adapt the launch by adding more examples to give students experience in using that material. Additionally, if you have to substitute a different manipulative because you don't have the one we suggest, be sure that the substitution allows for the mathematics to be modeled appropriately.

Some tasks recommend incorporating technology such as a graphing tool or calculator into the task. The technology you use may be dependent on what is easily accessible by the students, but you should also consider how the technology will enhance the task. In some cases, the use of a graphing tool, for example, eliminates any inaccuracies that students may have when they graph and allows them to focus on identifying patterns and making generalizations. As you do the task in your planning stage and are considering the needs of your students, you may identify technology that you feel will be beneficial in supporting them.

In the launch, students also need to know how and if they will be sharing the work they do on the task with the whole class when they are finished. This is where your planning (i.e., the anticipating stage) is important because you will have thought through how the solution process and solutions will be shared with the class. Some suggestions for ways to facilitate the whole-class discussion are given in the next section of this chapter. By giving students advance notice of the type of discussion, you will be holding them accountable for contributing to the discussion, and they will be able to structure their work on the task and feel prepared for the discussion as they provide meaningful contributions to the progress of building mathematical understanding in the class.

Finally, students need to know whether you will be grading the task and, if so, how you will grade it. You will find that the tasks are useful for formative assessments because they provide a lot of information that will be helpful in making instructional decisions. Feedback to students, however, is important because it helps students enhance their work to meet higher expectations. You can provide feedback to students in a variety of ways including, but not limited to, (1) writing comments on their task solution; (2) making oral comments to the group or individual, either privately or publicly during the class discussion; (3) assigning a score based on a rubric; and (4) eliciting (and vetting if you suspect it is needed) constructive comments from students about the mathematical solution or process.

Facilitating a Rich Algebra Task

Facilitating a rich algebra task has two parts: (1) monitoring students as they explore and complete the task and (2) organizing and facilitating a discussion of students' strategies and solutions.

The classroom structure and routines that you create for students as they engage in a rich algebra task are central to maximizing the learning that each task embodies. In classroom tests of the tasks, we learned that working in pairs or small groups helped to optimize the students' learning experience and build their confidence in sharing ideas with others. Heterogeneous pairs or small groups of three to four students provide opportunities for students to learn that (1) there are multiple ways to think about a problem and its solution, (2) everyone contributes something, and (3) sharing your thinking with someone else allows you to affirm or refute your ideas.

There are multiple strategies you can use to create a group. For example, strategies for groups of three or four students could include the following:

1. Using a deck of cards, have three or four kings, queens, jacks, tens, and so on that together make up the number of students in your class. Students draw a card and form a group of like cards.

2. Using postcards or pictures, cut them into three or four pieces until you have enough for each student in your class to choose one. Students draw a piece and find the other students whose pieces form a whole picture.

3. Using connecting cubes, have three or four in each color so that the total number of cubes matches the number of students in your class. Students draw a cube and form a group of like colors.

> The use of heterogeneous, randomly selected groups can often level the playing field and provide opportunities for students to demonstrate their strengths in different ways.

Using randomly selected groups creates opportunities for students to work with others they may not have the chance to work with if more deliberate group selection strategies are used. Additionally, in the middle and high school grades, students have often formed their own opinion about which students are the highest and lowest performing; this impacts how a student may be viewed in the group and the peers' expectations of this student's contributions. The use of heterogeneous, randomly selected groups can often level the playing field and provide opportunities for students to demonstrate their strengths in different ways. Liljedahl (2014) found that consistent use of randomly selected groups has an effect on students that is visible in the classroom:

- Students become agreeable to work in any group they are placed in.

- There is an elimination of social barriers within the classroom.

- Mobility of knowledge between students increases.

- Reliance on the teacher for answers decreases.

- Reliance on co-constructed intra- and inter-group answers increases.

- Engagement in classroom tasks increase[s].

- Students become more enthusiastic about mathematics class. (p. 5)

Getting Students to Talk More About Their Mathematics

If you are just starting to use group tasks in your classroom or your students need a boost to make their group discussions more robust, you can use an interview protocol to help them learn how to discuss mathematics. To implement an interview protocol, first place students in pairs and have them work independently on a task, preferably one from Chapter 4. Then, after they have worked for about 10 minutes, call time and have the students interview each other using questions such as those in Figure 3.1. As is typical in an interview, the interviewer should record the answers.

Figure 3.1 Example of an Interview to Promote Student Discourse

Name of interviewer: _____	Name of partner: _____
1. When you saw the problem, how did you decide what it was asking you to do?	2. Was there anything you were unsure about? If so, describe what that was.
3. What was your first idea about how to solve the problem?	4. Did your solution strategy work? If not, what did you do next?
5. How was this problem like or different from another problem you have solved?	6. Did you find more than one solution? Why or why not?
Interview checklist ☐ I did not interrupt while my partner responded. ☐ I read the questions in an understandable way. ☐ I repeated the questions if asked. ☐ I accurately recorded my partner's responses.	Interviewee checklist ☐ I responded to each question when asked. ☐ I used appropriate mathematical vocabulary. ☐ I listened carefully to the questions.

Having students work in groups or pairs is the first step, but it is also important to have students learn how to talk about the mathematics when they are working with a peer or in a group. You can promote more robust discussions by using an interview protocol that provides questions to prompt students to share their thinking.

Notice that the last row of the interview form asks students to review their performance as an interviewer or interviewee. The purpose of this row is to have students become aware of how they interact with others. You may want student pairs to exchange their checklists and decide if they agree with each other's assessment. It's important to remember that even for middle and high school students, there are learning opportunities to gain more skills to support their interactions in pairs and groups.

While students are working on a task or the partner interview, this is your opportunity to monitor their work by circulating around the room, observing their solution process and solution(s). If you see a group that is challenged by the problem, you can pose a scaffolding or prompting question, specific to that group. Examples of these questions are provided in every task.

If you do hear discussions that you feel should be redirected, it is often our instinct to interrupt the group. Rather than breaking into the group's discussion to ask a question, you can use a technique we call *cuing*. Cuing occurs when you give students a prompting or scaffolding question or a suggestion about using a representation on a sticky note that you drop in their group before walking away. This is the first step in supporting a group without interfering with their solution process. If cuing does not move the group forward, you can provide more support as appropriate. On the other hand, if a group is successful with a task and has completed it before other groups, you can extend the problem for them by cuing with an extension question. This technique promotes more student independence and does not disrupt the group dynamics. Extension questions are suggested in the tasks and are meant to push students' thinking or move students to conjectures and generalizations.

> " Cuing occurs when you give students a prompting or scaffolding question or a suggestion about using a representation on a sticky note that you drop in their group before walking away. "

As you monitor the groups, you will notice particular solution methods and solutions that you will want to highlight in the whole-class discussion of the task (Smith & Stein, 2018). Once you decide which groups' work you would like to share with the whole class, you can determine how you want to sequence the presentations (Smith & Stein, 2011). You may want to start with particular solution methods that highlight a specific strategy or that build in sophistication. Or, you may have a nonproductive approach shared to prompt discussion about how a method can be redirected. Regardless of the approach that you use for sharing, the discussions will be meaningful if they move beyond a show-and-tell presentation of the "steps" students used to solve the task without a description of why they chose the solution path, the patterns that they noticed, or generalizations they could make.

It is typical in these rich algebra tasks to see the recommendation to have groups come to the front of the class and share their process(es) and solution(s). This is a familiar approach that we call a collaborative group presentation. But, you may want to consider other ways of debriefing the task so that this process doesn't become boring. Four other methods you may want to consider are (1) poster sessions, (2) expert groups, (3) sharing, and (4) carousel.

Poster sessions. In a poster session, each group is given a sheet of chart paper and a marker. You assign one part of the rich algebra task to each group, and they write their solution process and solution for that part on the chart paper. You should allow about 4–6 minutes for them to complete this process, at which time you have groups rotate their chart paper.

As the chart paper goes to the next group, that group should review the process and solution and then write one comment that might include (1) an agreement with the process and answer, (2) the addition of another solution or a different process, (3) a question that they may have that is not answered by what is shown on the chart paper, or (4) a disagreement with a solution (but offering another). Groups may also answer a question that a previous group wrote. To keep the groups on task, limit the time they have with each chart paper to about 3–4 minutes, then rotate the chart paper to another group.

After you rotate the chart paper through the groups, you can initiate a brief whole-class discussion where you pinpoint particular aspects of the task that you want to highlight or use to extend the students' thinking. As you monitor the groups, you may identify some solution strategies that should be noted. Additionally, if the task has multiple solutions, perhaps you want to pull the students together to identify patterns or similarities in the solutions that could lead to a generalization.

Expert groups. If you grouped students by threes or fours, have the students number off from 1 to 3 or 4. The students then regroup so that all the 1s are together, as are all the 2s, 3s, and 4s, in a larger group in a different part of the classroom. These larger groups are assigned a part of the task to become an expert about the solution process and solution(s). This is an opportunity for the students to share their group's approach to the problem and to hear how other groups solved the problem. When students move to their expert group, it is helpful to assign a student in each group to be the facilitator who is responsible for making sure the discussion is productive. The facilitator ensures that anyone's questions are answered and that there is agreement within the group that the solutions and solution processes shared are accurate. You may want to allow approximately 5–6 minutes in the expert groups for their discussion before sending students back to their original groups.

When students return to their original groups, it is again helpful to assign a student to facilitate the small-group discussion. The facilitator will make sure that each person in the group has the opportunity to share their expert discussion and field any questions from the small group. Students should share the relevant points of their expert-group discussions with the expectation that every group member must contribute to this final phase of the process. If there are specific aspects of the task that you want to highlight or if there were questions from either the expert group or the small group that went unanswered, you can have a whole-class discussion with regard to the relevant questions.

Sharing. Sharing is very similar to the familiar collaborative group approach where groups share their solution process and solution. In the sharing technique, groups prepare a presentation for all or part of the rich algebra task. However, this is where sharing becomes different from the collaborative group method. The presentation sheets are collected and redistributed to different groups. Then, within a set time period, usually about 5 minutes, the new group must analyze what the original group wrote and determine if they agree or need to make changes. You can then select a group to present the solution and process.

Carousel. The carousel method, like sharing, is similar to another approach, the poster session. In addition to the chart paper and marker, each student in the group receives the number of sticky notes that corresponds to the number of chart papers they will review. The setup is the same where groups have about 4–6 minutes to prepare their problem on the chart paper. The chart papers are then rotated to the next group where the students have about 3–4 minutes to review the work. When the chart paper is rotated to a new group, each student responds individually rather than posting a group response on the chart paper. Similarly, students can respond in agreement with the solution or solution process, ask (or answer) a question, share a different solution or solution method, or disagree with the solution or solution process but offer another answer.

Each of these methods provides benefits and enhances the effectiveness of the debriefing. Figure 3.2 provides some of the benefits to class discussion that are afforded when you use a particular method. However, it is also important to consider the characteristics or demands of a task before choosing the method you will use for a whole-class discussion. Some of these considerations are also provided in Figure 3.2. Note that a collaborative group or sharing method can be used with any task and may be the easiest to start with at the beginning of the school year.

Figure 3.2 Methods for Structuring a Rich Algebra Task

Method	Characteristics of Tasks	Benefits
Poster session	1. Solution strategies are easily organized. 2. Task is focused on more procedural-type problems. 3. Problems in the task have one solution.	→ Is highly engaging → Provides a safe environment for students to address their own questions → Forces students to analyze their own and others' work → Allows for students to question in a nonthreatening way
Expert groups	1. There are multiple parts to the task. 2. Task has a variety of problem types (procedural, conceptual, or problem solving). 3. Task may have multiple possible solutions and/or solution methods.	→ Is highly engaging → Places the accountability on all students to contribute to the group discussion → Provides an opportunity for students to become confident about the problem → Creates a safe environment to ask questions
Sharing	1. Any task type can work with sharing.	→ Forces students to analyze their own and others' work → Provides additional solution strategies to bolster whole-class discussion
Carousel	1. Solution strategies are easily organized. 2. Task is focused on more procedural-type problems. 3. Problems in the task have one solution.	→ Is highly engaging → Provides a safe environment for students to address their own questions → Allows for students to question in a nonthreatening way → Places individuals accountable to analyze their own and others' work

With any of these methods, it is important to establish norms about the way students prepare a presentation sheet or chart paper that will be shared. For example, you may want to make clear that (1) the writing must be legible, (2) the only drawings to be included are those that contribute to the problem solution, and (3) the work should be organized so that someone can make sense of it. You may have others that you would like to include.

Close and Generalizations

> Even though the mathematical ideas may have come up in the small-group or whole-class discussion, it may not be the case that students grasped the explicit relationships or generalizations.

The closing of the rich algebra task discussion is the opportunity to make the mathematics more visible. Even though the mathematical ideas may have come up in the small-group or whole-class discussion, it may not be the case that students grasped the explicit relationships or generalizations. Now is your chance to make sure that they leave the task with a significant takeaway. You can do that by asking students to compare and contrast the solution methods. What do they notice that is similar about the methods? What is different? If the task has multiple solutions, ask students to identify any patterns that they see in the tasks. These patterns can lead to an important generalization that can build students' conceptual understanding and create a stronger foundation for future learning.

When you ask students these follow-up questions, it is often a verbal exchange of ideas. We have found that by recording students' ideas on a document camera, students feel that their ideas are valued, and they are more likely to focus on what is being shared and make sense of the concepts, solutions, or ideas. That leads to them offering more patterns or seeing connections, which makes their takeaways more robust.

Additionally, students can be asked to reflect on the task in a *Think-Pair-Share* activity. Ask them to consider all the solution strategies presented in the whole-class discussion and decide, if they were to solve a similar problem, which strategy they would choose, then share with their partner. Then, give them a similar problem and have them try the strategy they selected. Or, ask students to share one big idea they learned from the task. Record the big ideas on the document camera as they share so that students can see the diversity or homogeneity of their ideas.

This is also a time that you can use an exit ticket to gather formative assessment data that will assist you in planning the next lesson. An exit ticket should be short so that you do not give up a significant amount of instructional time at the end of the lesson. The questions can even be generated as you listen to groups' discussion and be put on a Google Form or another convenient survey tool.

Each of the rich algebra tasks has extension questions that can be posed so that the mathematical ideas introduced in the task build in a significant way. For example, in Stack 'em Up! (Chapter 5), students are introduced to exponents with a base of 2 in a task where they tear paper in half, stack it, tear it in half again, and repeat the process 20 times. They will notice a pattern that allows you to introduce exponential form, but the task can be extended to consider the effects of tearing the paper into thirds and doing that 20 times. By comparing the results from the tearing in half to the tearing into thirds or even fourths, students can quickly see the effect that exponential growth has in relation to the magnitude of the result.

The structure of the rich algebra tasks and the extension questions combined creates a path for students to form generalizations. In the case of the Stack 'em Up! task, students may conjecture that if the whole-number exponent greater than 0 remains the same but the base increases by 1, the result will be greater and will differ by an odd number. For example, $2^3 = 8$ and $3^3 = 27$, a difference of 19; $3^3 = 27$ and $4^3 = 64$, a difference of 37. The conjecture creates an opportunity for further investigation to see if this pattern holds and can be formed into a generalization.

As students form conjectures and generalizations, they should archive them in a journal or a shared class document, such as a Google Doc. The conjectures and generalizations can be revisited as students move forward in their learning to refine and reconsider the patterns they noticed. Generalizations in particular help students to determine the reasonableness of their answers, predict outcomes to problems, and make sense of the underlying mathematical ideas and concepts.

Post-Task Notes: Reflections And Next Steps

A lesson is not complete without the final step where, as teachers, we reflect on the implementation of the task to consider how it moved student thinking forward, the way students engaged, the instructional moves that we made, and so on. Reflecting on our implementation improves our professional practice and affords us the opportunity to make the next experience for students even more meaningful.

Sellars (2017) defines reflection as "the deliberate, purposeful, metacognitive thinking and/or action in which educators engage in order to improve their professional practice" (p. 2). This definition prompts us to intentionally replay the lesson and consider how we might change it the next time we use it.

Each task has a set of questions to guide the reflection process. In some tasks, the reflection may be more focused on the mathematics, and in others, the focus may be mostly on the pedagogical aspects. During your reflection, be sure that you write notes that you can refer to when you use the task again.

Summing Up

In this chapter, we focused on the implementation of the tasks by exploring the launch, facilitation, close and generalizations, and reflection parts of the rich algebra tasks. As you do each task yourself, you will gain further insights about the implementation that will maximize student learning. In Chapter 4, we will look at rich algebra tasks that invite students into a mathematical community.

Reflect

Read and discuss the following questions with colleagues in your department.

- What strategies have you used to start your lessons?

- What types of groupings have you used in your mathematics class?

- What advantages does each method for sharing solutions and solution strategies offer?

- How could the interview process support stronger student discourse?

- What type of closing have you used in the past? Are there others you would consider?

- How can you use the generalizations that come from tasks in future lessons?

PART 2

Rich Algebra Tasks

To guide your planning and use of the following chapters, this matrix provides a list of tasks and their associated standards. Keep in mind that even if a task is aligned with a lower grade level than the one you are teaching, it may still provide opportunities for you to (1) connect the new content to prior knowledge, (2) provide a problem-solving experience, or (3) focus on a concept that may not be well developed.

Chapter 4 Tasks to Establish Mathematical Community

	N/A	5. NF	6. RP	6. NS	6. EE	7. NS	7. EE	8. EE	8.F	8. SP	A-SSE	A-APR	A-CED	A-REI	F-IF	F-BF	F-LE
Seeing Squares	X																
The Symmetric Staircase	X																
Change Exchange	X																
Pondering Products		X				X											
Shapely Patterns															X		

Chapter 5 Rational Number Tasks

	N/A	5. NF	6. RP	6. NS	6. EE	7. NS	7. EE	8. EE	8.F	8. SP	A-SSE	A-APR	A-CED	A-REI	F-IF	F-BF	F-LE
See the Sign				X													
Subtraction Traction				X		X											
Integer Attraction				X		X											
If . . . Then											X						
Stack 'em Up!					X												
Powers of Prediction					X												
Berry Interesting											X						

Chapter 6 Expressions Tasks

	N/A	5.NF	6.RP	6.NS	6.EE	7.NS	7.EE	8.EE	8.F	8.SP	A-SSE	A-APR	A-CED	A-REI	F-IF	F-BF	F-LE
Trapezoid Figures					X		X				X						
Sticks and Squares					X		X				X						
Tile Expressions							X										
Be the Matchmaker!					X						X						
Faces, Edges, and Vertices					X		X				X						
Expression Challenge					X		X										
Expression Match-Up					X		X				X						

Chapter 7 Equations Tasks

	N/A	5.NF	6.RP	6.NS	6.EE	7.NS	7.EE	8.EE	8.F	8.SP	A-SSE	A-APR	A-CED	A-REI	F-IF	F-BF	F-LE
Pyramid Problems								X						X			
Cars and Trucks					X		X						X				
Riddle Me This!							X				X		X				
More Than or Less Than							X						X				

(Continued)

	N/A	5.NF	6.RP	6.NS	6.EE	7.NS	7.EE	8.EE	8.F	8.SP	A-SSE	A-APR	A-CED	A-REI	F-IF	F-BF	F-LE
And the Solution Is . . .								X						X			
Eggs-actly								X						X			X

Chapter 8 Linear and Nonlinear Relationship Tasks

	N/A	5.NF	6.RP	6.NS	6.EE	7.NS	7.EE	8.EE	8.F	8.SP	A-SSE	A-APR	A-CED	A-REI	F-IF	F-BF	F-LE
Guess My Rule					X				X						X		
Is It or Isn't It?									X						X	X	X
Reps and More Reps									X				X		X	X	
To the Slopes									X				X		X		
Not Fully Charged			X				X		X								
So Knotty									X						X	X	
Ratios Within									X				X		X	X	
Covered With Paint									X				X		X	X	X
If the Shoe Fits										X			X				

Chapter 9 Systems of Equations Tasks

	N/A	5.NF	6.RP	6.NS	6.EE	7.NS	7.EE	8.EE	8.F	8.SP	A-SSE	A-APR	A-CED	A-REI	F-IF	F-BF	F-LE
Shantelle's Special Number												X	X				
Baskets of Mangoes								X					X	X			
Sets of Systems														X			
Broken Plates								X					X	X			
Exploring Systems of Equations								X						X			

Chapter 10 Polynomial and Rational Expressions and Equations Tasks

	N/A	5.NF	6.RP	6.NS	6.EE	7.NS	7.EE	8.EE	8.F	8.SP	A-SSE	A-APR	A-CED	A-REI	F-IF	F-BF	F-LE
Square Up											X						
Sew, Sew											X		X				
Diagonals Galore														X	X	X	
Sticks and Marshmallows											X					X	X
Paying the Bill												X					
Ivone's Problem												X					

Tasks to Establish Mathematical Community

The tasks in this chapter provide nonroutine problem-solving experiences for your students. As such, they are especially useful in the first two weeks of school when you are establishing your classroom environment and need tasks to support high engagement and interesting discussions. They do not require a high level of procedural competency or fluency but instead focus on identifying patterns, making generalizations, using multiple solution strategies, and promoting creative thinking.

These tasks also offer an opportunity for your class as a whole to reflect on and monitor the norms for their pair or group work. During the closing and generalizations stage of the task, you can have students reflect on how their pair or group worked together and compare their process to the norms you have established. In the initial stages of using these tasks or at the beginning of the school year, the interview protocol introduced in Chapter 3 may provide a way for pairs or groups to document their process, which will enhance their reflection discussion.

The tasks begin with a geometric focus in Seeing Squares and The Symmetric Staircase, which provide a different context for students rather than starting with a numerical or algebraic task. Change Exchange has a unique context that involves patterns that incorporate number and a geometric approach. Students will next confront overgeneralizations they may have made about multiplication in Pondering Products where they have to determine the placement of digits in a three-digit factor times a two-digit factor to create the largest and smallest products possible. Finally, the tasks end with the most complex task of this type, Shapely Patterns, which asks students to generalize the patterns they see in pentagonal numbers that are represented geometrically.

Mathematics Focus

- Students design and apply multiple strategies to solve a problem.

Mathematics Content Standard(s)

- This task was designed to introduce students to problem solving through geometric patterns based on familiar mathematics content as a way to activate prior learning.

Mathematical Practice(s)

- Make sense of problems and persevere in solving them.
- Reason abstractly and quantitatively.
- Attend to precision.
- Look for and express regularity in repeated reasoning.

Vocabulary

- square number

Materials

- 1 Seeing Squares task per pair
- Calculator (optional)

Task 4.1
Seeing Squares

TASK

Seeing Squares

1. How many squares can you and your partner find on this BINGO card?

2. a. Describe the method you and your partner used to solve this problem.

   b. What patterns did you notice?

3. Using your patterns from the BINGO card, what prediction can you make about the number of squares on an ordinary chessboard?

4. a. How many squares did you find on the chessboard?

   b. What generalization can you make that would help you find the number of squares on any $n \times n$ board?

TASK PREPARATION CONSIDERATIONS

- How will I model the introduction of the task?

- Will some or all students need to continue modeling the action to see the patterns?

- What materials will I provide them to do the modeling?

SCAFFOLDING OR DIFFERENTIATING THE TASK

- Use a smaller card with fewer squares.

- Encourage students to use an organized method for counting and keeping track of their counts.

- Have students use highlighters to outline the squares they find (different colors for different sizes).

- Provide frames of squares that are 2 × 2, 3 × 3, and 4 × 4.

WATCH-FORS!

- Students may not think the squares can be overlapping. If they have trouble seeing overlapping squares, have them use a 2 × 2 or 3 × 3 square to overlay and translate across the BINGO card.

EXTEND THE TASK

- Consider a non-square rectangular game board and ask students how they would adjust their method, if at all, for counting and keeping track of the total number of squares.

- If students could use a different-shaped counting unit other than a square, what would be a "good unit" to use, and why?

LAUNCH

1. Show the BINGO card.

   » Tell students that the BINGO card contains a square made up of squares (trace your finger around the larger square).

   » Explain that they are going to determine how many total squares are on the BINGO card.

   » At this point, refrain from telling them that they should look for 2 × 2 and so on. Allow them the opportunity to figure that out.

2. Arrange students in pairs.

Task Type

	Conceptual
	Procedural
	Problem-Solving Application
X	Problem-Solving Critical Thinking

	Reversibility
X	Flexibility
X	Generalization

3. Distribute one student sheet to each pair and give the following directions:

   » Place the student sheet between you and your partner so you can work together.

   » Make sure that you understand each other as you share your ideas.

   » Agree on a shared written explanation.

4. Allow about 15–20 minutes for pairs to work.

FACILITATE

1. Without revealing the solution, identify a pair of students who used an interesting problem-solving method (e.g., an organized method of counting or a unique way of seeing the problem) to share their method.

2. Consider asking questions such as the following for class discussion:

   a. How does the presented method compare to the solution method you used?

   b. Did any pair use a different method?

3. Select a few pairs to share their solutions and discuss as needed.

4. Have students discuss the chessboard questions 3 and 4 and how they might link to strategies they used to solve the BINGO card questions.

EXPECTED SOLUTIONS

1. The BINGO card has 55 squares in all.

2. A chessboard has 204 squares in all.

CLOSE AND GENERALIZATIONS

1. Have the class make connections among the different methods and emphasize the importance of using a systematic and organized counting and recording system.

2. Focus on the generalizations students made so that they can find the number of squares on any $n \times n$ square.

3. Ask the class to reflect on their work in pairs. You may want to use the interview protocol shared in Chapter 3 to motivate their reflection. How can students improve on working together?

4. What organizational strategies did you use so that you could better detect patterns?

TASK 4.1: SEEING SQUARES

 Available to download at **resources.corwin.com/classroomreadymath/algebra**

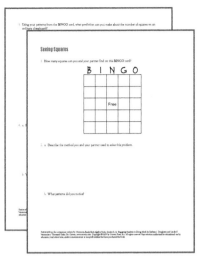

POST-TASK NOTES: REFLECTIONS AND NEXT STEPS

- How did the pairs interact? Do I need to develop a better understanding of how to have mathematics discussions?

- What problem-solving strategies did students use?

- Did students persevere?

- Were they open to considering more solutions than only counting the 1 × 1 squares?

- What were the strengths of their explanations in the whole-class discussion?

Mathematics Focus

- Students use multiple strategies to solve a problem with a geometric context.

Mathematics Content Standard(s)

- This task was designed to introduce students to problem solving through geometric patterns based on familiar mathematics content as a way to activate prior learning.

Mathematical Practice(s)

- Make sense of problems and persevere in solving them.
- Reason abstractly and quantitatively.
- Model with mathematics.
- Look for and make use of structure.
- Look for and express regularity in repeated reasoning.

Vocabulary

- symmetry

Materials

- 1 copy of The Symmetric Staircase task per student
- 30 square tiles per group of 4

Task 4.2
The Symmetric Staircase

TASK

The Symmetric Staircase

1. You would need 16 blocks to build a 4-step symmetric staircase like the one that follows.

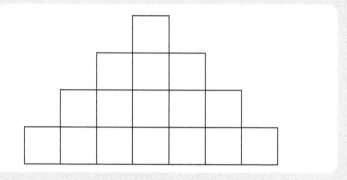

   a. How many blocks would be needed to build a symmetric staircase with 40 steps?

   b. Describe how you solved the problem.

2. a. If you had 360 blocks, what would be the maximum number of steps the staircase could have?

   b. Describe how you solved the problem.

3. a. What is the relationship between the number of blocks needed to build a symmetric staircase and the number of steps in the staircase?

   b. Why is this?

TASK PREPARATION CONSIDERATIONS

- How will I model the introduction of the task?
- Will some or all students need to continue modeling the action to see the patterns?
- What materials will I provide them to do the modeling?

SCAFFOLDING OR DIFFERENTIATING THE TASK

- Suggest students start with a staircase that is smaller. For example, what would a staircase look like if there were 5 tiles on the bottom row? Or 6 tiles on the bottom row? What pattern do you notice?

- Model how to create a table that organizes the number of rows or steps and the total number of tiles.

- Encourage students to use the tiles to model the staircase and physically build the next staircase so they can connect the action with the mathematical representation.

WATCH-FORS!

- Students may misread the problem and confuse the number of steps in a staircase with the number of blocks needed to build the staircase.

EXTEND THE TASK

- Create a geometric explanation to show and explain why the computational method (square the number of steps to find the number of blocks) makes sense.

LAUNCH

1. Using tiles, model a symmetric staircase.

   » Introduce the term *symmetric* as appropriate.

2. Arrange students in groups of 4.

3. Distribute one The Symmetric Staircase task to each student and the square tiles to each group.

4. Allow about 15 minutes for students to work. Students can use square tiles to model the staircase figures.

FACILITATE

1. Identify a variety of solution strategies used by students. Call out a solution strategy, starting with the most concrete, and invite students to share their work if they used the named strategy.

2. Have students discuss and justify their responses as time allows.

3. Have students write a generalization about the number of tiles in a staircase using an algebraic expression. Be sure to identify what the variable represents such as x = the number of steps.

EXPECTED SOLUTIONS

1. 1,600 blocks

2. 18 steps

3. a. The number of steps squared gives you the number of blocks needed to build the double staircase.

Task Type

	Conceptual
	Procedural
	Problem-Solving Application
X	Problem-Solving Critical Thinking

X	Reversibility
X	Flexibility
X	Generalization

CLOSE AND GENERALIZATIONS

1. Have the class make connections among the different solution strategies. Ask: How are they alike? How are they different?

2. Point out how students saw the staircase, how that led to what they counted, and how that was organized in their counting methods.

TASK 4.2: THE SYMMETRIC STAIRCASE

 Available to download at **resources.corwin.com/classroomreadymath/algebra**

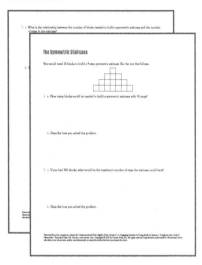

POST-TASK NOTES: REFLECTIONS AND NEXT STEPS

• How did modeling the task with tiles support student learning?

   » Did students model with a semi-concrete representation as well?

• Did students identify multiple patterns? If not, how can I motivate students to find multiple solutions?

• How can I align this task to others where students work with square numbers?

• Could this task be extended to use with functions where the number of steps is the *x*-value and the number of blocks is the *y*-value?

Task 4.3
Change Exchange

TASK

Change Exchange

1. Suppose 30 pennies are lined up on a table. Using a supply of nickels, dimes, quarters, and half-dollars, follow these instructions in the order given.

   a. Replace every second coin with a nickel.

   b. Replace every third coin with a dime.

   c. Replace every fourth coin with a quarter.

   d. Replace every fifth coin with a half-dollar.

2. How much money is on the table after all the exchanges have been made?

3. What patterns did you notice?

4. What exchanges were made if the amount on the table after all exchanges totaled $4.48?

TASK PREPARATION CONSIDERATIONS

- How will I model the introduction of the task?

- Will some or all students need to continue modeling the action to see the patterns?

- What materials will I provide them to do the modeling?

SCAFFOLDING OR DIFFERENTIATING THE TASK

- As a class, have student volunteers take turns to model each step of the original problem.

- Suggest that students model the problem with manipulatives such as chips or cubes.

- Have students use different colors to represent the coins and create a legend to help them remember which one is which.

- Make sure that students know how to count coins.

Mathematics Focus

- Students look for patterns as a strategy for solving nonroutine problems. Students persevere in problem solving through a nonlinear iterative process.

Mathematics Content Standard(s)

- The focus of this task is to introduce students to problem solving through sequencing and patterns based on familiar mathematics content as a way to activate prior learning.

Mathematical Practice(s)

- Make sense of problems and persevere in solving them.

- Reason abstractly and quantitatively.

- Attend to precision.

- Look for and express regularity in repeated reasoning.

Materials

- 1 Change Exchange task per student

- 30 chips or other counters per pair (optional)

Task Type

	Conceptual	
	Procedural	
	Problem-Solving Application	
X	Problem-Solving Critical Thinking	

X	Reversibility
X	Flexibility
X	Generalization

WATCH-FORS!

- Students may not be sure how to count to the ordinal position.

- Students may lose track of the coins they are swapping.

- Students may not be organized in their exchanges.

EXTEND THE TASK

Have students predict what would happen if a sixth coin exchange were added. Then have them test their prediction.

LAUNCH

1. Model the setup of the task with a lower number of coins.

   » Use a similar set of directions and demonstrate the exchange process.

2. Arrange students in pairs.

3. Distribute the Change Exchange task and chips/counters as needed.

4. Allow 10–15 minutes for students to work. Students may want to use chips or draw diagrams to model the actions in the task. Encourage students to devise ways to keep track of all their exchanges.

FACILITATE

1. Monitor the groups. If a group is having difficulty with the problem, consider these questions:

   a. Did you try using a different color or representation for each coin type?

   b. On problem 2, can you find a combination of coins that will give you that amount?

2. Have students share their strategies and solutions. Discuss as needed.

   a. What patterns did you notice as you solved the problem?

   b. How did you keep track of your exchanges?

EXPECTED SOLUTIONS

1. $5.38

2. Start with 30 pennies. Replace every second coin with a half-dollar. Replace every third coin with a nickel. Replace every fourth coin with a dime. Replace every fifth coin with a quarter.

CLOSE AND GENERALIZATIONS

1. Highlight the mathematical patterns students identified and have students share why those patterns make sense.

2. Have students discuss effective ways for keeping track of the exchanges.

3. Ask students to compare this task to Seeing Squares and The Symmetric Staircase. How are the problems alike? How are they different?

4. Have students identify connections in their solution strategies and highlight the mathematical practices that they are developing.

TASK 4.3: CHANGE EXCHANGE

 Available to download at **resources.corwin.com/classroomreadymath/algebra**

POST-TASK NOTES: REFLECTIONS AND NEXT STEPS

• Did students use any of the solution strategies from the previous tasks to get started with this one?

• Was modeling a simpler problem in the launch sufficient for students to understand the task?

• Were the manipulatives students used the best choice for the task?

• What strategies did students use when they were "stuck"?

Mathematics Focus

- Students generalize that the magnitude of the product is dependent on the place value of the digits in multidigit factors.

Mathematics Content Standard(s)

- 5.NF.5a: Interpret multiplication as scaling (resizing), by comparing the size of a product to the size of one factor on the basis of the size of the other factor, without performing the indicated multiplication.

- 7.NS.2: Apply and extend previous understandings of multiplication and division of fractions to multiply and divide rational numbers.

Mathematical Practice(s)

- Make sense of problems and persevere in solving them.
- Reason abstractly and quantitatively.
- Use appropriate tools strategically.
- Attend to precision.
- Look for and make use of structure.

Vocabulary

- product
- factor
- digit

Task 4.4
Pondering Products

TASK

Pondering Products

1. Of the digits 1–9, select any five different digits. For example, someone might select 2, 3, 6, 8, and 9. Record the digits you select in the space provided. Write each digit you selected on a sticky note or use number tiles with these digits.

2. Using each of your digits only once, form a two-digit number and a three-digit number whose product is as *large* as possible. Other groups may find a larger product using numbers formed with different digits, but your product should be as large as possible with *your* selected digits.

3. Kory arranged the digits 1, 2, 7, 8, and 9 into a two-digit factor. How might Kory have arranged the digits so that his product was the largest possible with these digits?

4. Using the digits from problem 3, arrange them into a two-digit number and a three-digit number whose product is the smallest possible.

5. What patterns do you notice for finding the smallest product?

TASK PREPARATION CONSIDERATIONS

- Will any students need support related to the general concepts of multidigit multiplication?

SCAFFOLDING OR DIFFERENTIATING THE TASK

- Demonstrate how to use the number tiles as tools to quickly form multidigit numbers and explore products.

- Assist the students in using a systematic process to keep track of their factors and products.

- Ask them how their previous experiences (e.g., solving the BINGO card problem) could help with a strategy to solve this problem.

- Be sure that students are using calculators to find the products rather than computing.

WATCH-FORS!

- Students may overlook the effects of multiplication with regrouping.

EXTEND THE TASK

- Have students select six digits from 1 to 9. How would they place the digits to form the largest product? The smallest product?

LAUNCH

1. Arrange students in groups of 4.

2. Distribute one Pondering Products task to each student and number tiles or small sticky notes and a calculator to each group.

3. Allow 10 minutes for students to work.

4. Monitor the groups. If a group is having difficulty with the problem, you may consider asking some of these questions:

   a. Have you tried putting the largest digit in different place value positions in the factors?

   b. How have you kept track of the arrangements of digits in the factors you have tried?

FACILITATE

1. After 10 minutes, do a check-in with all groups.

   a. Ask one or two groups to share their solution to the largest product.

   b. Ask other groups if it is possible to find a larger product with the digits the groups that shared used.

   c. If the factors are not arranged to get the largest product, tell them it is possible to get a larger product.

2. Allow 5 more minutes for students to work.

3. Allow at least 10 minutes to facilitate class discussion on the solution.

EXPECTED SOLUTIONS

2. Using *A* as the largest digit and *E* as the smallest digit, generalize the place value position of each digit to produce the largest product. The generalization for the largest product using five different digits is BCE × AD.

3. 871 × 92

Materials

- 1 Pondering Products task per student
- Number tiles 1–9 or 9 small blank sticky notes per group
- 1 calculator per group of 4

Task Type

X	Conceptual
X	Procedural
	Problem-Solving Application
	Problem-Solving Critical Thinking

X	Reversibility
	Flexibility
X	Generalization

4. 179 × 28

5. Students may notice that the placement of the smallest digit is in the tens place of the two-digit factor. Using *A* as the largest digit and *E* as the smallest digit, to generalize the place value position of each digit to produce the smallest product using five digits is DBA × EC.

CLOSE AND GENERALIZATIONS

1. Have the class focus on their strategies for finding the largest (smallest) products.

2. Make connections between strategies and discuss any concerns about efficiency and accuracy.

3. Have students discuss their pattern for finding the largest product of a two-digit number and a three-digit number. Describe the pattern with words and with algebraic symbols.

4. Assign each digit a variable, such as *A* as the largest digit, *B* as the next-largest digit, and so on through *E* as the smallest digit. Determine a generalization about the placement of the digits for the largest and the smallest products.

5. Ask students to compare the result with multiplication to a similar task\with addition. Would they place the digits in the same way in order to get the largest (smallest) sum? Why?

TASK 4.4: PONDERING PRODUCTS

 Available to download at **resources.corwin.com/classroomreadymath/algebra**

Pondering Products

1. Of the digits 1–9, select any five different digits. For example, someone might select 2, 3, 6, 8, and 9. Record the digits you select in the space provided. Write each digit you selected on a sticky note or use number tiles with these digits.

2. Using each of your digits only once, form a two-digit number and a three-digit number whose product is as large as possible. Other groups may find a larger product using numbers formed with different digits, but your product should be as large as possible with your selected digits.

3. Kory arranged the digits 1, 2, 7, 8, and 9 into a two-digit factor. How might Kory have arranged the digits so that his product was the largest possible with these digits?

4. Using the digits from problem 3, arrange them into a two-digit number and a three-digit number whose product is the smallest possible.

5. What pattern do you notice for finding the smallest product?

POST-TASK NOTES: REFLECTIONS AND NEXT STEPS

- What overgeneralizations did students have about the place value of digits and their effect on the product?

- What other ways could I facilitate the whole-class discussion?

- How have the discussions in pairs (or groups) evolved since the first task?

- How might I adapt the task to use it with division?

Mathematics Focus

- Students create and apply strategies to determine and describe nonlinear visual patterns.

Mathematics Content Standard(s)

- F-IF.9: Compare properties of two functions each represented in a different way (algebraically, graphically, numerically in a table, or by verbal descriptions).

Mathematical Practice(s)

- Make sense of problems and persevere in solving them.
- Reason abstractly and quantitatively.
- Model with mathematics.
- Look for and make use of structure.
- Look for and express regularity in repeated reasoning.

Vocabulary

- base
- exponent
- exponential notation

Task 4.5
Shapely Patterns

TASK

Shapely Patterns

1. a. Use the following diagrams to complete this table. Continue the pattern to find the number of dots for diagram numbers 3 through 7, 10, and 20.

Diagram number	Number of dots
1	1
2	5
3	
4	
5	
6	
7	
10	
20	

b. The pattern creates growing pentagons. The number of dots in each diagram represents a pentagonal number. What patterns did you notice to help you complete the table?

2. Triangular numbers can be shown with the following diagrams.

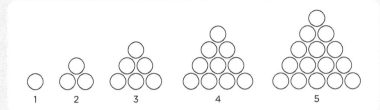

The table for triangular numbers looks like this:

Diagram number	Number of dots
1	1
2	3
3	6
4	10
5	15
10	55
20	210

a. What patterns do you notice about triangular numbers?

b. What do you notice about triangular numbers and their relationship to pentagonal numbers?

Materials

- 1 Shapely Patterns task per student
- 1 calculator per pair
- Round counters for each pair (optional)
- Colored pencils for each pair (optional)

Task Type

	Conceptual
	Procedural
	Problem-Solving Application
X	Problem-Solving Critical Thinking

	Reversibility
X	Flexibility
X	Generalization

TASK PREPARATION CONSIDERATIONS

- How will I introduce the task?

- How will I encourage students to move beyond counting the dots individually?

- How will I encourage more sophisticated thinking if students do not see patterns?

- What materials will I provide them to do the modeling?

SCAFFOLDING OR DIFFERENTIATING THE TASK

- Model how to complete the table by filling out the number of dots for the first three diagram numbers.

- Ask students to notice what stays the same and what changes from one figure to the next.

- Have students consider coloring each diagram in one color, then carrying that color over to the next diagram but using a different color to show the added part.

- Have students work in pairs so they can explain their thinking and discuss patterns before sharing out with the class.

- Provide isometric or grid papers to support building the figures.

- Change the task to triangles and triangular numbers.

WATCH-FORS!

- Students may fixate on the shape and overlook the dots that are not on the vertices of the pentagons.

- Students may only use one row or column in the table to create a generalization rather than use covariational thinking.

- Students may think that the generalization can only be linear.

EXTENDING THE TASK

- Develop algebraic expressions or equations to generalize the patterns students notice.

- Have students create their own growing patterns with different polygons and challenge their classmates to find the pattern.

LAUNCH

1. Build the first three figures in the pattern with students.

    » Ask them to describe what is happening as they move from figure 1 to figure 2, then from figure 2 to figure 3.

2. Arrange students in pairs.

3. Distribute one Shapely Patterns task to each student and a calculator to each pair.

4. Allow 15 minutes for students to work.

FACILITATE

1. Monitor the pairs. If a pair is having difficulty with the problem, you may consider making suggestions or asking these questions:

    » Try drawing a diagram or using round counters to model the problem.

    » Consider coloring each diagram in one color, then carrying that color over to the next diagram but using a different color to show the added part.

    What do you notice about the increase in the number of dots as the diagrams grow?

2. a. Have pairs compare their findings to the pentagon dots problem. Have at least one pair share their table. Ask students to compare their tables to the one shared and resolve any discrepancies.

    b. Have students in the whole class share patterns they see in the table or their responses to question 2a.

3. Have students discuss their findings.

   » What patterns do you notice about triangular numbers?

   » What do you notice about triangular numbers and their relationship to pentagonal numbers?

EXPECTED SOLUTION

Diagram number	Number of dots
1	1
2	5
3	**12**
4	**22**
5	**35**
6	**51**
7	**70**
10	**145**
20	**590**

Per diagram number, pentagonal numbers are larger than triangular numbers by $x(x - 1)$, where x is the diagram number.

CLOSE AND GENERALIZATIONS

1. Ask students if they found a way to represent a general solution for either the pentagon dots pattern or the triangular dots pattern. Have the class check each general solution (equation) to see if it yields the correct number of dots.

2. Ask students to compare the task structure to The Symmetric Staircase. How are the tasks alike? How are they different?

3. How did solving The Symmetric Staircase help the students solve this task?

4. Ask students, "How did your pair work together? Was it productive? If yes, what did you do to make it productive? If no, what could you do next time that would make your pair work more effectively together?"

TASK 4.5: SHAPELY PATTERNS

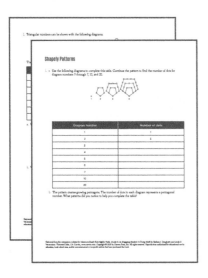

POST-TASK NOTES: REFLECTIONS AND NEXT STEPS

• What grouping structures are working well? What do I need to change?

• Are the whole-class discussions productive? If yes, what have I implemented that has supported them? If no, what can I do to make them more productive?

• How quickly did students engage in the task?

• Was the mathematics at the right level for the students?

• Could this task provide another context for a functions task by graphing the diagram number as the x-value and the number of dots as the y-value?

Rational Number Tasks

The tasks in this chapter focus on number, including integers and rational numbers. The integer tasks in this chapter focus on both conceptual understandings and procedural skills. Concrete materials such as two-color counters are used to provide visual representations of integers so that students think of them as more than numerical symbols. As students model with concrete materials, they should be drawing the representations and writing the mathematical symbols to create connections across the representations. In our classroom tests, we used two-color counters with red representing –1 and yellow representing +1 as the physical material. You can adapt the tasks for the materials you have available.

The first task, See the Sign, emphasizes the concrete representation of integers and models the "opposite" aspect so that students understand that, for example, –7 is the opposite of 7. From this conceptual task, the next two tasks, Subtraction Traction and Integer Attraction, move into integer addition and subtraction, and the following task, If . . . Then, provides students with the opportunity to generalize the results of computations without using specific values. From there, the tasks involve nonroutine contexts that include other representations of number with Stack 'em Up! and Powers of Prediction related to exponential growth and patterns with powers. The last task, Berry Interesting, is an engaging nonroutine problem that may bring out students' misconceptions about proportions and prompt the use of variables to represent a specific unknown quantity.

Mathematics Content Standard(s)

- 6.NS.5: Understand that positive and negative numbers are used together to describe quantities having opposite directions or values.

Mathematical Practice(s)

- Reason abstractly and quantitatively.
- Model with mathematics.
- Use appropriate tools strategically.
- Attend to precision.

Vocabulary

- integer
- representation
- zero pair
- identity property of addition

Materials

- 1 See the Sign task per student
- 25 counters, a mix of black and white, per pair (substitute as needed)

Task 5.1
See the Sign

TASK

See the Sign

1. a. Using integer units, make a model for 5. Draw a representation of your model.

   b. Draw two more different representations for 5.

   c. What is the minimum number of integer units you need to represent 5? Why?

   d. Draw a representation of 5 that uses each of the following.

1) 7 integer units	2) 9 integer units
3) 12 integer units	4) 15 integer units

   e. What do you notice about the representations you drew?

2. a. Draw a representation of –4 that uses each of the following:

1) 6 integer units	2) 8 integer units
3) 13 integer units	4) 16 integer units

   b. What do you notice about the representations you drew?

   c. What is the minimum number of integer units you need to represent –4? Why?

3. a. Show at least three ways to represent 0.

   b. Is 0 positive or negative? How does representing 0 with the integer units support your answer?

4. a. How are the representations for 6 and –6 alike?

   b. How are they different?

5. What have you noticed about representing positive and negative numbers?

TASK PREPARATION CONSIDERATIONS

- How will I introduce the concrete representations for integers and guide students to use the tools strategically?

- What other integer models have students used? How will these models help or hinder their work with the counters?

SCAFFOLDING OR DIFFERENTIATING THE TASK

- Provide additional practice in modeling integers before students move to the task.

- Have students place the minimal number of integer units to represent a number in a row and then add the zero pairs to create other representations.

Zero
pair

WATCH-FORS!

- Students may think a representation of 5 could be 3 positive and 2 negative units because the total number of unit pieces is 5.

- Students may say they are "canceling out" when they create a zero pair.

EXTEND THE TASK

Encourage students to think of different representations by asking questions such as the following:

- How many different ways can you represent 5 using a combination of positive and negative integer units?

- What integer units could you add to an arrangement so that its value remains the same?

LAUNCH

1. Arrange students in pairs.

2. Show various models for students to practice determining the values to familiarize themselves with the manipulative. Have them model with you. In this example, each black integer unit represents 1, and each white integer unit represents –1. You may need to adjust based on the manipulative you use. The convention of writing positive numbers without the preceding plus (+) symbol will be followed from the outset but should be verbalized in initial lessons during discussions.

Task Type

X	Conceptual
X	Procedural
	Problem-Solving Application
	Problem-Solving Critical Thinking

	Reversibility
	Flexibility
X	Generalization

Examples:

a. (-3)

b. (6)

c. (0)

d. (3) ●●●●○

3. Students may notice statements such as 4 + (–1) = 3 also fit a model where there are 4 black integer units and 1 white integer unit. These observations should be acknowledged, but the intent of this exploration is on integer representations. A subsequent exploration on representations for addition and subtraction focuses on the modeling of operations.

4. Distribute the See the Sign task to each student.

5. Allow about 20 minutes for students to work.

FACILITATE

1. Select several students to share their representations and discuss their solutions as time allows. Focus on patterns students notice and any generalizations they may make.

2. Accept models that represent the target integer—for example, a drawing of 5 positive integer units and a zero pair (6 positive and 1 negative units).

3. Encourage students to think of different representations by asking questions such as the following:

   » How can you represent the integer using a combination of positive and negative integer units?

   » What number added to another number will not change its sum? This is an opportunity to relate this to the identity property of addition.

   » What units could you add to an arrangement so that its value remains the same?

EXPECTED SOLUTIONS

1. c. Students need a minimum of 5 positive (black) integer units. Students may explain that since each black integer unit represents 1, then 5 of these units represent 5 (i.e., +5).

   e. Students should notice that to represent 5, an odd number of integer units are needed, with a minimum of 5 integer units.

2. b. Students should notice that to represent –4, an even number of integer units is needed. They cannot model –4 with an odd number of integer units.

   c. Four negative (white) integer units are required for the minimum number. Students may explain that since each white integer unit represents –1, then 4 of these units represent –4.

3. a. Answers will vary. Any representation should show equal numbers of positive (black) and negative (white) integer units. Students may refer to a white integer unit with a black integer unit (or vice versa) as a "zero pair." Students should be discouraged from saying that a red integer unit and a white integer unit "cancel each other out."

b. Zero is neither positive nor negative. Responses should include an observation that each positive integer unit is paired with a negative integer unit and there are no "extra" positive or negative integer units.

4. a. Answers will vary. Students often say that the minimum number of integer units needed to represent 6 and –6 is 6 integer units each. Any other representations require an even number of integer units greater than 6 since it must involve additional zero pairs.

   b. Answers will vary. Students often comment that to represent 6 requires more positive integer units than negative ones. To represent –6 requires more negative integer units than positive ones.

5. Answers will vary as students generalize about using the integer units.

CLOSE AND GENERALIZATIONS

1. Ask students to describe a zero pair. (The term *zero pairs* can be used to describe equal numbers of positive and negative integer units.)

2. What property of addition does the use of a zero pair demonstrate? (Identity property of addition. Any number of zero pairs can be added without changing the value of the represented integer.)

3. What big ideas are you taking away from the lesson?

TASK 5.1: SEE THE SIGN

online resources 🔍 Available to download at **resources.corwin.com/classroomreadymath/algebra**

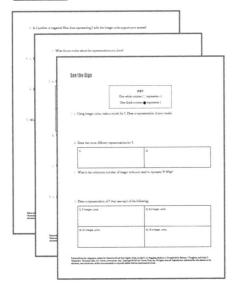

POST-TASK NOTES: REFLECTIONS AND NEXT STEPS

- How did the use of a concrete material support student learning?

- Were students familiar with the identity property of addition?

- Do students have sufficient conceptual understanding to move to semi-concrete or abstract? Which students would benefit from having concrete materials available?

Task 5.2
Subtraction Traction

TASK

Subtraction Traction

1. Draw negative and positive units that model the operation to find the difference and sum.

a. −4 − (−3)	−4 + 3
b. 2 − 7	2 + (−7)

2. Tyson said, "I think there's a pattern between the problems in 1.a and the problems in 1.b."

   a. What do you notice about the problems in 1.a?

   b. What do you notice about the problems in 1.b?

3. Draw negative and positive units to model the difference and sum indicated. Record the result of each operation.

−5 − 4	−5 + (−4)

4. Tyson thought he saw a pattern and began writing a statement. Complete what you think his statement might be.

   For any numbers a and b, a minus b is equal to a plus _____.

TASK PREPARATION CONSIDERATIONS

• How can negative and positive units be used to model subtraction?

• What other models for subtraction have students used? What challenges or opportunities do such prior experiences provide?

Mathematics Focus

• Students model subtraction with integer tiles to activate prior learning.

Mathematics Content Standard(s)

• 6.NS.7: Understand ordering and absolute value of rational numbers.

• 7.NS.1: Apply and extend previous understanding of addition and subtraction to add and subtract rational numbers.

Mathematical Practice(s)

• Reason abstractly and quantitatively.

• Model with mathematics.

• Use appropriate tools strategically.

• Attend to precision.

Vocabulary

• integer

• representation

• zero pair

• definition of subtraction

Materials

• 1 Subtraction Traction task per student

• 25 counters, a mix of black and white, per pair

Task Type

X	Conceptual
X	Procedural
	Problem-Solving Application
	Problem-Solving Critical Thinking

	Reversibility
	Flexibility
X	Generalization

SCAFFOLDING OR DIFFERENTIATING THE TASK

• Connect this model of subtraction to the takeaway model of subtraction with whole numbers.

• Relate the use of zero pairs to the identity property of addition.

• Ask students how they have previously modeled subtraction using manipulatives. Have them consider why a different model would be needed for subtraction with positive and negative integers.

WATCH-FORS!

• Students may not be familiar with different models of subtraction, including the takeaway model, finding a missing addend, and comparing the difference between two quantities.*

• Students may verbalize or read $-b$ as "negative b" rather than "the opposite of b" and thus think that $-b$ will be a negative value.

• Students may confuse the symbol – with the value of a number and the operation of subtraction.

• Students may try to model the subtraction by using the values of both the minuend and the subtrahend. They only need the representation for the minuend.

EXTEND THE TASK

• Construct more generalizations by asking students questions such as (1) Do you expect the difference between two negative numbers will always be negative? Why or why not?; (2) Is subtraction commutative?; (3) Do you expect the sum of two negative numbers will always be negative?; and so on.

LAUNCH

1. Distribute a set of positive (black) and negative (white) units to each pair and a Subtraction Traction task to each student.

---

* Examples of the types of subtraction include the following.

• Takeaway: Jon had 26 apples. He gave 14 to Maria. How many does he have left?

• Missing addend: Jon had 26 apples. Maria had 12 apples. How many more apples does Maria need to have as many as Jon?

• Comparison: Jon had 26 apples. Maria had 12 apples. How many more apples does Jon have than Maria?

2. Review the takeaway approach with problems such as 5 – 2 and –3 – (–4) by modeling with negative and positive units (see the examples that follow).

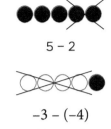

5 – 2

–3 – (–4)

Point out the strategy of adding one white and one black unit (–1 + 1 = 0, a zero pair) to create the needed conditions.

3. Have students work in pairs for about 15–20 minutes.

FACILITATE

1. Monitor to ensure students use the units to represent and solve the problems.

2. Discuss students' solutions as time allows.

EXPECTED SOLUTIONS

1. Students should describe the reasoning behind their models with negative and positive units. Students should note that when there are insufficient units to remove, they add in zero pairs.

2. a. Answers may vary. For example, students may say that subtracting –3 from –4 gives the same result (–1) as adding 3 to –4.

   b. Answers may vary. For example, students may say that subtracting 7 from 2 gives the same result (–5) as adding –7 to 2. Some students may describe that subtracting a number from another number gives the same result as adding its opposite to that number.

CLOSE AND GENERALIZATIONS

1. Discuss the generalization of the definition of subtraction by asking students to discuss question 4 on the task sheet.

   » For any numbers a and b, a minus b is equal to a plus the opposite of b.

   » Have students apply the definition to whole number or rational number subtraction such as 5 – 3 so that they see that it holds for any type of numbers.

TASK 5.2: SUBTRACTION TRACTION

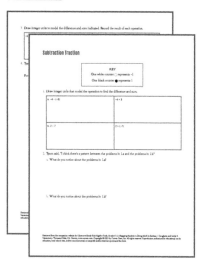

POST-TASK NOTES: REFLECTIONS AND NEXT STEPS

• How does this task support students' understanding of the definition of subtraction as opposed to only telling them the rule?

• How can this model be used with other physical materials to represent rational number subtraction?

Task 5.3
Integer Attraction

TASK

Integer Attraction

1. Kevin used integer units to show –5 + 8 = 3. Show how he may have done this and describe how you think he might explain his reasoning.

2. a. Shyla let  represent –1 and ● represent 1. What addition problem could she be showing? Explain your thinking.

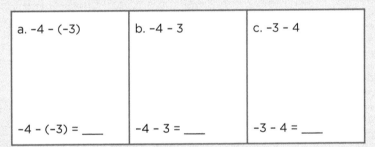

   b. Write an addition/subtraction fact team that Shyla's integer units represent.

   c. Shyla says that her integer units can show that 2 – (–4) = 6. Explain what you think she means.

3. Show how you would use integer units to model the subtraction and find each difference.

a. –4 – (–3)	b. –4 – 3	c. –3 – 4
–4 – (–3) = ___	–4 – 3 = ___	–3 – 4 = ___

4. Dex showed –4 – 3 in three steps. Write an explanation for each step that might describe her thinking.

Step 1   Step 2   Step 3

TASK PREPARATION CONSIDERATIONS

- How will I introduce the concrete representations for integers and guide students to use the tools strategically?

- Have we done sufficient modeling of integers?

- How will I help students make connections among the concrete, semi-concrete, and abstract representations?

Mathematics Focus

- Students model the addition and subtraction of integers using concrete, semi-concrete, and abstract representations.

Mathematics Content Standard(s)

- 6.NS.7: Understand ordering and absolute value of rational numbers.

- 7.NS.1: Apply and extend previous understanding of addition and subtraction to add and subtract rational numbers.

Mathematical Practice(s)

- Reason abstractly and quantitatively.

- Model with mathematics.

- Use appropriate tools strategically.

- Attend to precision.

- Look for and express regularity in repeated reasoning.

Vocabulary

- integer

- representation

- zero pair

- fact team or fact family

Materials

- 1 Integer Attraction task per student
- 25 counters, a mix of black and white, per pair

Task Type

X	Conceptual
X	Procedural
	Problem-Solving Application
	Problem-Solving Critical Thinking

	Reversibility
	Flexibility
X	Generalization

SCAFFOLDING OR DIFFERENTIATING THE TASK

- Connect this model of subtraction to the takeaway model of subtraction with whole numbers.

- Relate the use of zero pairs to the identity property of addition.

- Ask students how they have previously modeled subtraction using manipulatives. Have them consider why a different model would be needed for subtraction with positive and negative integers.

WATCH-FORS!

- Students may try to take away the number of tiles without regard for the available tiles in their models and may not think about adding sufficient zero pairs to be able to subtract the given integer.

- Students may use a set of tiles to represent the minuend and another set to represent the subtrahend in subtraction problems. They only need to represent the minuend.

EXTEND THE TASK

- Tell students you modeled an addition problem and got the sum of –7. What was the addition problem you modeled? Have them create the model and provide the equation.

- Tell students you modeled a subtraction problem and got the difference of 4. What was the subtraction problem you modeled? Have them create the model and provide the equation.

LAUNCH

1. Before distributing the exploration, have students define *addition*. Focus on notions of combining or joining. Display a sample representation of positive and negative units. Students should draw the representation and write an addition equation for that set of integers.

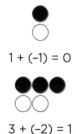

$$1 + (-1) = 0$$

$$3 + (-2) = 1$$

2. Have students define *subtraction*. They will likely be familiar with the takeaway model of subtraction. Other models they should discuss or be reminded of are subtraction as finding a missing addend and subtraction as comparing the difference between two quantities.

3. The takeaway approach will be used in this exploration. Begin with class discussion on problems such as 5 – 2 and –3 – (–4) by modeling with integer units.

4. Distribute the task following the discussion and allow about 20 minutes for students to work in pairs.

FACILITATE

1. Monitor the pairs as they work.

2. Discuss students' solutions as time allows by having pairs share the representations and explanations.

EXPECTED SOLUTIONS

1. Answers will vary. Responses should offer an explanation and accompanying visual representation with integer units. Students should notice that the combining action associated with addition gives 5 zero pairs with 3 positive integer units remaining.

2. a. Answers may vary. For example, they may say 6 + (–4) = 2 or 0 + 2 = 2.

   b. Answers may vary. For example,

$$6 + (-4) = 2$$
$$-4 + 6 = 2$$
$$2 - 6 = -4$$
$$2 - (-4) = 6$$

   c. Responses should indicate that to subtract 4 negative integer (white) units, zero pair integer units (1 white and 1 black) must be added to the 2 positive integer units (black) until there are 4 negative integer units to subtract or take away.

3. Example solutions are shown. Responses should clearly show an accurate model for each problem. Remind students to show the action used in each operation, such as to take away for subtraction. Answers should be clearly identified.

a. –4 – (–3)	b. –4 – 3	c. –3 – 4
Represent –4, then remove –3. The difference is –1.	See problem 4 in the task.	Represent –3. Add 4 zero pairs so the value remains –3, but 4 can be subtracted. The difference is –7. 

CLOSE AND GENERALIZATIONS

1. Have students make connections between the modeling and representing of integer addition and subtraction and modeling and representing along a number line. Be sure to note how the model with the integer units focuses on the strategic use of zero pairs.

2. Depending on students' experience with integers, ask if they noticed any patterns in subtraction. (They may notice that the difference in a subtraction problem is the same as the sum of adding the opposite.)

TASK 5.3: INTEGER ATTRACTION

 Available to download at **resources.corwin.com/classroomreadymath/algebra**

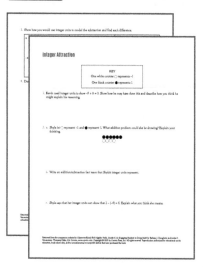

POST-TASK NOTES: REFLECTIONS AND NEXT STEPS

• How can I connect fact teams (or fact families) to other contexts such as solving linear equations?

• Is students' conceptual understanding sufficient, or is more modeling needed?

• How does this task support students' understanding of the definition of subtraction as opposed to only telling them the rule?

• How can this model be used with other physical materials to represent rational number subtraction?

Task 5.4
If . . . Then

TASK

If . . . Then

1. If $\square > 0$ and $\triangle > 0$, then what do you know about each of the following?

   a. $\square + \triangle$　　　　b. $\square \times \triangle$　　　　c. $\square - \triangle$

2. If $\square < 0$ and $\triangle > 0$, then what do you know about each of the following?

   a. $\square \times \triangle$?　　　　b. $\square + \triangle$?　　　　c. $\triangle - \square$?

3. If $\square > 0$ and $\triangle > 0$, then what do you know about $\square \div \triangle$?

4. Naomi said, "$\square$ and $\triangle$ are both positive when their difference is positive." Do you agree with Naomi? Explain why you agree or disagree.

TASK PREPARATION CONSIDERATIONS

- How will I remind students how to read and interpret the nonnumeric "greater than" and "less than" statements?

SCAFFOLDING OR DIFFERENTIATING THE TASK

- Provide an example with only whole numbers, such as the following: Let $a > 50$, and b is any number between 100 and 200. What can you say about the sum of $a + b$? The difference of $b - a$?

- Have students assign values to the variables and do the computations. Make sure they use multiple examples to see the pattern.

- Change the range of values for the variables to fit with students' needs.

WATCH-FORS!

- Students may substitute values for the variables that lead to inaccurate generalizations.

- Students may have trouble stating accurate generalizations, or they may create an inverse statement that is not true.

- Students may think that the values can only be integral, which may affect their responses.

Mathematics Focus

- Students generalize outcomes from operations with nonnumeric quantities.

Mathematics Content Standard(s)

- A-SSE.1: Interpret expressions that represent a quantity in terms of its context.

Mathematical Practice(s)

- Make sense of problems and persevere in solving them.
- Reason abstractly and quantitatively.
- Look for and make use of structure.

Vocabulary

- absolute value
- greater than
- less than

Materials

- 1 If . . . Then task per student

Task Type

X	Conceptual
	Procedural
	Problem-Solving Application
X	Problem-Solving Critical Thinking

	Reversibility
	Flexibility
X	Generalization

EXTEND THE TASK

- Have students write their arguments to convince a skeptic that the generalizations they found will always be true.

LAUNCH

- Arrange students in pairs.

- Distribute the If . . . Then task.

- Allow 10 minutes for students to solve the problems and write their reasoning.

FACILITATE

1. Have students describe their thinking to support their answers.

2. Invite students to refute an answer with a counterexample.

EXPECTED SOLUTIONS

1. a. The sum is greater than 0.

    b. The product is greater than 0.

    c. The difference will be greater than 0 if the first quantity is greater than the second. The difference will be less than 0 if the second quantity is greater than the first. The difference will be 0 if the quantities are equal.

2. a. The product is negative.

    b. The sum is greater than 0 if the absolute value of $\triangle$ is greater than the absolute value of $\square$. If the absolute value of $\square$ is greater than the absolute value of $\triangle$, then the sum is less than 0. If the absolute values of $\square$ and $\triangle$ are equal, then the sum is 0.

    c. The difference will always be positive.

3. If the first quantity is greater than the second, then the quotient will be greater than 1. If the first quantity is less than 1, then the quotient will be less than 1. If the quantities are equal, then the quotient is 1.

4. Naomi's statement is incorrect. A counterexample such as $2 - (-6) = 8$ proves that the statement is false.

CLOSE AND GENERALIZATIONS

1. Have students consider the outcomes of the computations. For example, if two integers are the divisor and dividend, will the quotient also be an integer? Connect this to the closure property.

2. Provide other generalized relationships and ask students to determine the expected response. For example, if $0 < a < \frac{1}{2}$ and $0 < b < \frac{1}{2}$, what do you know about ab?

TASK 5.4: IF . . . THEN

POST-TASK NOTES: REFLECTIONS AND NEXT STEPS

• How are we documenting the generalizations we make? Should we use a shared document such as a Google Doc to record them? Which, if any, should students record in their notebook?

• What other generalizations should I include moving forward so that students focus on the big idea?

• How can I use these generalizations to motivate students to predict the magnitude or type of answer they expect from a computation?

Mathematics Focus

- Students create the context, collect and analyze data, and articulate exponential growth as a consistent growth rate that increases rapidly as total growth numbers or quantities increase.

Mathematics Content Standard(s)

- 6.EE.1: Write and evaluate numerical expressions involving whole-number exponents.

Mathematical Practice(s)

- Make sense of problems and persevere in solving them.
- Reason abstractly and quantitatively.
- Model with mathematics.
- Look for and express regularity in repeated reasoning.

Vocabulary

- base
- exponent
- exponential notation

Task 5.5
Stack 'em Up!

TASK

Stack 'em Up!

1. Record the prediction you made about the expected height of the paper stack.

2. Use a sheet of paper and test your prediction. Record your findings in the table.

   a. What height did you find?

   b. Describe your method for determining the height of the stack.

No. of tears	No. of pieces	Height (inches)

3. a. What relationship do you notice between the number of tears and the number of pieces?

   b. What relationship do you notice between the number of pieces and the height?

   c. What relationship do you notice between the number of tears and the height?

4. a. How close to your prediction is the actual height you found?

   b. What might explain the difference between your prediction and the actual height you found?

TASK PREPARATION CONSIDERATIONS

- How will I model the introduction of the task?

- Will some or all students need to continue modeling the action to see the patterns?

- What materials will I provide them to do the modeling?

SCAFFOLDING OR DIFFERENTIATING THE TASK

• Allow students to model with tearing and stacking paper until they see the pattern.

• Model how to complete the table.

• Support students who struggle with computations by providing a calculator.

• Have students work in pairs so they can explain their thinking and discuss patterns before sharing out with the class.

WATCH-FORS!

• Students may assume an exponent of 2 is the same as multiplying by 2.

• Students may think 2^3 is the same as 2 + 2 + 2 because they think of multiplication as repeated addition.

EXTEND THE TASK

• Change the number of tears to produce thirds instead of halves.

• Reduce the number of tears.

• Have students make a prediction about tripling and then extending to n tears.

LAUNCH

• Place students in pairs.

• Show students a piece of paper.

  Tell them you are going to tear the paper in half and stack it.

  Ask them to predict how many pieces you will have.

  Then demonstrate the tearing and stacking (just once).

• Tell them you are going to tear the *new stack* in half.

  Ask them to predict how many pieces of paper you will have at the end of the tear.

  Demonstrate the tearing and stacking.

  Have students verify the number of pieces you have now.

• Tell students that you are going to keep doing this until you have torn and stacked the paper 20 times.

• Remind them about the information in the problem—the paper is about 0.003 inch thick.

Materials

• Calculator (1 per pair of students)

• 1 Stack 'em Up! task per student

• 8.5 × 11–inch paper (1 sheet per pair) and scissors (optional)

Task Type

X	Conceptual
	Procedural
	Problem-Solving Application
	Problem-Solving Critical Thinking

	Reversibility
	Flexibility
X	Generalization

- Ask them to predict how tall they think the stack of paper will be if you do the tearing and stacking 20 times. No paper-and-pencil or calculator computations allowed! Allow only about 10–15 seconds for students to think.

- Ask them to share with their partner, then have pairs share out their predictions.

- Record their predictions as they share but don't comment on them.

- Distribute calculators and task sheets to pairs.

- If needed, distribute an 8.5 × 11–inch sheet of paper and a pair of scissors for pairs to test their predictions.

FACILITATE

1. Have pairs compare their findings to their predictions. Typically, there are large discrepancies between the prediction and the actual calculation. Have at least one pair share their table. Ask students to compare their tables to the one shared and resolve any discrepancies.

   a. Ask students what caused the discrepancy.

2. Have students as a whole class share patterns they see in the table or their responses to questions 3 and 4. Students may notice any of the following:

   a. The number of pieces is 2 to the power of the number of tears. Students may wonder if $2^0 = 1$; this may come up later when properties of exponents are explored (e.g., $\frac{2^x}{2^x} = 2^{x-x}$).

   b. Students may point out a doubling pattern with consecutive heights or describe that the height is the product of 0.003 (thickness of paper) and the number of pieces.

   c. The height is the product of 0.003 (thickness of paper) and 2 to the power of the number of tears.

3. Introduce exponential form using student data and the vocabulary of *base* and *exponent*.

EXPECTED SOLUTION

If students calculate using the paper thickness of 0.003 inch, then the stack will be about 3,145.728 inches thick, or about 262 feet tall. A local reference helps students relate to the magnitude of the number (e.g., in Hawai'i, the Aloha Tower is 184 feet tall).

CLOSE AND GENERALIZATIONS

1. Ask, "How is raising a number to the power of 2 the same as or different from multiplying by 2?"

2. Extend the problem by changing the number of pieces with each tear. For example, if the paper had been torn into thirds instead of halves, how would that have affected the answer?

TASK 5.5: STACK 'EM UP!

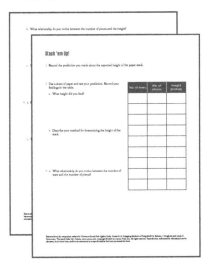

POST-TASK NOTES AND REFLECTIONS: NEXT STEPS

• How did the task support students' understanding of the growth resulting from raising a base to a power?

• Did students detect patterns in the table?

• Were the patterns robust? If not, how can I support students in identifying and describing patterns in a better way?

• How can I use students' learning from this task to connect it to negative or rational number exponents?

_____

_____

_____

_____

_____

_____

_____

- Make sense of problems and persevere in solving them.
- Reason abstractly and quantitatively.
- Use appropriate tools strategically.
- Attend to precision.
- Look for and express regularity in repeated reasoning.

Task 5.6
Powers of Prediction

TASK

Powers of Prediction

1. What digit will be in the ones place for each of the following?

   a. 3^{65}

   b. 3^{650}

2. What patterns do you notice about the digit in the ones place of the powers of 3?

3. What digit will be in the ones place for each of the following?

   a. 8^{65}

   b. 8^{650}

4. a. How are the powers of 3 and 8 alike?

   b. How are the powers of 3 and 8 different?

5. a. Consider the digits of the powers of 4. How are the powers of 4 and the powers of 8 alike?

   b. How are they different?

TASK PREPARATION CONSIDERATIONS

- How can I help students use their calculators strategically?

SCAFFOLDING OR DIFFERENTIATING THE TASK

- Have students start with smaller numbers as the exponent.

- Have students organize the outcomes of raising the base to smaller exponents in a table to see a pattern of the ones digits.

- Remind students, if they don't see a pattern, that the focus is on the ones digit. Have them make a list of the digits as they raise the base to successive powers.

WATCH-FORS!

- Students may misinterpret the exponential notation. They may treat it as multiplication between the base and the exponent. Use examples with smaller numbers to focus on how they differ.

- Students may focus on the product as a whole and not detect a pattern in the ones digits as they raise the base to successive powers.

- Students may be unsure how to use the cycle of the ones digits' pattern to find the solution.

EXTEND THE TASK

- Have students explore patterns in the powers of other bases.

- Use bases that are the result of a prime number raised to a power. For example, $8 = 2^3$. Compare the patterns in the ones digits to the results when the base is a composite number such as 6 where its prime factorization involves more than one prime number.

LAUNCH

- Display 3^4 and discuss with students the meaning of exponential notation.

- Distribute the Powers of Prediction exploration. Students should not access the internet for the task.

- Have students work in pairs for about 15–20 minutes.

FACILITATE

1. If students have difficulty with the problem, tell them that patterns are important in this problem. Organizing information in a table may be a helpful strategy for them to use.

2. An expert group discussion strategy could work well for this task.

3. After expert groups finish, discuss students' solutions as time allows.

EXPECTED SOLUTIONS

1. a. The digit in the ones place will be 3.

    b. The digit in the ones place will be 9.

2. Answers will vary. Students may comment on the cyclic nature (3, 9, 7, 1, etc.) of the ones digits in the powers.

3. a. The digit in the ones place will be 8.

    b. The digit in the ones place will be 4.

Task Type

	Conceptual
X	Procedural
X	Problem-Solving Application
	Problem-Solving Critical Thinking

	Reversibility
	Flexibility
X	Generalization

4. Students may notice that powers of 3 and 8 are similar in that they both have a cycle of four digits. They may notice that the powers of 3 have an odd number in the ones place while the powers of 8 have an even number in the ones place, or that the powers of 8 are larger than the respective powers of 3.

5. Students may notice that the powers of 4 have a cycle of two digits, 4 and 6, which also belong to the cycle of four digits, 8, 4, 2, 6, for the powers of 8.

CLOSE AND GENERALIZATIONS

1. Ask, "What do you notice about the ones digit when the base is an odd number? What do you notice about the ones digit when the base is even?"

2. Ask students what solution strategy or strategies helped them detect the patterns.

TASK 5.6: POWERS OF PREDICTION

 Available to download at **resources.corwin.com/classroomreadymath/algebra**

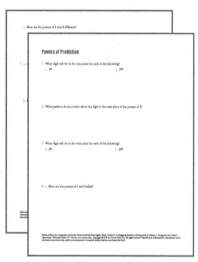

POST-TASK NOTES: REFLECTIONS AND NEXT STEPS

• How does this task support students' understanding of exponential expressions?

• What debriefing or discussion technique (collaborative, poster, and so on) best suits tasks such as this?

Task 5.7
Berry Interesting

TASK

Berry Interesting

There were 100 kg of berries at the market. The moisture in the berries was measured as 99%. What was the total mass of the berries when the moisture had become 98%?

TASK PREPARATION CONSIDERATIONS

- Although it may seem like a routine task, this is a nonroutine task that does not have an obvious solution path. Persuade students to persevere and to use creative thinking to find a successful solution path.

SCAFFOLDING OR DIFFERENTIATING THE TASK

- Have students talk about what the given percentages measure.

- If students prepare a proportion to solve the problem, review what assumptions they need to make when using a proportion.

WATCH-FORS!

- Students may not recognize that the *whole*, in this case the mass of the berries, changes and is not the same for both conditions. Thus, writing a proportion will not be a productive solution strategy.

EXTEND THE TASK

- Have students continue to investigate what happens to the mass of the berries if the moisture continues to drop. What would the mass be if it had no moisture?

LAUNCH

- Arrange students in pairs.

- Distribute 1 Berry Interesting task per student.

- Read the problem with the class to be sure students understand the context and what the problem is asking.

- Encourage them to work independently on the task before discussing with their partner.

- Allow about 15 minutes for students to work.

Mathematics Focus

- Students use equations with one variable to solve a nonroutine problem.

Mathematics Content Standard(s)

- A-SSE-1: Interpret expressions that represent a quantity in terms of its context.

Mathematical Practice(s)

- Make sense of problems and persevere in solving them.
- Reason abstractly and quantitatively.
- Construct viable arguments and critique the reasoning of others.
- Model with mathematics.
- Look for and make use of structure.

Vocabulary

- mass
- proportion
- ratio

Materials

- 1 Berry Interesting task per student

Task Type

X	Conceptual
	Procedural
	Problem-Solving Application
X	Problem-Solving Critical Thinking

	Reversibility
X	Flexibility
	Generalization

FACILITATE

1. Have students discuss the conditions in the problem that change and those that remain the same.

2. After that discussion, have them take another look at their solution process. Do they need to make any adjustments?

EXPECTED SOLUTION

$0.01 \times 100 = 1$ kg of berries (flesh) only

Thus, if x represents the weight of the berries after the moisture loss and $0.02x = 1$ kg of berries, then $x = 50$ kg.

When the moisture dropped to 98%, the berries weighed 50 kg.

CLOSE AND GENERALIZATIONS

1. Have students share productive solutions to the task.

2. Ask, "Why do strategies for solving real-world tasks become more complex than routine or manufactured mathematics tasks?"

TASK 5.7: BERRY INTERESTING

 Available to download at **resources.corwin.com/ classroomreadymath/algebra**

POST-TASK NOTES: REFLECTIONS AND NEXT STEPS

• How did students approach a nonroutine task?

• Were the assumptions the students made about the relationships in the task aligned with a strong understanding of ratio and proportion?

• How is this task similar to others I've used in my class? How is it different?

Expressions Tasks

In Chapter 6, the tasks focus on conceptual and procedural understanding of algebraic expressions. Central to this topic is the foundational understanding of the concept of variable including knowing the different roles that a variable can take and reasoning with generalized quantities. The concept of variable is central to any work with variables and algebraic expressions as a quantity rather than an object.

The beginning tasks use a geometric context that invites students to notice patterns and make generalizations using a variable. Trapezoid Figures and Sticks and Squares involve area and perimeter and counting partitions, respectively, in growing patterns that involve shapes. As students create a table, patterns should emerge that are directly linked to the building changes from one figure to the next.

Algebra tiles are introduced in Tile Expressions where students model algebraic expressions and are introduced to simplifying expressions. Be the Matchmaker! is a more procedural task that asks students to match symbolic representations with the words that describe them. Vocabulary is important in this task!

Faces, Edges, and Vertices uses three-dimensional shapes. Students are asked to find patterns among the faces, edges, and vertices that lead to Euler's formula.

In Expression Challenge, we introduce a model for students to organize their work when they simplify expressions. In our classroom tests, this method of using a table to record the property used in each step first helped students recapture their thinking when they explained the process, second prompted students to think about the mathematics in a deeper way, and third helped them to organize their work so that they made fewer inaccurate computations.

The last task, Expression Match-Up, is procedural in nature as students match expressions that are equivalent.

Mathematics Focus

• Students generalize area and perimeter patterns aligning geometric and algebraic representations.

Mathematics Content Standard(s)

• 6.EE.2: Write, read, and evaluate expressions in which letters stand for numbers.
• 7.EE.4: Use variables to represent quantities in a real-world or mathematical problem, and construct simple equations and inequalities to solve problems by reasoning about the quantities.
• A-SSE.1: Interpret expressions that represent a quantity in terms of its context.

Mathematical Practice(s)

• Make sense of problems and persevere in solving them.
• Reason abstractly and quantitatively.
• Model with mathematics.
• Look for and make use of structure.
• Look for and express regularity in repeated reasoning.

Task 6.1
Trapezoid Figures

TASK

Trapezoid Figures

1. Measure and record the area of the trapezoid using the area of one triangle as 1 area unit. Sketch the trapezoid and label the triangles to indicate its area.

2. Using the length of one side of the triangle as 1 length unit, measure the length of each side of the trapezoid. Sketch the trapezoid and label the length of each side.

3. a. Make a line of trapezoids. Each time you add a trapezoid, record the perimeter and area in the table.

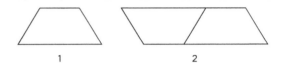

Figure number	1	2	3	4	5	6	10	n
Area of figure in area units	3							
Perimeter of figure in length units	5	11						

b. In words, describe any patterns you notice in the area as you add a trapezoid.

c. Write what n represents. Then, using n as your variable, write an algebraic expression to describe the pattern you notice for area.

$$n =$$

d. In words, describe any patterns you notice in the perimeter as you add a trapezoid.

e. Write what n represents. Then, using n as your variable, write an algebraic expression to describe the pattern you notice for perimeter.

$$n =$$

4. a. Build a line of equilateral triangles and trapezoids as shown in this pattern. Record the perimeter and area for each figure in the table.

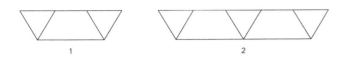

Figure number	1	2	3	4	5	6	10	n
Area of figure in area units								
Perimeter of figure in length units								

b. In words, describe any patterns you notice in the area as you add a trapezoid and a triangle.

c. Write what n represents. Then, using n as your variable, write an algebraic expression to describe the pattern you notice for area.
$n =$

d. In words, describe any patterns you notice in the perimeter as you add a trapezoid and a triangle.

e. Write what n represents. Then, using n as your variable, write an algebraic expression to describe the pattern you notice for perimeter.
$n =$

TASK PREPARATION CONSIDERATIONS

• How will I use concrete, semi-concrete, or abstract representations to demonstrate measuring the area and perimeter?

• Will some or all students need to continue modeling the action to see the patterns?

SCAFFOLDING OR DIFFERENTIATING THE TASK

• Encourage students to model the figures that are not included in the table.

• Demonstrate how to complete the table and have students explain the organization of the table.

• Have students work in pairs so they can explain their thinking and discuss patterns before sharing out with the class.

Vocabulary

• area
• perimeter
• variable
• generalization

Materials

• 1 Trapezoid Figures task per student

• 10 red trapezoid and 10 green triangle pattern blocks per pair

Task Type

X	Conceptual
	Procedural
	Problem-Solving Application
X	Problem-Solving Critical Thinking

	Reversibility
X	Flexibility
X	Generalization

- Use questions like "What do you notice about the perimeter each time you add a block?" and "What do you notice about the area each time you add a block?"

- Modify the table by separating area and perimeter.

WATCH-FORS!

- Students may not notice that the table skips to 10 and will continue the numerical pattern they found.

- Students may use the variable *n* to represent blocks, not the *number* of blocks. They see the variable as an object and not a quantity.

EXTEND THE TASK

- Reverse the task by giving the number of blocks and having students determine (1) the largest figure they can make *or* (2) the greatest number of figures they can make. For example, tell students they have 50 trapezoids and 50 triangles. What is the largest figure they can make using the pattern in 4.a? Beginning with building figure 1 and then building each consecutive figure, how many figures can you make with 50 trapezoids and 50 triangles?

LAUNCH

1. Place students in pairs.

2. Tell students that they will be measuring area and perimeter but not in the same way they usually measure them.

3. Show the trapezoid and tell them that the area of the trapezoid will be measured by the area of the equilateral triangle.

4. Model laying three triangles on the face of the trapezoid.

5. Show the table and model recording the area for the first task.

6. Model perimeter by running your finger around the edge of the trapezoid.

7. Lay equilateral triangles around the edge so students can see that the perimeter of the trapezoid measured by these length units is 5.

8. Show how a trapezoid is placed next to the first trapezoid to determine the pattern they will use.

9. Distribute the Trapezoid Figures task to pairs.

10. Allow about 15 minutes for the students to work together.

FACILITATE

1. Monitor the pairs as they work.

2. Watch for students who notice a pattern and then fill in the table with the values without building the line. Remind them to build the pattern so that they understand why and how the change in the perimeter and area happens.

3. Select some pairs to share their responses, with a focus on the alignment between the geometric representation and the numerical pattern.

   a. As they share a pattern, make sure they link it to the geometric representation. This will help students better understand how it is represented algebraically.

   b. Their descriptions may vary, but the expressions they generate should be equivalent to those that follow.

EXPECTED SOLUTIONS

First pattern:

Figure number	1	2	3	4	5	6	10	n
Area of figure in area units	3	6	9	12	15	18	30	$3n$
Perimeter of figure in length units	5	8	11	14	17	20	32	$3n + 2$

Second pattern:

Figure number	1	2	3	4	5	6	10	n
Area of figure in area units	5	9	13	17	21	25	41	$4n + 1$
Perimeter of figure in length units	7	11	15	19	23	27	43	$4n + 3$

CLOSE AND GENERALIZATIONS

1. Summarize the importance of the variable in patterns. In this role, variables can assume many different values. They are efficient because the generalization provides a way to find information without building the pattern.

2. Emphasize the concept that variables represent quantities (the *number* of trapezoids), not objects (the trapezoid).

TASK 6.1: TRAPEZOID FIGURES

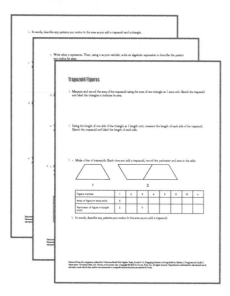

POST-TASK NOTES: REFLECTIONS AND NEXT STEPS

• How can I modify the task using different shapes? For example, what if I exchanged the trapezoid with a hexagon? How would that change the task?

• How did using physical materials support students in detecting the patterns?

• Did I prompt students to link the numerical patterns in the table to the physical materials? How can I motivate students to not rely solely on the numerical patterns?

Task 6.2
Sticks and Squares

TASK

Sticks and Squares

1. Without counting each stick individually, find a way to determine how many sticks are needed to make this arrangement of 5 squares.

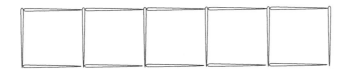

2. a. Without actually building it, how many sticks would you need to build a row of 18 squares?

   b. Describe the method you and your partner used.

3. Cameron made a row of squares in the same arrangement on his desk, but he forgot to count the number of sticks he used. Write an algebraic representation that will help him know how many sticks he used.

   n = number of squares

4. Mazie has 750 sticks.

   a. What is the largest number of squares she can make by extending the arrangement in problem 1?

   b. Show your process or describe your thinking.

TASK PREPARATION CONSIDERATIONS

• How will I use concrete, semi-concrete, or abstract representations to demonstrate the pattern?

• Will some or all students need to continue modeling more figures to see the patterns?

• If students have not generalized patterns, can I use this task to introduce the idea of representing geometric patterns with algebraic expressions?

SCAFFOLDING OR DIFFERENTIATING THE TASK

• Encourage students to model the figures prior to and after the given one.

• Demonstrate how to make a table to better see a pattern.

Mathematics Focus

• Students generalize patterns aligning geometric and algebraic representations.

Mathematics Content Standard(s)

• 6.EE.2: Write, read, and evaluate expressions in which letters stand for numbers.

• 7.EE.4: Use variables to represent quantities in a real-world or mathematical problem, and construct simple equations and inequalities to solve problems by reasoning about the quantities.

• A-SSE.1: Interpret expressions that represent a quantity in terms of its context.

Mathematical Practice(s)

• Make sense of problems and persevere in solving them.

• Reason abstractly and quantitatively.

• Construct viable arguments and critique the reasoning of others.

• Model with mathematics.

• Look for and make use of structure.

• Look for and express regularity in repeated reasoning.

Vocabulary

- variable
- generalization

Materials

- 1 Sticks and Squares task per student
- 30 toothpicks (or other stick manipulative) per pair (optional)

Task Type

X	Conceptual
	Procedural
	Problem-Solving Application
X	Problem-Solving Critical Thinking

X	Reversibility
X	Flexibility
X	Generalization

- Have students work in pairs so they can explain their thinking and discuss patterns before sharing out with the class.

- Use questions like "What do you notice about the total number of sticks every time you add a square?"

WATCH-FORS!

- Students may create a different arrangement of the sticks rather than maintaining the given pattern.

- Students may use the variable *n* to represent sticks, not the *number* of sticks, seeing the variable as an object and not a quantity.

- Students may notice a pattern that indicates that there is a square of 4 sticks, then 2 sticks, then 4 sticks, and so on, creating a generalization that may only apply to arrangements that have an odd number of squares.

EXTEND THE TASK

- Reverse the task by giving the number of sticks and having students determine (1) the largest figure in the pattern they can make *or* (2) the greatest number of figures in the pattern they can make. For example, tell students they have 150 sticks. What is the largest figure they can make using the pattern? Beginning with building figure 1 and then building each consecutive figure, how many figures can you make with 150 sticks?

LAUNCH

1. Place students in pairs.

2. Tell students that they will be creating a pattern using sticks.

3. Show them the 5 squares arranged in a row.

4. Tell them that the task is to determine the total number of sticks in the figure.

5. Indicate that the easiest way to find the total number is to count one by one, but there are other ways to find the total. Their goal is to find as many ways to count the sticks as they can without counting them one by one.

6. Distribute the Sticks and Squares task to pairs.

7. Allow about 15 minutes for the students to work together.

FACILITATE

1. Monitor the pairs as they work.

2. Watch for students who change the pattern by rearranging the sticks.

3. Select some pairs to share their responses, with a focus on the alignment between the geometric representation and the numerical pattern.

   a. Begin the sharing with patterns that students will share in words, and move toward those where students have used algebraic expressions or equations.

   b. As they share a pattern, make sure students link it to the geometric representation. This will help students better understand how it is represented algebraically as you create generalized expressions.

   c. Their descriptions may vary in words, but the expressions they generate should be equivalent to $3n + 1$ where n = number of squares.

4. Have students share their algebraic expressions. Watch for those that are equivalent.

EXPECTED SOLUTIONS

1. To make the arrangement of 5 squares, 16 sticks are needed.

2. a. You would need 55 sticks.

3. Any expression equivalent to $3n + 1$.

4. a. She can make an arrangement of 249 squares.

CLOSE AND GENERALIZATIONS

1. Ask students which method of counting they would use if you gave them a figure that had 30 squares in this pattern.

   » Have them share why they chose that method.

2. Summarize the importance of the variable in patterns. In this role, variables can assume many different values. They are efficient because the generalization provides a way to find information without building the pattern.

3. Emphasize the concept that variables represent quantities (the *number* of squares), not objects (the square).

4. Discuss the equivalent algebraic expressions that students shared with a focus on what it means to be equivalent.

TASK 6.2: STICKS AND SQUARES

Sticks and Squares

1. Without counting each stick individually, find a way to determine how many sticks are needed to make this arrangement of 5 squares.

2. a. Without actually building it, how many sticks would you need to build a row of 10 squares?

   b. Describe the method you and your partner used.

3. Cameron made a row of squares in the same arrangement on his desk, but he forgot to count the number of sticks he used. Write an algebraic representation that will help him know how many sticks he used.

   n = number of squares

4. Mazie has 750 sticks.
   a. What is the largest number of squares she can make by extending the arrangement in problem 1?

   b. Show your process or describe your thinking.

POST-TASK NOTES: REFLECTIONS AND NEXT STEPS

- Did I introduce the task in a way that helped students understand what to do?

- Would physical materials have made the task more robust?

- Did students find the counting strategies I anticipated?

- How well did we as a class align the numerical and algebraic patterns with the geometric pattern?

Task 6.3
Tile Expressions

TASK

Tile Expressions

1. Select one each of the following tiles from your set of algebra tiles, then complete the table.

	Length in units	Width in units	Area in sq. units
a. Small square tile	1		
b. Long tile	x		
c. Big square tile			

2. a. Describe how you would use tiles to represent –5. Sketch a representation.

   b. What is the minimum number of tiles you need to model –5? Sketch a representation.

   c. What is the maximum number of tiles you need to model –5? Sketch a representation.

   d. What do you notice about your models?

3. a. Describe how you would use tiles to model $4x$. Sketch your representation.

   b. Can you model $4x$ using 6 tiles? If yes, sketch the model. If no, explain why.

   c. Can you model $4x$ using 8 tiles? 9 tiles? Sketch your models or explain why you cannot make the model.

4. a. Show a model for $5x + 2$.

   b. Show two more models for $5x + 2$.

   c. Write algebraic expressions that more accurately represent your two models in 4.b.

   d. Are the two expressions equivalent to $5x + 2$? Why or why not?

5. a. Use tiles to show a model for twice the sum of $2x + (-3)$.

   b. What is the minimum number of tiles needed? Justify your answer.

6. What does it mean for two algebraic expressions to be equivalent? Explain by using tiles.

Mathematics Focus

- Students model algebraic expressions with algebra tiles (or similar area models).

Mathematics Content Standard(s)

- 7.EE.1: Apply properties of operations as strategies to add, subtract, factor, and expand linear expressions with rational coefficients.

Mathematical Practice(s)

- Model with mathematics.
- Use appropriate tools strategically.
- Look for and make use of structure.

Vocabulary

- algebraic expression
- equivalent

Materials

- 1 Tile Expressions task per student
- 1 set of algebra tiles (or similar manipulative) per pair

Task Type

X	Conceptual
	Procedural
	Problem-Solving Application
	Problem-Solving Critical Thinking

	Reversibility
	Flexibility
X	Generalization

TASK PREPARATION CONSIDERATIONS

- Have students modeled integers using a two-color chip or algebra tile model? If not, what should I do to introduce the task?

- If algebra tiles are not available, what manipulative could be substituted for the task?

SCAFFOLDING OR DIFFERENTIATING THE TASK

- Complete problem 1 as a whole class.

- Model how to represent an integer with the unit tiles, then model how to represent, for example, $2x$.

- Remind students of the "zero pair" model and connect it to the identity property of addition.

- Extend the task to model more complex algebraic expressions and simplify them.

WATCH-FORS!

- Students may read $-x$ as "the opposite of x" but interpret that as indicating the value will always be a negative number.

- Students may not think about using zero pairs and connecting them to the identity property of addition.

- Students may line up 5 unit tiles next to the x tile and think that the x tile has a numerical value of a little more than 5.

EXTEND THE TASK

- Show students the tile representation for an algebraic expression such as $3x + (-5)$. Have them write algebraic expressions that represent the model.

LAUNCH

1. Place students in pairs.

2. Tell students that they are going to use an area model to represent algebraic expressions.

3. Depending on their experience modeling with algebra tiles, indicate that each tile (show the tiles) represents area. (At this point, you may want to scaffold the task by completing problem 1 of the exploration with the whole class. Stress that the dimensions form the area of the tile such that x, for example, represents the area of the tile that is x units long and 1 unit wide.)

4. Model as many examples of integer or algebraic expressions as needed.

5. Distribute the Tile Expressions task to each student and algebra tiles to each pair.

6. Allow about 30 minutes for students to work.

FACILITATE

1. Monitor the pairs as they work.

2. Watch for limited use of zero pairs and for inaccurate mathematical language, such as negative x.

3. Select some student pairs to share their answers.

    a. Discuss alternative representations or expressions as appropriate.

    b. Focus on the expressions that are connected to the models.

EXPECTED SOLUTIONS

1.

	Length in units	Width in units	Area in sq. units
a. Small square tile	1	1	1
b. Long tile	x	1	x
c. Big square tile	x	x	x^2

2. b. Five –1 tiles.

   c. Any odd number greater than five –1 tiles.

   d. Students should notice that any model that uses more than five tiles will have an odd number and include zero pairs.

3. a.

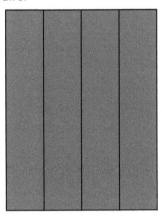

   b. There are multiple models for $4x$ that include only x tiles or four x tiles and a zero pair of any tiles.

c. *4x* cannot be modeled with 9 tiles, but there are multiple models that can be created with 8 tiles.

4. a. Other models are possible by using zero pairs.

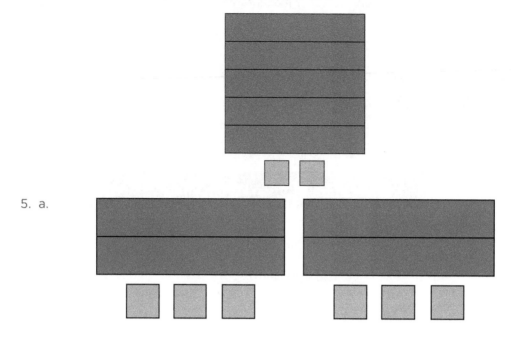

5. a.

b. The minimum number of tiles is 10: four *x* tiles and six –1 tiles.

CLOSE AND GENERALIZATIONS

1. Point out that algebraic expressions can be modeled in multiple ways and that the algebraic expressions that represent the models are all equivalent.

2. Focus on the concept of equivalency with algebraic expressions.

3. Ask students how using the physical materials helped them "see" algebraic expressions.

TASK 6.3: TILE EXPRESSIONS

online resources Available to download at **resources.corwin.com/classroomreadymath/algebra**

POST-TASK NOTES: REFLECTIONS AND NEXT STEPS

- How does the physical material help students understand the conceptual aspect of algebraic expressions?

- How can I build on the modeling of algebraic expressions to support students' understanding of simplifying?

- Was the amount of physical materials sufficient for students so they could work productively and effectively in a group?

Mathematics Focus

- Students match algebraic expressions with the words that describe them.

Mathematics Content Standard(s)

- 6.EE.2: Write, read, and evaluate expressions in which letters stand for numbers.
- A-SSE.1: Interpret expressions that represent a quantity in terms of its context.

Mathematical Practice(s)

- Reason abstractly and quantitatively.
- Model with mathematics.
- Look for and make use of structure.

Vocabulary

- algebraic expression

Materials

- 1 set of Be the Matchmaker! cards per pair of students
- 1 sheet of chart paper per pair of students
- Tape per pair of students

Task 6.4
Be the Matchmaker!

TASK

See Facilitate 3.

TASK PREPARATION CONSIDERATIONS

- How many sets of Be the Matchmaker! cards are needed?
- What strategies will I use with nonreaders?

SCAFFOLDING OR DIFFERENTIATING THE TASK

- Modify the task to include only the expressions that have a match with the word card.
- Identify any vocabulary that students may not be familiar with, and have examples of the meaning or refer them to anchor charts or a word wall.
- Generate vocabulary that may be used to describe an expression in words.

WATCH-FORS!

- Students may confuse the order of the terms in word descriptions that deal with division or subtraction.
- Students may think that in a matching task, every expression must have a match.

EXTEND THE TASK

- Have students create three expressions and the matching word descriptions to trade with another student to match up.
- In each pair, have one student write an expression and one student write a word description. They swap with each other and write either an expression or a word description to match.

LAUNCH

1. Place students in pairs.

2. Show an expression such as $3x - 4$.

3. Ask students how they would translate the expression into words.

   a. As they share, record their phrases.

4. Discuss the different ways they used words, focusing on descriptions such as the difference of the product of 3 and x and 4 rather than the literal translation (3 times x minus 4). Ask them in how many different ways they can represent the expression with words (e.g., the difference of the product of 3 and x and 4, 4 subtracted from the product of 3 and x, the product of 3 and x less 4).

5. Tell them that they are going to match algebraic expressions with their associated word descriptions.

6. Remind them that some word descriptions or algebraic expressions may not have a match, so they will need to record on the card an appropriate matching expression or description.

7. Distribute the Be the Matchmaker! cards to each pair.

8. Allow about 20 minutes for students to work.

FACILITATE

1. Monitor the pairs as they work.

2. Put two pairs together and have them share their chart papers.

   a. Ask students to record any questions, discrepancies, or issues they could not resolve in their pairs.

3. Have students share any questions, discrepancies, or issues they could not resolve with the whole class.

Task Type

	Conceptual
X	Procedural
	Problem-Solving Application
	Problem-Solving Critical Thinking

	Reversibility
X	Flexibility
X	Generalization

EXPECTED SOLUTIONS

Word description	Expression
W1 The sum of six and the product of two and n	**E4** $2n + 6$
W2 The square of the product of three and n	**E7** $(3n)^2$
W3 Twice the product of six and n	**No match** $2(6 \times n)$
W4 The quotient of the sum of n and six, and two	**E1** $\frac{n+6}{2}$
W5 Twice the sum of n and three	**E5** $2(n + 3)$
W6 The square of the sum of n and six	**E8** $(n + 6)^2$
W7 The sum of the product of two and n, and twelve	**E3** $2n + 12$
W8 The sum of six and the quotient of n and two	**E6** $\frac{n}{2} + 6$
W9 The sum of the square of n and six	**E11** $n^2 + 6$
W10 The product of the square of n and six	**No match** $6n^2$ or $n^2 \times 6$
The product of three and the square of n	**E2** $3n^2$
The quotient of the sum of three and n, and two	**E9** $\frac{3+n}{2}$
The sum of three and the quotient of n and two	**E10** $\frac{n}{2} + 6$
The sum of the square of n and the square of six	**E12** $n^2 + 6^2$

4. Discuss the unmatched cards and student responses to address those.

CLOSE AND GENERALIZATIONS

1. Summarize the properties and vocabulary used by groups.

TASK 6.4: BE THE MATCHMAKER!

online resources Available to download at **resources.corwin.com/classroomreadymath/algebra**

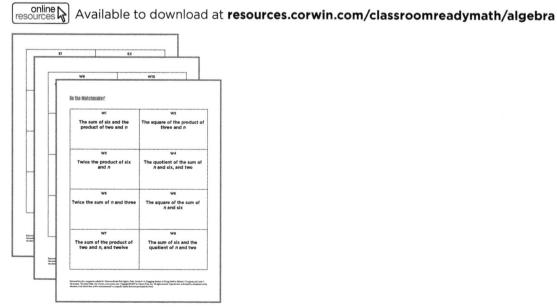

POST-TASK NOTES: REFLECTIONS AND NEXT STEPS

- In how many different ways did students describe the algebraic expressions? How can I expand their vocabulary?

- What expressions were easiest, and which provide some opportunities to learn?

Mathematics Focus

- Students generalize the relationships among the number of faces, edges, and vertices in polyhedra (Euler's formula).

Mathematics Content Standard(s)

- 6.EE.2: Write, read, and evaluate expressions in which letters stand for numbers.

- 7.EE.2: Understand that rewriting an expression in different forms in a problem context can shed light on the problem and how the quantities in it are related.

- 7.EE.4: Use variables to represent quantities in a real-world or mathematical problem, and construct simple equations and inequalities to solve problems by reasoning about the quantities.

- A-SSE.1: Interpret expressions that represent a quantity in terms of its context.

- A-SSE.2: Use the structure of an expression to identify ways to rewrite it.

- A-SSE.3: Choose and produce an equivalent form of an expression to reveal and explain properties of the quantity represented by the expression.

Task 6.5
Faces, Edges, and Vertices

TASK

Faces, Edges, and Vertices

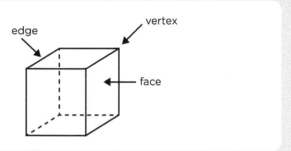

A polyhedron is a three-dimensional shape that has polygons as its faces. The faces meet to form edges; the edges meet to form vertices.

1. Write the names of at least five polyhedra in the table.

2. Count the number of faces, edges, and vertices for each polyhedron and record it in the table. Be sure that your group verifies your count.

Polyhedron	Number of Faces (f)	Number of Vertices (v)	Number of Edges (e)

3. a. What relationships do you see among the number of faces, edges, and vertices? Describe what you notice in words.

   b. Write algebraic equations to generalize the relationships. Be sure to identify what your variable represents.

TASK PREPARATION CONSIDERATIONS

- How many different polyhedra will be needed for students to detect the patterns?

- How will I introduce faces, edges, and vertices?

- Can virtual polyhedra be used to provide more opportunities to see the patterns? If so, will students be able to accurately count the faces, edges, and vertices?

SCAFFOLDING OR DIFFERENTIATING THE TASK

- Have students show their understanding of faces, edges, and vertices on a polyhedron, individually or in pairs with you.

- Demonstrate how to complete the table, and have students explain the organization of the table.

- Have students work in pairs so they can explain their thinking and discuss patterns before sharing out with the class.

- Focus students' attention on relationships between only faces and vertices first.

WATCH-FORS!

- Students may use *f*, *e*, and *v* to represent the faces, edges, and vertices but may not recognize that they represent the *number* of faces, edges, and vertices.

- Students may use *F*, *E*, and *V* rather than *f*, *e*, and *v* to represent the number of faces, edges, and vertices.

- Students may call a face a side or call a vertex a corner rather than using accurate mathematical vocabulary.

EXTEND THE TASK

- Reverse the task by giving students the number of faces, edges, and vertices and asking them questions. For example, if you tell them there are 7 faces, 12 edges, and 7 vertices, what could the polyhedron be? (Answer: a hexagonal pyramid.)

- Ask students if their generalizations will be true for concave polyhedra.

LAUNCH

1. Place students in groups of 4.

2. Discuss the names of each polyhedron that you have for students to use.

Mathematical Practice(s)

- Make sense of problems and persevere in solving them.
- Reason abstractly and quantitatively.
- Model with mathematics.
- Use appropriate tools strategically.
- Look for and make use of structure.
- Look for and express regularity in repeated reasoning.

Vocabulary

- polyhedron
- face
- edge
- vertex
- prism
- pyramid
- the names of additional polyhedra that you will use in the task

Materials

- 1 Faces, Edges, and Vertices task per student
- A classroom set of polyhedra

Task Type

X	Conceptual
	Procedural
	Problem-Solving Application
X	Problem-Solving Critical Thinking

	Reversibility
X	Flexibility
X	Generalization

3. Select one of the polyhedra, such as a cube, and have students identify the number of faces, edges, and vertices.

4. Verify that they know and can identify faces, edges, and vertices.

5. Show the table and model recording the information for the cube.

6. Distribute the Faces, Edges, and Vertices task to the small groups.

7. Allow about 20 minutes for the students to work together.

FACILITATE

1. Monitor the small groups as they work.

2. Listen for the use of accurate mathematical language such as *vertex* instead of *corner* or *face* instead of *side*.

3. Have students find the counts for at least five polyhedra.

4. Ask students to share the relationships that they noticed without focusing on writing algebraic equations or expressions.

   a. Students may notice that the number of edges is two less than the sum of the number of vertices and the number of faces.

   b. They may express the pattern in different ways, but they should have equivalent meanings.

5. Have students share their generalizations. Watch for those that are equivalent.

   a. $e = f + v - 2$ or any equivalent ones such as $f + v = e + 2$; $v - 2 = e - f$; $f = e - v + 2$; or $f + v - e = 2$.

   b. Be sure to identify the variables as e = *number* of edges; f = *number* of faces; and v = *number* of vertices.

CLOSE AND GENERALIZATIONS

1. Summarize the importance of the variable in generalizing patterns.

2. Tell students that the generalizations they created are related to Euler's (pronounced *oilers*) formula. This formula is credited to Leonhard Euler, an 18th century Swiss mathematician. For more information, see www.ams.org/publicoutreach/feature-column/fcarc-eulers-formula (Malkevitch, 2004).

3. Extend the task by asking if their patterns hold for *all* polyhedra. Explore that idea with concave polyhedra if none was included in their investigation.

TASK 6.5: FACES, EDGES, AND VERTICES

online resources ⌖ Available to download at **resources.corwin.com/classroomreadymath/algebra**

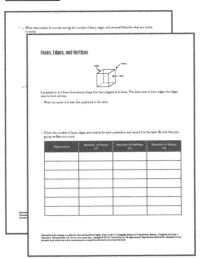

POST-TASK NOTES: REFLECTIONS AND NEXT STEPS

• Did students have enough polyhedra for the task to determine the patterns?

• Did I organize the sharing of the polyhedra in a way that allowed the groups to work productively?

• Was the task accessible for all students? If not, how could I adapt it?

Mathematics Focus

- Students analyze worked examples to provide the justification for simplifying algebraic expressions.

Mathematics Content Standard(s)

- 6.EE.2: Write, read, and evaluate expressions in which letters stand for numbers.
- 7.EE.1: Apply properties of operations as strategies to add, subtract, factor, and expand linear expressions with rational coefficients.

Mathematical Practice(s)

- Reason abstractly and quantitatively.
- Construct viable arguments and critique the reasoning of others.
- Look for and make use of structure.

Vocabulary

- algebraic expression
- simplify
- commutative property
- definition of subtraction
- distributive property of multiplication over addition/subtraction
- combine like terms
- order of operations

Task 6.6
Expression Challenge

TASK

Expression Challenge

1. Eric and Kara challenged each other to simplify an algebraic expression. Their process appears in the following tables. Analyze their work and write the justification for each step in their process by considering the order of operations and properties of operations.

a. Eric's table

Expression	Justification
$4x + 3b - 2x + 5b$	Given
$4x + 3b + (-2x) + 5b$	
$4x + (-2x) + 3b + 5b$	
$2x + 8b$	

b. Kara's table

Expression	Justification
$6(2x - 4) - 6x$	Given
$6[2x + (-4)] + (-6x)$	
$12x + (-24) + (-6x)$	
$12x + (-6x) + (-24)$	
$6x + (-24)$	

2. Michaela simplified the expression $5x - 2(3x - 8)$. Do you agree with her process and explanation? If you agree, explain why. If you do not agree, explain why not.

Expression	Justification
$5x - 2(3x - 8)$	Given
$5x + (-2)[3x + (-8)]$	Definition of subtraction
$5x + (-6x) + (-8)$	Distributive property of multiplication over addition (DPMA)
$-x + (-8)$	Combine like terms

3. Andrew has a challenge for you with the expression $8 + 3(-2 + x) - 2(4 - x)$. He has included the justifications for the process in the table. Your challenge is to complete the table using these justifications.

Expression	Justification
$8 + 3(-2 + x) - 2(4 - x)$	Given
	Definition of subtraction
	Distributive property of multiplication over addition (DPMA)
	Commutative property of addition
	Combine like terms

4. Complete Jadon's similar challenge with his expression $-3(5 - x) - 7(-2)$.

Expression	Justification
$-3(5 - x) - 7(-2)$	Given
	Definition of subtraction
	Commutative property of addition
	Distributive property of multiplication over addition (DPMA)
	Combine like terms

Materials

- 1 Expression Challenge task per student

Task Type

	Conceptual
X	Procedural
	Problem-Solving Application
	Problem-Solving Critical Thinking

X	Reversibility
X	Flexibility
	Generalization

TASK PREPARATION CONSIDERATIONS

- Are students familiar with the properties of operations?

- Do students have sufficient skill with order of operations?

- Have students had some experience simplifying algebraic expressions?

SCAFFOLDING OR DIFFERENTIATING THE TASK

- Model the completion of a table with a simpler algebraic expression.

- List the properties of operations for students to refer to.

- Use GEMS (grouping, exponents, multiplication and division, subtraction and addition) or GEMA (grouping, exponents, multiplicative structures, additive structures) to support remembering the order of operations.

- Rewrite expressions to be addition only by applying the definition of subtraction to any subtraction computations.

WATCH-FORS!

- Students may confuse the subtraction symbol (−) for a negative sign.

- Students may have difficulty subtracting accurately with integers, so encourage them to use the definition of subtraction to rewrite expressions as addition.

EXTEND THE TASK

- Have students create an algebraic expression and set up a table like the ones in the exploration. Trade expressions with other students in the class and complete.

LAUNCH

1. Place students in pairs.

2. Select an algebraic expression to introduce using a table to simplify an expression. An expression such as $4y + 3(5y − 1)$ would be a good choice.

3. Call on students to provide the process they would use.

4. Record the process including the justification in the table.

Expression	Justification
$4y + 3(5y − 1)$	Given
$4y + 3[5y + (−1)]$	Definition of subtraction
$4y + 15y + (−3)$	Distributive property of multiplication over addition (DPMA)
$19y + (−3)$	Combine like terms

5. Note that in this example, the subtraction expression was changed to addition by using the definition of subtraction. This step helps students be more accurate, especially when the distributive property is involved.

6. Distribute the Expression Challenge task to each student.

7. Allow about 10 minutes for students to work on problems 1 and 2.

FACILITATE

1. Monitor the pairs as they work.

2. Listen for the use of accurate mathematical language.

3. Select some pairs to share their tables.

4. Discuss their entries as appropriate.

EXPECTED SOLUTIONS

1. a. Eric's table

Expression	Justification
$4x + 3b - 2x + 5b$	Given
$4x + 3b + (-2x) + 5b$	Definition of subtraction
$4x + (-2x) + 3b + 5b$	Commutative property of addition
$2x + 8b$	Combine like terms

b. Kara's table

Expression	Justification
$6(2x - 4) - 6x$	Given
$6[2x + (-4)] + (-6x)$	Definition of subtraction
$12x + (-24) + (-6x)$	Distributive property of multiplication over addition (DPMA)
$12x + (-6x) + (-24)$	Commutative property of addition
$6x + (-24)$	Combine like terms

2. Michaela's table

Expression	Justification
$5x - 2(3x - 8)$	Given
$5x + (-2)[3x + (-8)]$	Definition of subtraction
$5x + (-6x) + (-8)$	Distributive property of multiplication over addition (DPMA)
$-x + (-8)$	Combine like terms

Students should disagree with the third step.

Have pairs complete the rest of the exploration.

a. Select some pairs to share their tables.

b. Discuss alternate solutions to problem 4.

3. Andrew's table

Expression	Justification
8 + 3(–2 + x) – 2(4 – x)	Given
8 + 3(–2 + x) + (–2)[4 + (–x)]	Definition of subtraction
8 + (–6) + 3x + (–8) + 2x	Distributive property of multiplication over addition (DPMA)
8 + (–6) + (–8) + 3x + 2x	Commutative property of addition
–6 + 5x	Combine like terms

4. Jadon's table

Expression	Justification
–3(5 – x) – 7(–2)	Given
–3[5 + (–x)] + (–7)(–2)	Definition of subtraction
–3[(–x) + 5] + (–7)(–2)*	Commutative property of addition
3x + (–15) + 14	Distributive property of multiplication over addition (DPMA)
3x + (–1)	Combine like terms

* Alternate solution: –7(–2) + –3[5 + (–x)]

CLOSE AND GENERALIZATIONS

1. Provide another algebraic expression such as 2(x – 3) + 4(6 + x). Have students create a table and simplify the expression in more than one way. They should notice that they can apply the distributive property before they use the definition of subtraction and combine like terms in different orders. The result is still the same.

2. Summarize the importance of the definition of subtraction and the order of operations.

3. Discuss how tables can be helpful to organize your thinking and explanations for describing the process.

TASK 6.6: EXPRESSION CHALLENGE

Available to download at **resources.corwin.com/classroomreadymath/algebra**

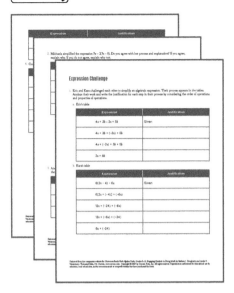

POST-TASK NOTES: REFLECTIONS AND NEXT STEPS

• Are students using PEMDAS (parentheses, exponents, multiplication, division, addition, subtraction), GEMS, or GEMA?

• How does students' procedural understanding of real number operations impact their work with algebraic expressions?

• How does the use of a table to organize the simplifying process support students?

- Students identify algebraic expressions that are equivalent.

Mathematics Content Standard(s)

- 6.EE.3: Apply the properties of operations to generate equivalent expressions.

- 6.EE.4: Identify when two expressions are equivalent.

- 7.EE.1: Apply properties of operations as strategies to add, subtract, factor, and expand linear expressions with rational coefficients.

- A-SSE.1: Interpret expressions that represent a quantity in terms of its context.

- A-SSE.2: Use the structure of an expression to identify ways to rewrite it.

- A-SSE.3: Choose and produce an equivalent form of an expression to reveal and explain properties of the quantity represented by the expression.

Mathematical Practice(s)

- Reason abstractly and quantitatively.
- Model with mathematics.
- Look for and make use of structure.

Task 6.7
Expression Match-Up

TASK
Expression Match-Up

A. $7x + 8(2 - x)$	B. $12x - 7 + 4(6 - x)$	C. $2(18 - x)$
D. $-x + 16$	E. $-(8 - 4)^2x - 3(2x - 2)$	F. $36 - 2x$
G. $2 - 5(3 - x)$	H. $-6x + 6$	I. $10 + 2(3 + x) - 4(x - 5)$
J. $-22x + 6$	K. $4 + (-8x) - 3x^2$	L. $4 + x(3 - 5)^3 - x(3x)$
M. $-6(x - 1)$	N. $-2(11x - 3)$	O. $-10x + 2x + 4 - 3x^2$
P. $5x - 13$	Q. $8x + 17$	R. $-3(x - 1) + 3(1 - x)$

TASK PREPARATION CONSIDERATIONS

- How many sets of Expression Match-Up cards are needed?

- Should students work in pairs or small groups of 4?

- Do students have some procedural understanding of simplifying expressions and order of operations?

SCAFFOLDING OR DIFFERENTIATING THE TASK

- Modify the task to include only the expressions that match with exactly one other expression.

- Suggest that all expressions be simplified before trying to do the matches.

WATCH-FORS!

- Students may misapply the order of operations when simplifying the expressions.

- Students may think that a matching task only allows an expression to be paired with one other expression or that every expression must have a match.

EXTEND THE TASK

- Give students an expression and have them generate two or more equivalent expressions.

LAUNCH

1. Place students in pairs or small groups.

2. Show three expressions, such as $3x + 2$, $5x + 8 + (-6) - 2x$, and $2(x - 4) + 10 + x$.

3. Ask students what they notice about the three expressions. (They should notice they are equivalent.)

4. Tell them that they will be given a set of cards in their pair or small group and their task is to find all the equivalent expressions.

5. Remind them that there may be more than two expressions that match.

6. Distribute an Expression Match-Up task sheet to each student and a set of Expression Match-Up cards to each pair or small group.

7. Allow about 20 minutes for students to work.

FACILITATE

1. Monitor the pairs or small groups as they work.

2. Have students exchange their exploration paper with someone they did not work with.

3. Display the solutions.

4. Have students circle any sets that are not correct when compared to the displayed solutions.

5. Return the papers back to the original students.

6. Have students double-check their solutions and make any corrections.

7. Ask students to share how they decided which expressions were equivalent for any sets of which they were unsure.

   a. What properties did they use to simplify expressions?

   b. How did they use the order of operations?

Vocabulary

- algebraic expression
- equivalent

Materials

- 1 Expression Match-Up task per student
- 1 set of Expression Match-Up cards per pair of students

Task Type

	Conceptual
X	Procedural
	Problem-Solving Application
	Problem-Solving Critical Thinking

	Reversibility
X	Flexibility
X	Generalization

EXPECTED SOLUTIONS

Matches: A and D; G and P; K, L, and O; B and Q; C, F, and I; H, M, and R; E, J, and N

Table can be in any order.

Group 1	A. $7x + 8(2 - x)$	D. $-x + 16$	
Group 2	G. $2 - 5(3 - x)$	P. $5x - 13$	
Group 3	K. $4 + (-8x) - 3x^2$	L. $4 + x(3 - 5)^3 - x(3x)$	O. $-10x + 2x + 4 - 3x^2$
Group 4	B. $12x - 7 + 4(6 - x)$	Q. $8x + 17$	
Group 5	C. $2(18 - x)$	F. $36 - 2x$	I. $10 + 2(3 + x) - 4(x - 5)$
Group 6	H. $-6x + 6$	M. $-6(x - 1)$	R. $-3(x - 1) + 3(1 - x)$
Group 7	E. $-(8 - 4)^2x - 3(2x - 2)$	J. $-22x + 6$	N. $-2(11x - 3)$

CLOSE AND GENERALIZATIONS

1. Tell students you simplified an expression and got $2x - 3$. Have them write two expressions you could have simplified.

   » Have students share the process they used to generate the expression.

2. Summarize the properties used by groups.

TASK 6.7: EXPRESSION MATCH-UP

online resources ⟶ Available to download at **resources.corwin.com/classroomreadymath/algebra**

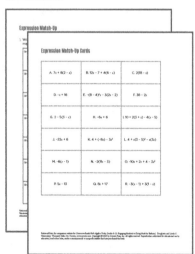

POST-TASK NOTES: REFLECTIONS AND NEXT STEPS

• Do students recognize that there are an infinite number of equivalent expressions?

• Did students use the definition of subtraction to simplify the expressions?

• Which expressions were the easiest for them to simplify? Which expressions were challenging?

Equations Tasks

Now that students have developed the building blocks for algebraic equations in the previous chapters, in Chapter 7 students are ready to work with equations. The tasks in this chapter invite students to create equations to represent the relationships within a particular context, solve equations using multiple strategies, and push their thinking beyond application problems.

In Pyramid Problems, students work within given layouts to solve for missing values. This task engages students in practicing basic computation skills in a game-like context. In a similar playful manner, the Riddle Me This! task draws students into solving problems posed as puzzles by correctly applying properties of operations to modify algebra riddles.

In the Cars and Trucks task, an urban context is used to elicit connection to mathematics that can be modeled using an equation with two variables. The class will be able to find multiple possible solutions to this task.

The More Than or Less Than task reminds students that variables are sometimes used to represent a range of possible solutions and not just one number.

In the task And the Solution Is . . ., students notice the structural aspects of equations that provide insights into the solution process and type of solution.

Eggs-actly involves a nonroutine problem. Students typically choose to work backward or use an equation to solve the task. This generates opportunities for making connections between solution strategies, and fuel for a rich class discussion.

Pyramid Problems

Mathematics Focus

- Students use relationships and equations to solve for missing values.

Mathematics Content Standard(s)

- 8.EE.7: Solve linear equations in one variable.
- A-REI.3: Solve linear equations and inequalities in one variable, including equations with coefficients represented by letters.

Mathematical Practice(s)

- Reason abstractly and quantitatively.
- Construct viable arguments and critique the reasoning of others.
- Model with mathematics.
- Attend to precision.
- Look for and make use of structure.

Vocabulary

- equation

Materials

- 1 Pyramid Problems task per student

TASK

Pyramid Problems

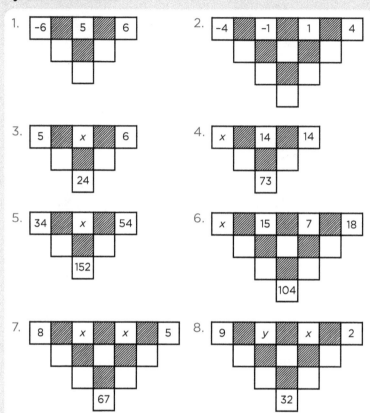

TASK PREPARATION CONSIDERATIONS

- What solution methods have students experienced for solving linear equations?
- How comfortable are students with working backward?

SCAFFOLDING OR DIFFERENTIATING THE TASK

- Have students write the values in each blank square before they try to solve the problems.
- Suggest that students predict the magnitude of the missing values to determine if their solutions are reasonable.
- Change the problems with variables to numerical values.

WATCH-FORS!

- Students may write an equation using only the information in the top row.

- Students may think that if the variable (such as x) is repeated in the pyramid, it cannot represent the same value.

- Students may think that if there are two different variables (such as x and y) in the pyramid, they must be the same value.

EXTEND THE TASK

- Have students create their own pyramid with missing values and trade with other students in the class to solve.

LAUNCH

1. Show an example pyramid such as the one that follows.

   a. Explain that the value of each box is found by adding the values of the two boxes above it.

   b. Use the example pyramid to work with students to complete it.

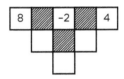

2. Distribute the Pyramid Problems task.

3. Have students independently solve the problems.

4. Allow about 10 minutes.

FACILITATE

1. Monitor students as they work.

2. When the class is finished, put students in pairs.

3. Have them compare their solutions and rectify any discrepancies.

4. Allow about 10 minutes.

5. Ask some pairs to share the process they used to find the missing values.

6. Focus on problem 8, which has multiple solutions.

Task Type

	Conceptual	
X	Procedural	
X	Problem-Solving Application	
	Problem-Solving Critical Thinking	

X	Reversibility	
X	Flexibility	
	Generalization	

EXPECTED SOLUTIONS

1.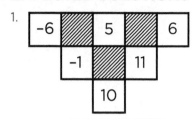

2.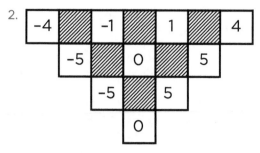

3.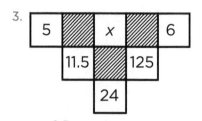

   $x = 6.5$

4.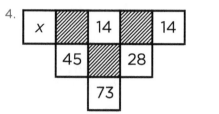

   $x = 31$

5.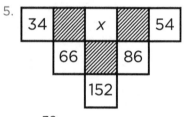

   $x = 32$

6.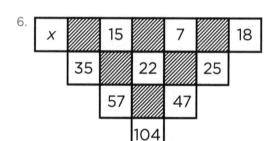

   $x = 20$

7.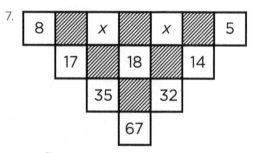

   $x = 9$

8.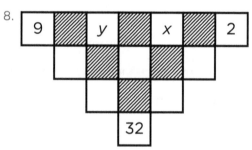

   x and y = any values whose sum is 7

CLOSE AND GENERALIZATIONS

1. Compare and contrast the different processes that students used to find the missing values.

2. Determine equations that could have been used to solve for each of the missing values if they were part of the processes that students described.

3. As time allows, extend the task by asking students to create their own pyramids to exchange with other students to solve.

TASK 7.1: PYRAMID PROBLEMS

 Available to download at **resources.corwin.com/classroomreadymath/algebra**

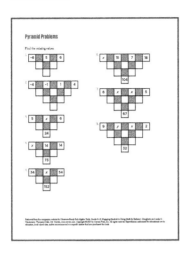

POST-TASK NOTES: REFLECTIONS AND NEXT STEPS

• Did students use a "working backward" strategy?

• Did I extend the problem? Were the student-constructed pyramids robust?

• Should I change the grouping strategies?

Mathematics Focus

- Students model a contextual problem with an equation using two variables and determine multiple solutions.

Mathematics Content Standard(s)

- **6.EE.6:** Use variables to represent numbers and write expressions when solving a real-world or mathematical problem; understand that a variable can represent an unknown number, or, depending on the purpose at hand, any number in a specified set.

- **6.EE.7:** Solve real-world and mathematical problems by writing and solving equations of the form $x + p = q$ and $px = q$ for cases in which p, q, and x are all nonnegative rational numbers.

- **7.EE.4:** Use variables to represent quantities in a real-world or mathematical problem, and construct simple equations and inequalities to solve problems by reasoning about the quantities.

- **A-CED.2:** Create equations in two or more variables to represent relationships between quantities; graph equations on coordinate axes with labels and scales.

Task 7.2
Cars and Trucks

TASK

Cars and Trucks

You may have seen devices called *traffic counters* that count the vehicles passing along a street. You can recognize the devices as thin black cords stretched across a street or highway and connected to a "brain box" at the side of the road. The traffic counter is usually pressure activated. It registers a count each time a set of wheels (wheels on a single axle) rolls over the tube. A normal car registers two counts: one for the front wheels and one for the rear wheels. A truck with three axles (front wheels plus a double set of rear wheels) registers three counts. A large semi-truck with more axles might register four or five counts.

1. Suppose that during a one-hour period, a particular traffic counter registered 35 counts on a residential street where heavy trucks are prohibited. (That is, only two-axle vehicles like cars or three-axle vehicles like light trucks are allowed.) How many cars and light trucks passed over the traffic counter?

   a. Describe your solution process.

   b. Is there one unique answer? If yes, support your answer. If no, find other possible solutions.

TASK PREPARATION CONSIDERATIONS

- Will students understand what a traffic counter is from the description in the problem?

- What solution methods will students use to solve the problem?

- How many different solution methods are possible?

SCAFFOLDING OR DIFFERENTIATING THE TASK

- Suggest that students take a guess-and-test approach if they have difficulty starting on a solution.

- Recommend headings for their table to record guesses.

- Ask if there is a reasonable range for the number of cars and light trucks. For example, it has to be fewer than 20 cars.

WATCH-FORS!

- Students may consider only one solution.

- Students may label the variables (if they use them) as *c* and *t* to represent cars and trucks rather than the *number* of cars and trucks.

- Students may think they cannot use any other variables besides *c* and *t* to represent the number of cars or trucks.

EXTEND THE TASK

- Change the number recorded from the traffic counter to allow larger trucks. For example, suppose that the traffic counter recorded 54 counts.

- Use the equation $2b + 3h = 35$ and graph potential ordered pairs on a coordinate grid. Focus on reasonable solutions, noting that all solutions will be in quadrant I and the graph will be a discrete graph.

LAUNCH

1. Place students in pairs.

2. As needed, explain what a traffic counter is or show a video of a traffic counter. Students may have seen these devices in their own town.

3. Distribute a Cars and Trucks task to each student.

4. Have students think independently for 1 minute about how they will attack the problem.

5. Have them share their strategy with their partner and then begin work on the solution.

6. Allow about 15 minutes for students to work.

FACILITATE

1. Monitor the pairs as they work.

2. Select pairs to first share their solution strategy.

   a. Did any pairs write an equation?

   b. How were their tables organized if they used guess-and-test?

3. Have pairs share their solutions.

   a. What do students notice about the solutions? Do they see any patterns?

Mathematical Practice(s)

- Make sense of problems and persevere in solving them.
- Reason abstractly and quantitatively.
- Model with mathematics.
- Attend to precision.
- Look for and express regularity in repeated reasoning.

Vocabulary

- mathematical modeling
- variable

Materials

- 1 Cars and Trucks exploration per student

Task Type

	Conceptual
	Procedural
X	Problem-Solving Application
	Problem-Solving Critical Thinking

	Reversibility
X	Flexibility
	Generalization

EXPECTED SOLUTION

b	16	13	10	7	4	1
h	1	3	5	7	9	11

b = number of cars; *h* = number of light trucks

CLOSE AND GENERALIZATIONS

1. Summarize the solution strategies used.

2. Discuss the value of making a table to organize information when using guess-and-test as a solution strategy.

3. Focus on writing an equation with two variables such as $2b + 3h = 35$, allowing the value of each variable to vary. Have students discuss how the equation represents the relationship and supports a solution approach.

TASK 7.2: CARS AND TRUCKS

 Available to download at **resources.corwin.com/classroomreadymath/algebra**

POST-TASK NOTES: REFLECTIONS AND NEXT STEPS

• How did the context of the problem impact students' solution process and solution?

• Were students comfortable with accepting multiple solutions?

• How effective and productive was having students think independently before they worked in a pair?

Task 7.3
Riddle Me This!

Mathematics Focus

- Students use properties of operations to modify algebraic riddles.

Mathematics Content Standard(s)

- 7.EE.1: Apply properties of operations as strategies to add, subtract, factor, and expand linear expressions with rational coefficients.

- 7.EE.2: Understand that rewriting an expression in different forms in a problem context can shed light on the problem and how the quantities in it are related.

- 7.EE.4: Use variables to represent quantities in a real-world or mathematical problem, and construct simple equations and inequalities to solve problems by reasoning about the quantities.

- A-SSE.3: Choose and produce an equivalent form of an expression to reveal and explain properties of the quantity represented by the expression.

- A-CED.1: Create equations and inequalities in one variable and use them to solve problems.

TASK

Riddle Me This!

1. a. Follow the steps in the riddle.

   Think of a number between 1 and 30.

   Multiply the number by 3.

   Add 8 more than the original number.

   Divide by 4.

   Subtract the original number.

   b. How could you change the final step so you end up with your original number?

2. a. Follow the steps in the riddle.

   Enter the first three digits of your phone number (not your area code).

   Multiply by 80.

   Add 1.

   Multiply by 250.

   Add the last four digits of your phone number.

   Add the last four digits of your phone number again.

   Subtract 250.

   Divide by 2.

   b. Describe the number that you got as your result.

3. a. Follow the steps in the riddle.

   Think of a number.

   Subtract 7.

   Add 3 more than the original number.

   Add 4.

   Multiply by 3.

   Divide by 6.

Mathematical Practice(s)

- Reason abstractly and quantitatively.
- Construct viable arguments and critique the reasoning of others.
- Model with mathematics.
- Attend to precision.
- Look for and make use of structure.

Vocabulary

- opposite
- commutative property of multiplication
- commutative property of addition

Materials

- 1 Riddle Me This! task per student
- 1 calculator per student or pair of students

Task Type

X	Conceptual
X	Procedural
	Problem-Solving Application
X	Problem-Solving Critical Thinking

X	Reversibility
X	Flexibility
X	Generalization

b. Describe the number that you got as your result.

c. Look at the steps in the riddle. Which steps can you reverse without changing the result?

4. a.   This riddle is missing the last step.

Think of a number.

Take its opposite.

Multiply by 2.

Subtract 2.

Divide by 2.

b. Create a final step so that the result is one more than the original number.

c. Create a final step so that the result is the opposite of the original number.

d. Create a final step so that the result is always 0.

e. Create a final step so that the result is always –1.

TASK PREPARATION CONSIDERATIONS

- Have students had experience with number riddles and generalizing them?
- Are students familiar with the properties of operations?

SCAFFOLDING OR DIFFERENTIATING THE TASK

- Have students try more than one number in the riddles to better detect patterns.
- Provide algebra tiles or other manipulatives to assist students in understanding why each riddle gets a particular result.
- Suggest that students organize their results from the riddles' steps in a table so they can more easily see the results.
- Provide a calculator for students so that their results are accurate.

WATCH-FORS!

- Students may consider only whole number values and not realize that the riddles work for any numbers.

EXTEND THE TASK

- Have students create their own riddles and share them with the class.

LAUNCH

1. Place students in pairs.

2. Do an example riddle with the class.

   Think of a number between 1 and 30.

   Multiply the number by 3.

   Add 8 more than the original number.

   Divide by 4.

   Subtract the original number.

3. Have students share their results.

   a. Students should notice that the result is 2 no matter what number they start with.

   b. To extend the problem as time allows, you can ask students to try it with other numbers, such as a fraction, a decimal, 0, or a negative number.

   c. You may want to work through a generalization with the class if they have not had experience in doing one.

   Let x = starting number.

   First step: $3x$

   Second step: $3x + x + 8$

   Third step: $\dfrac{4x + 8}{4} = x + 2$

   Final step: $x + 2 - x = 2$

4. Tell the students that they are going to be working with riddles like this as they try to determine why they get the results they do or how to change the riddle for a different or the same result.

5. Allow about 30 minutes for students to work.

FACILITATE

1. Monitor the pairs as they work.

2. Have pairs share their solutions by selecting a different pair for each riddle.

EXPECTED SOLUTIONS

1. b. Subtract 2 for the final step.

2. b. The result should be the student's phone number.

3. b. The result should be the original number.

   c. Steps 2 and 3; steps 3 and 4; and steps 2 and 4 can be reversed.

4. b. Add 2 more than twice the original number.

    c. Add 1.

    d. Add 1 more than the original number.

    e. Add the original number.

CLOSE AND GENERALIZATIONS

1. Select a riddle and work through the algebraic expressions to create a generalization. Be sure to identify the variable.

TASK 7.3: RIDDLE ME THIS!

 Available to download at **resources.corwin.com/classroomreadymath/algebra**

POST-TASK NOTES: REFLECTIONS AND NEXT STEPS

• How did the task contribute to students' understanding of the concept of variable?

• What riddles could I incorporate in future lessons that would build on this experience?

• What properties of operations did students explicitly discuss as part of their solution process?

Task 7.4
More Than or Less Than

Mathematics Focus

- Students substitute values into inequality statements to determine the solution set.

Mathematics Content Standard(s)

- 7.EE.4: Use variables to represent quantities in a real-world or mathematical problem, and construct simple equations and inequalities to solve problems by reasoning about the quantities.
- A-CED.1: Create equations and inequalities in one variable and use them to solve problems.

Mathematical Practice(s)

- Reason abstractly and quantitatively.
- Model with mathematics.
- Attend to precision.
- Look for and make use of structure.

Vocabulary

- inequality
- solution set
- substitute
- equivalent inequalities

Materials

- 1 More Than or Less Than task per student

TASK

More Than or Less Than

1. Substitute the values for x in each inequality. State whether the value makes a true or false inequality.

x	–3	–2	–1	0	1	2
$2x < 4$	True	True	True	True	True	False
$1 > x$						
$-2 > 5x + 3$						
$8x + 3 < 3x - 2$						
$3 < 3 + x$						
$3x + 5 > 2x + 5$						

2. Use the preceding table to graph the solution set for each of the following inequalities on a number line.

a. $2x < 4$

b. $1 > x$

c. $-2 > 5x + 3$

d. $8x + 3 < 3x - 2$

e. $3 < 3 + x$

f. $3x + 5 > 2x + 5$

3. How does the table in problem 1 help you understand the graph of each inequality?

4. Zoie said, "I am trying to solve the inequality $2x + 3 < 7$. I know if I substitute 2 for x, $2 \cdot 2 + 3$ *equals* 7. I think 0 and the negative numbers will be a solution for the inequality. The solution must be $x < 1$ because that includes numbers that are less than 2."

   Do you agree with Zoie's thinking? Why or why not? Be specific in your explanation.

Task Type

X	Conceptual
	Procedural
	Problem-Solving Application
	Problem-Solving Critical Thinking

	Reversibility
	Flexibility
X	Generalization

TASK PREPARATION CONSIDERATIONS

- Can students read inequality symbols ($<$, $\leq$, $>$, $\geq$)?

- What experience have students had in graphing points on a number line?

SCAFFOLDING OR DIFFERENTIATING THE TASK

- Provide a calculator if students have difficulty substituting values into the inequality.

- Have students look for patterns in the table to determine the point where the expressions on both sides of the inequality sign are equal.

- Suggest that students try values that are not integers.

WATCH-FORS!

- Students may say "plug in" when they substitute the values for the variable. Restate their language using "substitute" instead of "plug in."

- Students may think that the solution to an inequality contains only integral values.

- Students may use the "alligator mouth" to read the inequality symbols. Restate their language using "greater than" or "less than."

EXTEND THE TASK

- Give students a solution to an inequality such as $x > -2$ and ask them to create an inequality for which this would be a solution.

LAUNCH

1. Place students in pairs.

2. Distribute a More Than or Less Than task per student.

3. Review the directions. Check students' understanding of the inequality signs.

4. Allow about 15 minutes for students to work.

FACILITATE

1. Monitor the pairs as they work.

2. Select a pair to share their table responses.

   a. Does everyone agree with the responses?

3. Have another pair share their graphs.

   a. Does everyone agree with the graphs?

   b. What do students notice about questions 2.c, 2.d, 2.e, and 2.f? Use these graphs to discuss equivalent inequalities.

   c. Discuss graphs as needed.

4. Ask two other pairs to share their responses for questions 3 and 4.

EXPECTED SOLUTIONS

1.

x	-3	-2	-1	0	1	2
$2x < 4$	True	True	True	True	True	False
$1 > x$	T	T	T	T	F	F
$-2 > 5x + 3$	T	T	F	F	F	F
$8x + 3 < 3x - 2$	T	T	F	F	F	F
$3 < 3 + x$	F	F	F	F	T	T
$3x + 5 > 2x + 5$	F	F	F	F	T	T

2. a. $2x < 4$

   b. $1 > x$

   c. $-2 > 5x + 3$

   d. $8x + 3 < 3x - 2$

   e. $3 < 3 + x$

   f. $3x + 5 > 2x + 5$

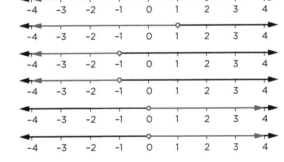

4. Disagree. The solution is $x < 2$. Nonintegral numbers less than 2 such as 1.9 or $\frac{7}{4}$ are also solutions.

CLOSE AND GENERALIZATIONS

1. Discuss the difference between an open and a closed circle on the number line.

2. Extend the discussion by asking students questions such as "If the solution to an inequality is $x > 4$, what is the smallest value x could be?"

TASK 7.4: MORE THAN OR LESS THAN

POST-TASK NOTES: REFLECTIONS AND NEXT STEPS

• Were students relying on the "alligator mouth" or another nonmathematical mnemonic to read the inequality signs?

• How important is students' understanding of rational numbers in solving algebraic inequalities? Do I need to adjust instruction to build on that understanding?

• Is the number line a sufficient representation to support students' understanding of the solution to an inequality?

Task 7.5
And the Solution Is . . .

TASK

And the Solution Is . . .

You are solver A.

You and your partner (solver B) will each solve three equations from the And the Solution Is . . . equation sheet.

1. Choose one equation labeled *L*, one labeled *M*, and one labeled *R*.

2. Do not choose any of the same equations as your partner.

3. Solve one of the equations by guess-and-test.

4. Solve a second equation using equivalent equations.

5. Solve the third equation by a method of your choice, excluding solving by inspection.

Guess-and-test method: Write the number next to the label of the equation you are solving by the guess-and-test method.

L＿＿   M＿＿   R＿＿＿

Write the left-hand expression of the equation in the heading of the middle column (LHE). Write the right-hand expression of the equation in the heading of the third column (RHE). For each value of *x* you decide to use, record the value of each expression in the respective column. You may add rows as needed.

x	LHE	RHE

Mathematics Focus

- Students notice structural aspects of equations that provide insights into the solution process and the type of solution.

Mathematics Content Standard(s)

- 8.EE.7: Solve linear equations in one variable.
- A-REI.3: Solve linear equations and inequalities in one variable, including equations with coefficients represented by letters.

Mathematical Practice(s)

- Reason abstractly and quantitatively.
- Model with mathematics.
- Attend to precision.
- Look for and make use of structure.

Vocabulary

- equivalent equations
- guess-and-test
- solving by inspection
- solution of an equation

Materials

- 1 And the Solution Is . . . set of equations per pair
- 1 And the Solution Is . . . set of solver sheets A and B per pair

Task Type

	Conceptual
X	Procedural
X	Problem-Solving Application
	Problem-Solving Critical Thinking

	Reversibility
X	Flexibility
	Generalization

I agree/disagree with the solution of the equation.

_____

Equivalent equations method: Write the number next to the label of the equation you are solving by using equivalent equations. (Remember, you must select an equation labeled with a different letter from the equation you chose for the guess-and-test method.)

L___   M___   R___

Write the equations in the left-hand column and the property or reason in the right-hand column. You may add rows as needed for your work.

Equivalent Equations	Reasoning/Property
	Given

I agree/disagree with the solution of the equation.

_____

Your solution choice: Write the number next to the label of the equation you are solving using a method of your choice, excluding solving by inspection. You must select an equation labeled with the letter of an equation you have not yet solved.

L___   M___   R___

Clearly show or describe your work in an organized manner in the area provided so anyone can understand your reasoning.

I agree/disagree with the solution of the equation.

_____

And the Solution Is . . .

You are solver B.

You and your partner (solver A) will each solve three equations from the And the Solution Is . . . equation sheet.

1. Choose one equation labeled *L*, one labeled *M*, and one labeled *R*.

2. Do not choose any of the same equations as your partner.

3. Solve one of the equations by guess-and-test.

4. Solve a second equation using equivalent equations.

5. Solve the third equation by a method of your choice, excluding solving by inspection.

Guess-and-test method: Write the number next to the label of the equation you are solving by the guess-and-test method.

L___   M___   R___

Write the left-hand expression of the equation in the heading of the middle column (LHE). Write the right-hand expression of the equation in the heading of the third column (RHE). For each value of *x* you decide to use, record the value of each expression in the respective column. You may add rows as needed.

x	LHE	RHE

I agree/disagree with the solution of the equation. _____

Equivalent equations method: Write the number next to the label of the equation you are solving by using equivalent equations. (Remember, you must select an equation labeled with a different letter from the equation you chose for the guess-and-test method.)

L___   M___   R___

Write the equations in the left-hand column and the property or reason in the right-hand column. You may add rows as needed for your work.

Equivalent Equations	Reasoning/Property
	Given

I agree/disagree with the solution of the equation. _____

Your solution choice: Write the number next to the label of the equation you are solving using a method of your choice, excluding solving by inspection. You must select an equation labeled with the letter of an equation you have not yet solved.

L___   M___   R___

Clearly show or describe your work in an organized manner in the area provided so anyone can understand your reasoning.

I agree/disagree with the solution of the equation. _____

TASK PREPARATION CONSIDERATIONS

- What solution methods have students experienced for solving linear equations?

- Should concrete manipulatives such as algebra tiles be provided for students?

SCAFFOLDING OR DIFFERENTIATING THE TASK

- Suggest that students select a different equation if they have difficulty solving their original choice or that they switch the equation to a different solution method.

- Consider providing algebra tiles to support solving an equation.

WATCH-FORS!

- Students may think that an equation can have only one solution.

- Students may solve an equation in only one way, by creating equivalent equations.

EXTEND THE TASK

- Have students create an equation that could most efficiently be solved by a specific strategy, such as solving by inspection (e.g., $3 + x = 1$) or guess-and-test.

LAUNCH

1. Place students in pairs and designate one student to be solver A and the other student to be solver B.

2. Distribute the And the Solution Is . . . solver sheets A and B to each pair and have the respective student take the appropriate one.

3. Distribute the And the Solution Is . . . set of equations to each pair.

4. Discuss the directions for And the Solution Is . . . For example:

   a. Each of you will solve three equations. You will select one equation labeled *L*, one labeled *M*, and one labeled *R*. You may not choose the same equation as your partner. You must use guess-and-test to solve one of your equations and equivalent equations to solve a second equation. For your third equation, you can solve it using any strategy you choose, except solving by inspection.

5. Allow about 25 minutes for students to work.

FACILITATE

1. Monitor the pairs as they work.

   a. Make sure students are solving the equations independently.

2. Have students in each pair exchange their recording sheets.

   a. Ask students to check their partner's work.

   b. If they agree with the solution, they should circle *agree* and initial it.

   c. If they disagree with the solution, they should explain why.

   d. Students then return the recording sheets to the original solver.

   e. Have the original solver make any needed corrections.

3. Have students share the solutions with the whole class for each equation.

EXPECTED SOLUTIONS

For equations in group *L*: $\frac{11}{3}$

For equations in group *M*: No solution

For equations in group *R*: −8

CLOSE AND GENERALIZATIONS

1. Ask students what they notice about the equations and their solutions.

2. Discuss why all the equations in each of the three groups have the same solution. You may want to focus on the equivalency of the equations in each group.

3. Discuss how students decided which solution method to use to solve the equations in each of the groups.

TASK 7.5: AND THE SOLUTION IS . . .

 Available to download at **resources.corwin.com/classroomreadymath/algebra**

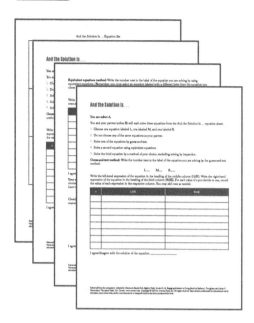

POST-TASK NOTES: REFLECTIONS AND NEXT STEPS

• What different methods of solving equations did my students use?

• Are students noticing the structure of the equations to help them consider an efficient method for solving an equation, or do they automatically go to an equivalent equation method?

• Have students had experience with equations that have more than one solution or have no solution?

Task 7.6
Eggs-actly

TASK

Eggs-actly

An egg vendor sold half her supply of eggs and half an egg to Jared. She then sold half of her remaining supply and half an egg to Staci. Then Kyra bought half the eggs she had left and half an egg. Finally, Kenni bought the rest of her supply of 33 eggs. The vendor did not sell any broken eggs. How many eggs did the egg vendor have to start with?

TASK PREPARATION CONSIDERATIONS

- How many different strategies could be used to solve the problem?

- Should students work individually, in pairs, or in small groups?

- How will students handle the half of an egg?

SCAFFOLDING OR DIFFERENTIATING THE TASK

- Have students use a guess-and-test approach to establish parameters for the numerical solutions.

- Ask students to predict if the number of eggs is odd or even.

- Provide two-color counters or other manipulatives so that students can model the problem using simpler amounts.

- Suggest students start with the ending amount to see if that provides a solution strategy.

WATCH-FORS!

- Students may think the problem is not solvable with the information given.

- Students may try to write an equation to solve the problem as their first strategy.

EXTEND THE TASK

- Present the problem: Mac will be three times Jae's present age in three years. Jae will then be half as old as Mac. How old is Jae now? How are the two problems similar? How are they different?

- Have students solve the problem.

Mathematics Focus

- Students solve a nonroutine problem by using a "working backward" strategy or writing an equation.

Mathematics Content Standard(s)

- 8.EE.7: Solve linear equations in one variable.

- A-REI.3: Solve linear equations and inequalities in one variable, including equations with coefficients represented by letters.

Mathematical Practice(s)

- Make sense of problems and persevere in solving them.

- Reason abstractly and quantitatively.

- Construct viable arguments and critique the reasoning of others.

- Model with mathematics.

- Attend to precision.

- Look for and express regularity in repeated reasoning.

Vocabulary

- discrete variable

Materials

- 1 Eggs-actly task per student
- Calculator (optional)

Task Type

X	Conceptual
	Procedural
	Problem-Solving Application
X	Problem-Solving Critical Thinking

X	Reversibility
X	Flexibility
	Generalization

LAUNCH

1. Place students in pairs.

2. Distribute the Eggs-actly task.

3. Have students read through the problem to make sure they understand it.

4. Tell students to work with their partner to find a solution.

5. Allow about 20 minutes for students to work.

FACILITATE

1. Monitor the pairs as they work.

2. Have pairs share the solution method or strategy they used.

   a. How are the solution methods alike? How are they different?

   b. How did the students use the information about half an egg to help them solve the problem? Introduce the term *discrete values* in talking about counting by egg units.

   c. Why is that important information?

3. Select pairs to share their answers.

EXPECTED SOLUTION

The vendor started with 271 eggs.

CLOSE AND GENERALIZATIONS

1. Summarize the similarities and differences between solution approaches.

2. Ask students which solution approach they would use if they were to do a similar problem.

TASK 7.6: EGGS-ACTLY

Eggs-actly

An egg vendor sold half her supply of eggs and half an egg to Jared. She then sold half of her remaining supply and half an egg to Staci. Then Kyra bought half the eggs she had left and half an egg. Finally, Kenni bought the rest of her supply of 35 eggs. The vendor did not sell any broken eggs. How many eggs did the egg vendor have to start with?

POST-TASK NOTES: REFLECTIONS AND NEXT STEPS

- Were students open to trying solution approaches other than using an equation?

- Did students persevere as they solved the problem?

- Was the support of working in a pair sufficient for this problem?

CHAPTER 8

Linear and Nonlinear Relationship Tasks

Functions and relationships are the focus of this chapter. The tasks provide opportunities for you to develop conceptual understandings and explore multiple contexts that involve relationships between two variables. Students have the opportunity to build their understanding of these relationships as they use multiple representations to model them.

Guess My Rule is an introductory task that can be modified to use as a warm-up for any class. It supports students in developing covariational thinking.

Is It or Isn't It?, Reps and More Reps, and To the Slopes coalesce the relationship among equations, graphs, and tables. These tasks emphasize the characteristics of functions, multiple representations of functions, and the concept of slope, respectively.

A familiar context for students is that of charging a cell phone or computer. Not Fully Charged uses that context to focus on dependent and independent variables.

So Knotty presents a context that requires students to measure and record data. This is a great problem to use to help students visualize the meaning of slope because they can "see" where the slope comes from in the physical materials. It also provides an opportunity to distinguish between discrete and continuous data and see how the data type may impact the graph. Ratios Within continues with a measurement context, but in this task, students are measuring their own arms, hands, and fingers and determining the relationships that approximate the Golden Ratio.

Covered With Paint is a familiar painted-cube problem with a twist. Students graph the relationships between the total number of cubes and the number of cubes painted on certain sides.

The tasks in this chapter end with If the Shoe Fits where students explore the relationship between their height and shoe size. This provides a real-world context that also emphasizes the imprecision of measurement.

- Students use values in a table to predict the shape of a graph and graph the values on a Cartesian coordinate plane.

Mathematics Content Standard(s)

- 6.EE.9: Use variables to represent two quantities in a real-world problem that change in relationship to one another; write an equation to express one quantity, thought of as the dependent variable, in terms of the other quantity, thought of as the independent variable. Analyze the relationship between the dependent and independent variables using graphs and tables, and relate these to the equation.

- 8.F.2: Compare properties of two functions, each represented in a different way (algebraically, graphically, numerically in tables, or by verbal descriptions).

- 8.F.4: Construct a function to model a linear relationship between two quantities. Determine the rate of change and initial value of the function from a description of a relationship or from two (x, y) values, including reading these from a table or from a graph. Interpret the rate of change and initial value of a linear function in terms of the situation it models, and in terms of its graph or a table of values.

Task 8.1
Guess My Rule

TASK

Guess My Rule

Anna was playing Guess My Rule with Ray. As Anna gave numbers, Ray applied his rule to them. They entered their numbers into a table.

Before (Anna)	After (Ray)
–1	–1
2	2
0	0
–4	–4
3	3
1	1

Anna thought that it would be possible to graph the information from the table on a Cartesian coordinate system.

1. a. Use Anna's number as the x-value and Ray's number as the y-value. Write an equation that shows Ray's rule.

   b. Graph the ordered pairs (x, y).

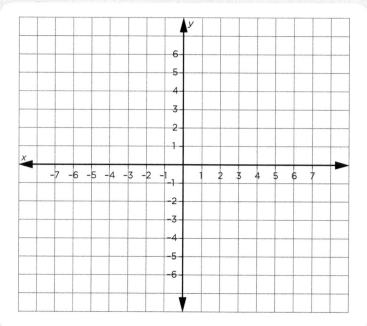

c. Connect the points on your graph. What do you notice?

d. In Anna and Ray's graph, the y-value is equal to the x-value. What do you think the graph would look like if the y-value was equal to the opposite of the x-value? Why? Justify your answer.

e. Complete a table of values to represent $y = -x$.

x	y
–4	4

f. Graph your points.

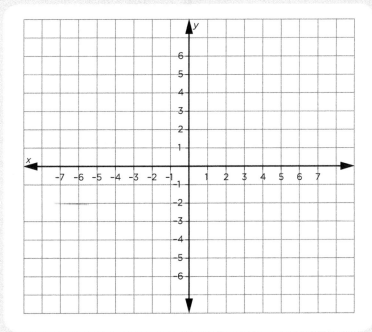

g. How does your graph compare to the graph you made in problem 1.b?

• F-IF-4: For a function that models a relationship between two quantities, interpret key features of graphs and tables in terms of the quantities, and sketch graphs showing key features given a verbal description of the relationship.

Mathematical Practice(s)

• Make sense of problems and persevere in solving them.
• Model with mathematics.
• Look for and make use of structure.

Vocabulary

• independent variable
• dependent variable
• slope
• slope-intercept form
• function

Materials

• 1 Guess My Rule task per student

	Conceptual
X	Procedural
	Problem-Solving Application
	Problem-Solving Critical Thinking

X	Reversibility
	Flexibility
X	Generalization

2. It was Anna's turn to make a rule. Here is the table from this version of the game.

Before (Ray)	After (Anna)
2	2
4	3
1	$1\frac{1}{2}$
–4	–1
0	1
–1	$\frac{1}{2}$

a. Use Ray's number as the *x*-value and Anna's number as the *y*-value. Write an equation that shows Anna's rule.

b. Graph the ordered pairs (*x*, *y*).

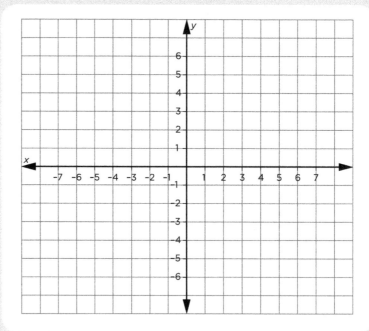

c. Connect the points on your graph. What do you notice about your graph?

d. How does your graph in problem 2.b compare to your graphs in problems 1.b and 1.f?

TASK PREPARATION CONSIDERATIONS

• What rules should I choose for the launch portion of the task?

• What is students' skill level in graphing?

• Will students differentiate between proportional and nonproportional relationships?

SCAFFOLDING OR DIFFERENTIATING THE TASK

• Review how to graph points and how to find the coordinate of points on a graph.

WATCH-FORS!

• Students may use only positive integer input values to identify the rule.

• Students may look for patterns in only one column or one row rather than thinking covariationally.

EXTEND THE TASK

• If you were to continue the table and graph with many more points, in what quadrants would you expect to find the points?

• How do you think the graph would change if the equation was $y = \frac{1}{2}x + 2$?

• How do you think the graph would change if the equation was $y = x + 1$?

LAUNCH

1. Arrange students in pairs.

2. Display a two-column table with the headers Before and After.

3. Tell students you are going to play a game called Guess My Rule.

4. Tell them that you have decided on a rule. They will take turns giving you a number. You'll record the number in the Before column of the table. You will then apply your rule and record the result in the After column of the table. When students think they know the rule, they are to raise their hand but not reveal the rule. Continue soliciting numbers until several students have their hands raised.

5. Have students tell the rule in words.

6. Record n in the Before column and ask students what will go in the After column.

7. Record their expressions. Discuss as appropriate.

8. Tell students they are going to be working with Guess My Rule tables in this task.

9. Distribute a Guess My Rule task to each student.

10. Allow 15 minutes for students to work.

FACILITATE

1. Monitor students as they work.

2. Have pairs share their solutions to each of the problems.

3. During debriefing, ask questions to focus students' attention on the steepness of the lines and the relationship to the equation. This may also be an opportunity to introduce proportional relationships and slope-intercept form, depending on students' needs.

EXPECTED SOLUTIONS

1. a. $x = y$ or $y = x$. If students write it as $x = y$, offer $y = x$ to focus on the independent and dependent variable ideas. This will also set up writing equations in slope-intercept form and using function notation.

    b.

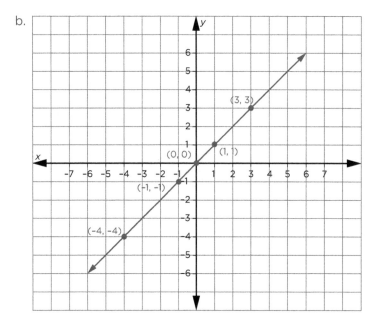

    c. Students should notice that the points suggest a line. What other points would belong on this line? Be sure students recognize that other points such as $\left(\frac{1}{2}, \frac{1}{2}\right)$ are on the line. Focus on the linear relationship. They may also notice that the line goes through the origin and passes through quadrants I and III. The graph of a line that goes through the origin represents a proportional relationship.

    d. Answers will vary, but the value of x should be opposite the value of y.

e.

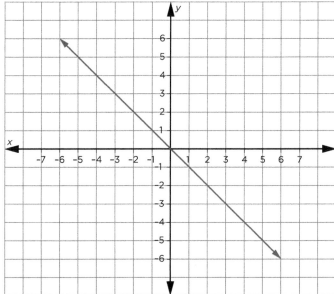

f. Answers will vary, but students should notice that this graph goes down from left to right. Both lines pass through the origin.

2. a. $y = \frac{1}{2}x + 1$

b.

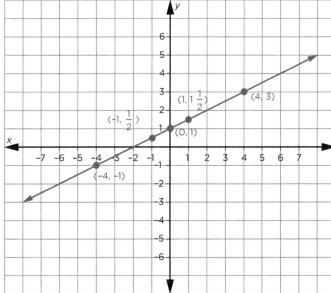

c. Students should notice that the points suggest a linear relationship. Through what quadrants does the line go? (Quadrants I, II, and III.) Why do you think this line does not go through the origin? (It is not a proportional relationship.) Students may notice that the line is shifted or translated up 1 unit.

d. Answers will vary, but look for opportunities to discuss the steepness, the shape of the graph, and the intersection with the origin.

CLOSE AND GENERALIZATIONS

1. Continue to focus on other generalizations. For example, is it possible for a line to go through all four quadrants?

2. Summarize the characteristics of a proportional relationship versus one that is not.

TASK 8.1: GUESS MY RULE

online resources — Available to download at **resources.corwin.com/classroomreadymath/algebra**

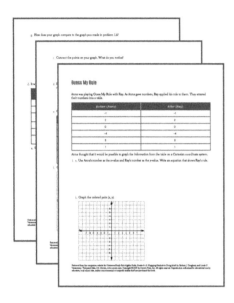

POST-TASK NOTES: REFLECTIONS AND NEXT STEPS

• What evidence do I have that students are using covariational thinking?

• How can I use Guess My Rule as a warm-up for my lessons that involve polynomials or quadratics?

• Are there graphing skills that need to be developed further to support students' access to functions?

Task 8.2

Is It or Isn't It?

TASK

Is It or Isn't It?

Cruz and his friends are trying to find which graphs represent a function. They have determined that two of the following graphs are functions and one is not a function.

Function

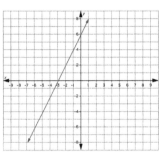

Not a function

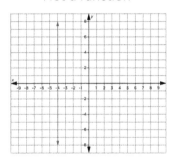

Function

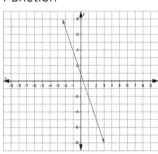

1. They must decide which of these two graphs represents a function. Which graph do you think represents a function? Why?

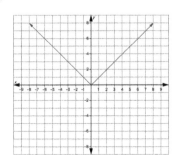
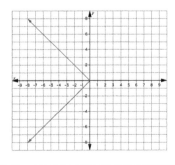

Mathematics Focus

- Students identify relationships that are functions and note that they can be represented with function notation [$f(x)$].

Mathematics Content Standard(s)

- 8.F.1: Understand that a function is a rule that assigns to each input exactly one output. The graph of a function is the set of ordered pairs consisting of an input and the corresponding output.

- 8.F.4: Construct a function to model a linear relationship between two quantities. Determine the rate of change and initial value of the function from a description of a relationship or from two (x, y) values, including reading these from a table or from a graph. Interpret the rate of change and initial value of a linear function in terms of the situation it models, and in terms of its graph or a table of values.

- F-IF-1: Understand that a function from one set (called the domain) to another set (called the range) assigns to each element of the domain exactly one element of the range. If f is a function and x is an element of its domain, then $f(x)$ denotes the output of f corresponding to the input

2. Cruz decides that it would be helpful to make a table to show some of the points found on the graphs.

Graph and Table A

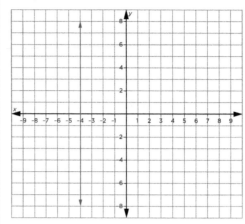

x = –4	
x	y
–4	5
–4	3
–4	7
–4	9
–4	1
–4	11
–4	–1

Graph and Table B

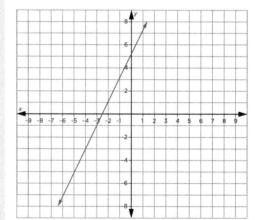

y = 2x+5	
x	y
–3	–1
–2	1
–1	3
0	5
1	7
2	9
3	11

Graph and Table C

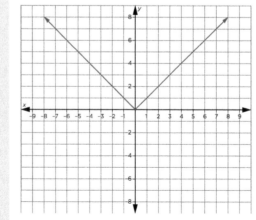

y = |x|	
x	y
0	0
–1	1
1	1
2	2
–2	2
3	3
–3	3

Graph and Table D

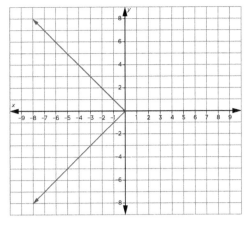

-|y| = x	
x	y
0	0
-1	1
-1	-1
-2	2
-2	-2
-3	3
-3	-3

Graph and Table E

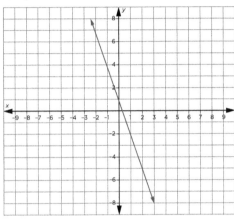

y = -3x+1	
x	y
-1	4
0	1
1	-2
2	-5
3	-8
4	-11
5	-14

Task Type

X	Conceptual
X	Procedural
	Problem-Solving Application
	Problem-Solving Critical Thinking

X	Reversibility
	Flexibility
X	Generalization

a. What do you notice about the values of x and y in Tables A and E?

b. What do you notice about the values of x and y in Tables D and A?

c. What conjectures can you make about the relationship between the x- and y-values and functions?

3. A relationship can be a function if every x-value has a unique (or different) y-value. The relationship $y = 2x + 1$ is a function. This means that each value of y is paired with only one value of x. We say that y is a function of x. When a relationship is a function, we can write it using function notation: $f(x) = 2x + 1$. We read this as "f of x equals 2x + 1."

Take turns reading the following functions to your partner.

a. $f(x) = 3x - 1$

b. $f(x) = 5 - 4x$

c. $f(x) = 2 - x$

d. $f(x) = \frac{1}{2}x + 2$

4. Cruz's teacher said that the disappearance of the rainforest was a "function of the people's choices." He showed a table that made the point that there is a consistent relationship between time and the diameter of the rainforest's disappearance.

Number of Years Since Beginning	Diameter of Barren Area (km)
500	750
475	712.5
450	675
425	637.5
400	600
375	562.5
350	525
325	487.5
300	450
275	412.5
250	375
225	337.5
200	300
175	262.5
150	225
125	187.5
100	150
75	112.5
50	75
25	37.5
0	0

Use the information in the table to write an equation that represents the pattern in the table. Write it using function notation [$f(x)$]. Let x = number of years since beginning.

TASK PREPARATION CONSIDERATIONS

- How will students interpret the function notation? What can you say to help them recognize that this notation is different from multiplication notation?

SCAFFOLDING OR DIFFERENTIATING THE TASK

- Encourage students to notice and articulate the characteristics of the graph or values in the table.

- Have students share their descriptions with their peers.

WATCH-FORS!

- Students may think the *f* in the function notation is a variable being multiplied.

- Students may consider all straight lines as functions.

- Students may confuse lines with undefined slopes and lines with a slope of 0.

EXTEND THE TASK

- Have students generate additional examples of functions and nonfunctions. Select a few and use them in the closure to a class discussion.

LAUNCH

1. Distribute the Is It or Isn't It? task.

2. Have students do problems 1 and 2.

3. Allow about 10 minutes.

FACILITATE

1. Discuss students' ideas for problems 1 and 2. Do not come to any resolution at this time.

2. Have students complete the task.

3. Discuss their solutions as appropriate for your class. Focus on the function notation. Be sure that students understand that $y = 2x + 8$ is the same as $f(x) = 2x + 8$, and y is a function of x. That is, the value of y depends on the value of x.

EXPECTED SOLUTIONS

1. The first graph is a function. The second graph is not a function.

2. a. Students may notice that x-values that repeat have different y-values in Table A, but x-values do not repeat in Table E.

   b. Students may notice that x-values that repeat have different y-values in both tables.

3. Answers may vary. Note:

   a. *f* of *x* equals $3x$ minus 1

   b. *f* of *x* equals 5 minus $4x$

   c. *f* of *x* equals 2 minus *x*

   d. *f* of *x* equals $\frac{1}{2}$ *x* plus 2

4. $f(x) = 1.5x$ or an equivalent form

CLOSE AND GENERALIZATIONS

1. Have students summarize observations and effective strategies they used to determine whether a graph or table of values represents a function.

2. Focus on the concept of function related to the uniqueness of the *y*-value for every *x*-value.

TASK 8.2: IS IT OR ISN'T IT?

 Available to download at **resources.corwin.com/classroomreadymath/algebra**

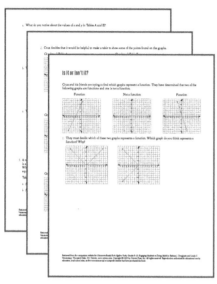

POST-TASK NOTES: REFLECTIONS AND NEXT STEPS

• Were the patterns in the table robust enough that students could detect characteristics of functions?

• Does the function notation confuse students? Will they see the relationship between function notation and slope-intercept form of an equation?

Task 8.3
Reps and More Reps

TASK

Reps and More Reps

1. Use the information from each graph that follows to write an equation in slope-intercept form. Show your process for finding the equation.

a.
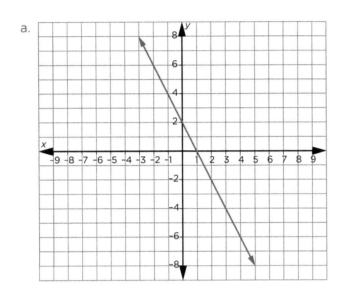

b.
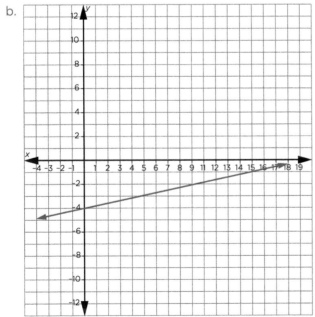

Mathematics Focus

- Students find a linear relationship that can be described by its graph, a set of ordered pairs, and an equation in slope-intercept form.

Mathematics Content Standard(s)

- 8.F.4: Construct a function to model a linear relationship between two quantities. Determine the rate of change and initial value of the function from a description of a relationship or from two (x, y) values, including reading these from a table or from a graph. Interpret the rate of change and initial value of a linear function in terms of the situation it models, and in terms of its graph or a table of values.

- A-CED-4: Rearrange formulas to highlight a quantity of interest, using the same reasoning as in solving equations.

- F-IF-4: For a function that models a relationship between two quantities, interpret key features of graphs and tables in terms of the quantities, and sketch graphs showing key features given a verbal description of the relationship.

- F-BF-1: Write a function that describes a relationship between two quantities.

Mathematical Practice(s)

- Model with mathematics.
- Attend to precision.
- Look for and make use of structure.

Vocabulary

- ordered pairs
- slope-intercept form

Materials

- 1 Reps and More Reps task per student

Task Type

	Conceptual
X	Procedural
	Problem-Solving Application
	Problem-Solving Critical Thinking

X	Reversibility
	Flexibility
	Generalization

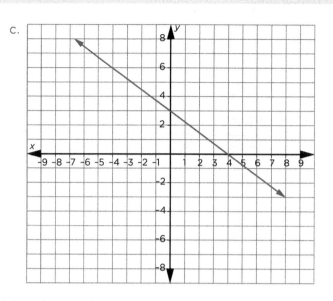

c.

2. Each pair of ordered pairs is on a line. Use the ordered pairs to write an equation in slope-intercept form for each line. Show your process for finding the equation.

   a. (3, 0) and (0, –6)

   b. (–1, 0) and (5, 1)

   c. (–3, 4) and (3, –4)

   d. (4, 5) and (1, 2)

TASK PREPARATION CONSIDERATIONS

- To what extent have students worked with linear relationships?

SCAFFOLDING OR DIFFERENTIATING THE TASK

- Have students describe the pertinent features of the graph.
- Suggest that students consider the slope-intercept form of an equation and relate the needed information to the graph.

WATCH-FORS!

- Students may think they must use two neighboring points to create an equation.

- Students may think a negative slope is less steep than a positive slope.

- Students may think the slope will change if two different points on the same line are used to compute slope.

EXTEND THE TASK

- Tell the class that two students, Aiysha and Chloe, were trying to decide which line had the steeper slope, the line represented with $y = \frac{3}{4}x + 8$ or the line represented by $y = -\frac{3}{4}x - 3$. Which line would you select? Why?

LAUNCH

1. Arrange students in pairs.

2. Distribute the Reps and More Reps task to each student.

3. Remind students to explain or show the process they used to create their equations.

4. Allow about 15 minutes for students to work.

FACILITATE

1. Students who finish before time is called should write their equations in both slope-intercept form and standard form.

2. Have students compare their processes with another pair (i.e., groups of 4).

3. Discuss as a class how students determined the equations of the lines.

EXPECTED SOLUTIONS

1. a. $y = -2x + 2$

   b. $y = \frac{1}{4}x - 4$

   c. $y = -\frac{3}{4} + 3$

2. a. $y = 2x - 6$

   b. $y = \frac{1}{6}x + \frac{1}{6}$

   c. $y = -\frac{4}{3}x$

   d. $y = x + 1$

CLOSE AND GENERALIZATIONS

1. Ask students to discuss the relationships between problems 1 and 2. Which format was the easier one to use, graphs or ordered pairs? Why?

2. Discuss why a specific equation format can be useful in mathematics. For example, compare and contrast the standard form of an equation with the slope-intercept form. What is an advantage of the standard form? What is an advantage of the slope-intercept form?

TASK 8.3: REPS AND MORE REPS

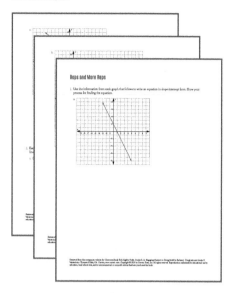

POST-TASK NOTES: REFLECTIONS AND NEXT STEPS

• Is students' conceptual understanding of slope sufficient?

• What methods did students use to write the equation of the line? Were they efficient methods?

• What Watch-Fors! did I note in the lesson that need to be addressed?

Task 8.4
To the Slopes

TASK

To the Slopes

1. Make sets of related cards. Each set consists of a graph, a table, and a slope card. If a set is incomplete, create the missing card to complete it. Record your sets by row in the table.

Graph	Table	Slope

2. Describe the process you used to determine what went into a set of related cards.

3. a. What are some new understandings for you?

   b. What questions do you have about graphing, finding slope, or identifying intercepts?

TASK PREPARATION CONSIDERATIONS

- What experience do students have in finding slope of a line in multiple ways?

- Do students have sufficient graphing skills?

- Do students need a reminder of group behavior norms and expectations before you distribute the task?

SCAFFOLDING OR DIFFERENTIATING THE TASK

- Ask, "How could you use the ordered pairs in the table to find the matching graph and slope?"

Mathematics Focus

- Students recognize that a linear relationship can be described by its graph, a set of ordered pairs, and its slope.

Mathematics Content Standard(s)

- **8.F.4:** Construct a function to model a linear relationship between two quantities. Determine the rate of change and initial value of the function from a description of a relationship or from two (x, y) values, including reading these from a table or from a graph. Interpret the rate of change and initial value of a linear function in terms of the situation it models, and in terms of its graph or a table of values.

- **A-CED-4:** Rearrange formulas to highlight a quantity of interest, using the same reasoning as in solving equations.

- **F-IF-4:** For a function that models a relationship between two quantities, interpret key features of graphs and tables in terms of the quantities, and sketch graphs showing key features given a verbal description of the relationship.

Mathematical Practice(s)

- Make sense of problems and persevere in solving them.
- Construct viable arguments and critique the reasoning of others.
- Model with mathematics.
- Attend to precision.

Vocabulary

- slope
- intercepts

Materials

- 1 To the Slopes task per student
- 1 set of To the Slopes cards, cut apart and shuffled, per pair of students (These need to be prepared prior to class.)

Task Type

X	Conceptual	
	Procedural	
X	Problem-Solving Application	
	Problem-Solving Critical Thinking	

X	Reversibility	
	Flexibility	
X	Generalization	

WATCH-FORS!

- Students may consider only one method for finding the slope of the line.
- Students may think all straight lines are functions.
- Students may think that any graph of an equation in slope-intercept form will be a function and linear.

EXTEND THE TASK

- Have groups change one of the cards in a way that still maintains the match.

LAUNCH

1. Arrange students in pairs.

2. Give students an equation such as $y = 3x + 2$.

   a. Ask them to describe the characteristics of the graph of the equation.

   b. Have them describe what part of the equation relates to that characteristic. For example, they may note that the graph will go up from left to right because the coefficient of the x is positive.

3. Distribute the To the Slopes task to each student and a card set to each pair.

4. Tell students they will be matching three different representations: a graph, a table of values, and the slope of a line.

5. Allow about 15 minutes for students to work.

FACILITATE

1. Have students rotate tables to see what other pairs matched as sets. Do they agree?

2. Have students discuss how they determined which representations went together.

3. Have students share their methods for finding slope.

EXPECTED SOLUTIONS

1. There are 8 sets of related cards.

Graph	Table	Slope
A	2	b
B	4	c
C	6	d
D	8	e
E	1	f
F	3	g
G	5	h
H	7	a

CLOSE AND GENERALIZATIONS

1. Ask, "How could you use the slope to determine the matching graph and table?"

2. Ask students which is most helpful to them in providing information about the shape of a graph: a table or an equation. Why?

3. Do students recognize that the relationship given by graph F is not a function?

TASK 8.4: TO THE SLOPES

online resources Available to download at **resources.corwin.com/classroomreadymath/algebra**

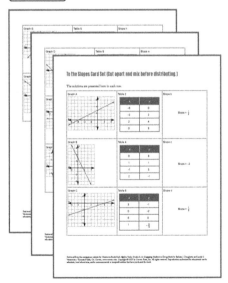

POST-TASK NOTES: REFLECTIONS AND NEXT STEPS

- Can students predict characteristics of a graph from a given equation? Can they predict characteristics of an equation given a graph or a table?

- How can I make the relationships among a table, a graph, and an equation more meaningful for students?

- Have students had enough opportunities with multiple representations of other algebraic concepts to be comfortable using them?

Task 8.5
Not Fully Charged

TASK

Not Fully Charged

1. Marta has a dilemma. She forgot to charge her phone and her computer overnight. It is only an hour before she must leave for school, and her phone is completely dead. She knows that her phone charges at the rate of 10% for every 5 minutes she charges it.

   a. If she charges her phone for 20 minutes, what will be the percentage of charge her phone has?

   b. If she wants to have *at least* 80% charge, how long will she have to charge her phone? Will she have enough time to charge it before she leaves for school?

   c. This table represents the rate at which her phone charges.

Number of minutes charging	0	5	10	15	20	x
Percentage of charge	0	10	20	30	40	y

   Write an equation that represents the relationship in the table, where x is the number of minutes charging and y is the percentage of charge.

2. Marta is not sure how fast her computer charges. She plugged it in and noticed that it already had 12% charge. She recorded information about the time it was plugged in and the corresponding increase in the charge.

Number of minutes charging	0	10	20	30	40
Percentage of charge	12	22	32	42	52

   a. Explain the relationship between the number of minutes charging and the percentage of charge.

   b. If x represents the number of minutes charging, and y represents the percentage of charge, what equation could you write to show this relationship?

Mathematics Focus

- Students use a table to organize data between two quantities, analyze the data, and use symbolic representations to generalize the patterns they notice.

Mathematics Content Standard(s)

- 6.RP.3: Use ratio and rate reasoning to solve real-world and mathematical problems, e.g., by reasoning about tables of equivalent ratios, tape diagrams, double number line diagrams, or equations.

- 7.EE.3: Solve multi-step real-life and mathematical problems posed with positive and negative rational numbers in any form (whole numbers, fractions, and decimals), using tools strategically. Apply properties of operations to calculate with numbers in any form; convert between forms as appropriate; and assess the reasonableness of answers using mental computation and estimation strategies.

- 7.EE.4: Use variables to represent quantities in a real-world or mathematical problem and construct simple equations and inequalities to solve problems by reasoning about the quantities.

- 8.F.4: Construct a function to model a linear relationship between two quantities. Determine the rate of change and initial value of the function from a description of a relationship or from two (x, y) values, including reading these from a table or from a graph. Interpret the rate of change and initial value of a linear function in terms of the situation it models, and in terms of its graph or a table of values.

Mathematical Practice(s)

- Reason abstractly and quantitatively.
- Model with mathematics.
- Look for and express regularity in repeated reasoning.

Vocabulary

- independent variable
- dependent variable
- covary

Materials

- 1 Not Fully Charged task per student

TASK PREPARATION CONSIDERATIONS

- How will I use the context to draw students into the mathematical representation and algebraic reasoning?

- Is the context accessible and appropriate for my students? If not, how can I change the context?

- Will it be helpful for students to graph the data in the tables when we discuss the solutions?

- How can I motivate students to use covariational thinking?

- What other examples can we discuss at the end of the lesson that allow students to easily distinguish between the dependent and independent variables?

SCAFFOLDING OR DIFFERENTIATING THE TASK

- Have students scan the data to make useful predictions before they engage in the formulation of a solution.

WATCH-FORS!

- Students may use a series of computations to produce a single solution, overlooking the generalization that focuses on the relationship between the independent and dependent variables.

- Students may focus on the numerical patterns without considering the generalization.

EXTEND THE TASK

- Have students identify similar scenarios for which covariational data can be collected and used to create an equation.

LAUNCH

1. Arrange students in pairs.

2. Discuss the context of the problem as needed.

3. Distribute the Not Fully Charged task to each student.

4. Allow 10–15 minutes for students to work.

FACILITATE

1. Have pairs share their findings for each problem.

2. During their presentations, focus on language that would indicate covariational thinking. This will help students identify the independent and dependent variables.

3. What are the dependent and independent variables in the equation?

4. Have students describe the relationship in words as you debrief.

   a. Why is there a coefficient of 2 in the equation?

   b. Focus on covariational language such as "As the number of minutes of charging increases by 5 minutes, the percentage of charge increases by 10%."

EXPECTED SOLUTIONS

1. a. 40%

   b. 40 minutes; yes

   c. $y = 2x$

2. a. Answers will vary. For example, students may say that as the number of minutes of charging increases by 10 minutes, the percentage of charge increases by 10%.

   b. $y = x + 12$

CLOSE AND GENERALIZATIONS

1. Have students make explicit connections between the values in the table and the representation of the relationship as an algebraic equation.

2. If time permits, have students graph the points in the table and discuss the shape of the graph.

TASK 8.5: NOT FULLY CHARGED

 Available to download at **resources.corwin.com/classroomreadymath/algebra**

Task Type

	Conceptual
	Procedural
X	Problem-Solving Application
	Problem-Solving Critical Thinking

	Reversibility
X	Flexibility
X	Generalization

POST-TASK NOTES: REFLECTIONS AND NEXT STEPS

• How did the context of the problem support students' engagement?

• Do I see evidence of covariational thinking?

• Did I focus on the relationships between the table and the equation?

Task 8.6
So Knotty

TASK

So Knotty

1. You will collect data showing how the length of a rope changes with each additional knot tied in it. Before your group begins, discuss what you expect to find out. Write your group's prediction about what you think will happen.

2. Measure the length of the rope before you tie any knots, and record the length in the following table. Tie one knot in the rope, measure the new length, and record it in the data table. Continue tying knots in the rope, measuring, and recording data until you have nine knots.

Number of Knots	Length of Rope (cm)
0	
1	
2	
3	
4	
5	
6	
7	
8	
9	

4. What patterns do you notice in the table?

4. a. You will plot the data on graph paper. What quadrant(s) do you need to use? Why?

   b. You will need to decide what scaling to use on the x- and y-axes. Then, plot your data.

   c. What are the dependent and independent variables?

5. Without tying another knot, but using the patterns you noticed in your data, make a prediction for the length of the rope if you were to tie a 10th knot. Explain your reasoning to support that prediction.

Mathematics Focus

- Students find generalizations regarding rate of change that can be applied to real-world experiences.

Mathematics Content Standard(s)

- 8.F.4: Construct a function to model a linear relationship between two quantities. Determine the rate of change and initial value of the function from a description of a relationship or from two (x, y) values, including reading these from a table or from a graph. Interpret the rate of change and initial value of a linear function in terms of the situation it models, and in terms of its graph or a table of values.

- F-IF-4: For a function that models a relationship between two quantities, interpret key features of graphs and tables in terms of the quantities, and sketch graphs showing key features given a verbal description of the relationship.

- F-BF-1: Write a function that describes a relationship between two quantities.

Mathematical Practice(s)

- Reason abstractly and quantitatively.

- Construct viable arguments and critique the reasoning of others.
- Model with mathematics.
- Look for and express regularity in repeated reasoning.

Vocabulary

- rate of change
- diameter
- independent variable
- dependent variable
- proportional relationship
- quadrant

Materials

- 1 So Knotty task per student
- 1 piece of rope per pair or group of 4 (ropes of various diameters, about 55–60 inches in length)
- 1 meter stick or metric measuring tape per pair or group of 4

Task Type

	Conceptual
	Procedural
X	Problem-Solving Application
	Problem-Solving Critical Thinking

	Reversibility
	Flexibility
X	Generalization

6. Does this appear to be a proportional relationship? Why or why not?

7. a. What is the rate of change in your data? Write your answer as a ratio (change in y:change in x).

   b. Write it as a fraction: $\frac{\text{change in } y}{\text{change in } x}$.

8. What is the y-intercept?

9. Using the y-intercept and your rate of change, write an equation that models the relationship of your data.

TASK PREPARATION CONSIDERATIONS

- How many different diameters of rope do I want to use?

- What skills do students have to determine the scaling on a graph for a data set like this one?

- What prior experiences have students had with measuring and producing real-world data?

- If students are inaccurate in their measurements, how will that affect their data?

- How will I handle it if students reverse the dependent and independent variables?

SCAFFOLDING OR DIFFERENTIATING THE TASK

- Ask students by how much their rope length changes as they add more knots. How do they think that will affect their graph?

- Have students graph some of the ordered pairs and notice the trend of the graph.

WATCH-FORS!

- Students may measure with customary units rather than metric.

- Students may think that all data points on a coordinate grid should be connected, regardless of what the data are.

- Students may think that the rate of change across all tables and graphs should be the same because the same number of knots are being tied.

- Students may reverse the dependent and independent variables.

EXTEND THE TASK

- Consider other data collection contexts that could be used to create a table and graph with "messy" real-world data. For example, if it is possible to take students outside, have the groups record the time it takes for each group member to walk a certain distance.

LAUNCH

1. Tell students they are going to be measuring a rope in their pair or group.

   a. Set any norms needed such as that the rope is not to be used for anything except as a tool that is measured in this task.

2. Demonstrate the measuring of the rope and the tying of a knot so that there is some uniformity across the groups. The individual knots should be tied separately on the rope and not stacked on each other.

3. Distribute the So Knotty task to each student.

4. Place students in pairs or groups of 3 or 4.

5. Give pairs or groups a length of rope and a meter stick or measuring tape.

6. Have students share observations of the rope types and make predictions about their findings depending on rope type.

7. Allow about 30 minutes for students to complete the task.

FACILITATE

1. When students have completed the task, put two groups together to compare their graphs and to discuss conjectures that could be made based on similarities and differences that they notice in their tables and graphs.

2. Use a graphing software or application for students to input their data and compare their graphs.

EXPECTED SOLUTIONS

3. a. Only Quadrant I is needed as there will not be any negative values for either the length of the rope or the number of knots.

   b. Scaling of the y-axis will probably vary depending on the original length of the rope.

   c. The number of knots is the independent variable, and the length of the rope is the dependent variable.

4. Answers will vary.

5. No, it is not a proportional relationship because there is not a multiplicative relationship between the number of knots and the length of the rope.

6. Answers will be negative but vary depending on the thickness of the rope.

7. The y-intercept should be the original length of the rope.

8. Answers will vary. For example, students may write the equation $y = 85 - 5x$ if the original length of their rope was 85 cm and each knot shortened its length by 5 cm.

CLOSE AND GENERALIZATIONS

1. Discuss the graphs. Are the graphs all the same?

2. Discuss the rate of change. Is it the same for all tables and graphs?

   It is not, if students use different diameters of rope. The larger the diameter, the greater the rate of change since the knot will use more length of the rope.

Graphs will vary depending on the length and diameter of the rope used, the accuracy of the measurements, and/or the scaling used on the graph. The shape of the graphs should approximate a linear relationship.

3. Ask students what affects the slope. They should notice that the slope is related to the length of the rope that is in the knot. This is also affected by the diameter of the rope. They may notice that the thicker the diameter, the larger the slope.

4. Show students a rope that they did not have in their groups. Based on their data, what would they expect the shape of the graph to be?

5. Ask, "Are the graphs of the data discrete or continuous graphs?" Students should recognize that even though they are dealing with continuous data with the length measures, the knots are discrete data.

TASK 8.6: SO KNOTTY

 Available to download at **resources.corwin.com/classroomreadymath/algebra**

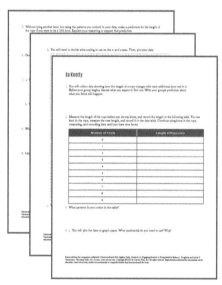

POST-TASK NOTES: REFLECTIONS AND NEXT STEPS

• Did I introduce the task sufficiently so that students were productive with their use of materials?

• Were students familiar with metric units?

• Was their measurement accurate enough to show the patterns?

• How does the context of the problem support students' understanding of discrete data? Of a physical representation of slope?

Task 8.7
Ratios Within

TASK

Ratios Within

1. In your group, measure and record the information in the table. *Use centimeters.* Measure the distances A, B, and C between your index finger joints.

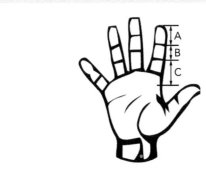

Source: OpenClipart-Vectors/pixabay.com

Measure the distances D and E on your arm.

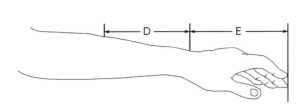

Source: OpenClipart-Vectors/pixabay.com

Name	A	B	C	D	E

2. Graph the sets of ordered pairs on *different* Cartesian coordinate grids.

   a. 1) Graph the ordered pairs (A, B):

Mathematics Focus

- Students explore ratios between their fingers, wrists, and elbows and find instances of the Golden Ratio.

- *Note for teachers:* In this task, students are just approximating the equation of the line, so the term *line of best fit* is not used. That term is used when the equation is calculated through linear regression.

Mathematics Content Standard(s)

- 8.F.4: Construct a function to model a linear relationship between two quantities. Determine the rate of change and initial value of the function from a description of a relationship or from two (x, y) values, including reading these from a table or from a graph. Interpret the rate of change and initial value of a linear function in terms of the situation it models, and in terms of its graph or a table of values.

- A-CED-4: Rearrange formulas to highlight a quantity of interest, using the same reasoning as in solving equations.

- F-IF-4: For a function that models a relationship between two quantities, interpret key features of graphs and tables in terms of the quantities, and

Mathematical Practice(s)

- Model with mathematics.
- Attend to precision.

Vocabulary

- ratio
- slope
- approximate
- Golden Ratio

Materials

- 1 Ratios Within task
- 1 metric tape measure or ruler per group

Task Type

	Conceptual
X	Procedural
X	Problem-Solving Application
	Problem-Solving Critical Thinking

	Reversibility
	Flexibility
X	Generalization

sketch graphs showing key features given a verbal description of the relationship.

- F-BF-1: Write a function that describes a relationship between two quantities.

  2) Draw a line you think best approximates the data you graphed. What is the slope?

  b. 1) Graph the ordered pairs (B, C):

  2) Draw a line you think best approximates the data you graphed. What is the slope?

  c. 1) Graph the ordered pairs (E, D):

  2) Draw a line you think best approximates the data you graphed. What is the slope?

TASK PREPARATION CONSIDERATIONS

- What prior experiences have students had with measuring and producing real-world data?

- How familiar are students with using a ruler to measure lengths?

- What experience have students had in identifying slope from graphs?

SCAFFOLDING OR DIFFERENTIATING THE TASK

- Have students discuss the importance of measuring and recording accurate data. If necessary, review how to accurately use a ruler to measure in centimeters.

- Remind students that slope represents the ratio of the change in y-values compared to the change in x-values.

WATCH-FORS!

- Students may use customary units instead of metric units.

- Students may record inaccurate data.

- Students may determine slope by comparing the change in x-values to the change in y-values.

EXTEND THE TASK

- Have students look for other examples of this special proportion, which is often noted in works of art, architecture, and nature.

LAUNCH

1. Tell students they will measure parts of their hand and arm using centimeters and record the data in a table.

2. Demonstrate how to measure with a student, emphasizing the use of centimeters.

3. Place students in groups of 3 or 4.

4. Distribute the Ratios Within task to each student.

5. Tell them that when they measure, one student will be the measurer, one will be the recorder, and one will be measured.

6. Allow time for students to make their measurements and record their data.

FACILITATE

1. How does each set of data correlate? When values of both sets increase, it is a *positive correlation*. When values in one set decrease as those in the other increase, it is a *negative correlation*.

2. Discuss the three graphs students made.

   a. How did students label their axes?

   b. How did students determine the line of best fit?

   c. What is the slope of each graph? Do students notice anything special about the slope?

EXPECTED SOLUTIONS

The data collected will not be the same across groups. Their ratios should be close to 1.618, the Golden Ratio.

CLOSE AND GENERALIZATIONS

1. Relate the slopes of the graphs to the Golden Ratio. Provide some history of the Golden Ratio as appropriate for your class.

2. Play the video www.pbs.org/video/music-from-the-golden-ratio-and-fibonacci-sequence-afdd5k/ (PBS Digital Studios, 2019). This clip explores the Golden Ratio and the Fibonacci Sequence through music.

3. As time allows, discuss error measurement and the effect on data.

TASK 8.7: RATIOS WITHIN

online resources Available to download at **resources.corwin.com/classroomreadymath/algebra**

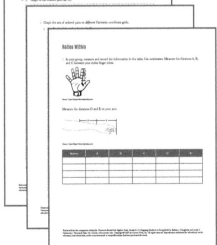

POST-TASK NOTES: REFLECTIONS AND NEXT STEPS

• What are other contexts that use the Golden Ratio that I can incorporate into my future lessons?

• Were the group sizes appropriate for the task?

• What supports would be appropriate to help students find the line that approximates the data?

• Were there computations that were difficult for students? Would a calculator support be beneficial?

Task 8.8
Covered With Paint

TASK

Covered With Paint

1. Selena made a foam cube that measured 3 inches on an edge. She dipped it into paint to completely cover it. When the paint dried, she cut the large cube into 1-inch cubes.

   a. How many 1-inch cubes were in the large cube?

   b. Of the 1-inch cubes, how many had *only* 1 face painted?

   c. How many had *only* 2 faces painted?

   d. How many had *only* 3 faces painted?

2. Devon made a foam cube that measured 4 inches on an edge. He dipped it into paint to completely cover it. When the paint dried, he cut the large cube into 1-inch cubes.

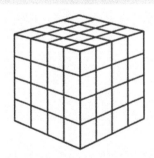

   a. How many 1-inch cubes were in the large cube?

   b. Of the 1-inch cubes, how many had *only* 1 face painted?

   c. How many had *only* 2 faces painted?

   d. How many had *only* 3 faces painted?

Mathematics Focus

- Students create functions to model patterns found in geometric and table representations and identify rate of change (slope).

Mathematics Content Standard(s)

- 8.F.4: Construct a function to model a linear relationship between two quantities. Determine the rate of change and initial value of the function from a description of a relationship or from two (x, y) values, including reading these from a table or from a graph. Interpret the rate of change and initial value of a linear function in terms of the situation it models, and in terms of its graph or a table of values.

- A-CED-4: Rearrange formulas to highlight a quantity of interest, using the same reasoning as in solving equations.

- F-IF-4: For a function that models a relationship between two quantities, interpret key features of graphs and tables in terms of the quantities, and sketch graphs showing key features given a verbal description of the relationship.

- F-LE-1: Distinguish between situations that can be modeled with linear functions and with exponential functions.

- F-BF-1: Write a function that describes a relationship between two quantities.

Mathematical Practice(s)

- Make sense of problems and persevere in solving them.
- Reason abstractly and quantitatively.
- Model with mathematics.
- Use appropriate tools strategically.
- Attend to precision.
- Look for and express regularity in repeated reasoning.

Vocabulary

- cube
- face
- edge
- vertex
- rate of change
- coefficient

Materials

- 1 Covered With Paint task per student
- At least 27 wood or connecting cubes per group of 4 students (64 cubes is optimal)

3. Record your information in each of the following tables. Build additional cubes as you need to help you see patterns.

Table 1

Number of cubes on one edge (x)	Total number of 1-inch cubes (y)
2	8
3	27
4	
5	
6	
x	

In Table 1, as x increases by 1, what do you notice about the values of y?

Table 2

Number of cubes on one edge (x)	Number of 1-inch cubes painted on 3 faces (y)
2	
3	
4	
5	
6	
x	

In Table 2, as x increases by 1, what do you notice about the values of y?

Table 3

Number of cubes on one edge (x)	Number of 1-inch cubes painted on 2 faces (y)
2	
3	
4	
5	
6	
x	

In Table 3, as x increases by 1, what do you notice about the values of y?

Table 4

Number of cubes on one edge (x)	Number of 1-inch cubes painted on 1 face (y)
2	
3	
4	
5	
6	
x	

In Table 4, as x increases by 1, what do you notice about the values of y?

TASK PREPARATION CONSIDERATIONS

• Can students identify linear and nonlinear patterns in a table?

• How much experience have students had with three-dimensional shapes—in particular, building a cube?

• Will students be able to visualize the cubes that are not on the faces of the larger cube?

Task Type

X	Conceptual
	Procedural
	Problem-Solving Application
X	Problem-Solving Critical Thinking

	Reversibility
X	Flexibility
X	Generalization

SCAFFOLDING OR DIFFERENTIATING THE TASK

- Remind students to build the cubes with their concrete materials.

- Demonstrate how to count the number of painted cubes on a face by using a think-aloud approach or providing different-colored stickers to place on the smaller cube faces.

- Have students focus on the linear relationships before moving to the nonlinear relationships.

WATCH-FORS!

- Students may have inefficient counting strategies.

- Students may forget that there are smaller cubes "inside" the larger cube.

- Students may think that all functions are linear.

- Students may focus on relationships but not use covariational thinking.

EXTEND THE TASK

- Have students graph the relationships in each table and note the similarities and differences of the graphs as they compare to the values in the tables and geometric models.

LAUNCH

1. Place students in groups of 3 or 4.

2. Use wooden or connecting cubes to create a 2 × 2 × 2 cube.

   a. Have students identify the number of faces, edges, and vertices.

   b. Demonstrate dipping the cube into paint.

   c. Ask, "How many of the smaller cubes will have 0 faces painted? 1 face painted? 2 faces painted? 3 faces painted? 4 faces painted? 5 faces painted? 6 faces painted?"

   d. Record students' responses for them to refer to as they work through the task.

3. Build a 3 × 3 × 3 cube and follow the same pattern of questioning.

   a. Record the responses for students to refer to as they work through the task.

4. Distribute the Covered With Paint task.

5. Allow about 25–30 minutes for students to work.

FACILITATE

1. Monitor the groups as they work.

2. Select a group to share their answers to problems 1 and 2.

3. Select a group to share their table entries to verify the data recorded.

   a. Does everyone agree with the entries?

   b. Continue with each table and a different group sharing.

4. Discuss the relationships as *x* increases by 1.

    a. Focus on the covariational aspects of the relationships using the language "As *x* increases by 1, *y* . . ."

EXPECTED SOLUTIONS

1. a. 27 cubes
   b. 6 cubes
   c. 12 cubes
   d. 8 cubes

2. a. 64 cubes
   b. 24 cubes
   c. 24 cubes
   d. 8 cubes

3. Table 1

Number of cubes on one edge (x)	Total number of 1-inch cubes (y)
2	8
3	27
4	64
5	125
6	216
x	x^3

Table 2

Number of cubes on one edge (x)	Number of 1-inch cubes painted on 3 faces (y)
2	8
3	8
4	8
5	8
6	8
x	8

Table 3

Number of cubes on one edge (x)	Number of 1-inch cubes painted on 2 faces (y)
2	0
3	12
4	24
5	36
6	48
x	$12(x - 2)$

Table 4

Number of cubes on one edge (x)	Number of 1-inch cubes painted on 1 face (y)
2	0
3	6
4	24
5	54
6	96
x	$6(x - 2)^2$

CLOSE AND GENERALIZATIONS

1. As time allows, use these questions to extend the task discussion.

   a. If the entries in the tables were graphed as ordered pairs, what could you predict about the shape of the graphs? (Answers will vary.) What would it mean if a curve were drawn through the points?

   b. What quadrant(s) are appropriate for the graphs? (Only Quadrant I.) Why?

   c. Which of the tables represent functions? (All tables.)

   d. Which tables represent a linear relationship? (Tables 2 and 3.) Why?

   e. What did you notice about the rate of change in Tables 2 and 3 as compared to Tables 1 and 4? (Answers will vary. The rates of change in Tables 2 and 3 are each consistent, and the rates of change in Tables 1 and 4 are not.)

   f. Discuss how the rate of change is determined. Write the rate of change as a ratio. (For Table 2, the rate of change, or ratio, is 0:1; for Table 3, it is 12:1 [change in y as compared to change in x].)

   g. Have students graph the points in Tables 2 and 3 on coordinate grids. Use a separate grid for each table.

h. Focus on Table 3. Select two points on the line. Demonstrate how to find the change in x and the change in y from these two points. Write it as a ratio. Simplify the ratio to show it is the same ratio as they found on the table.

i. Have students select two different points. Ask them to find the rate of change in a similar way. Write it as a ratio and simplify it. What do they notice? They should notice that the rate of change is the same no matter what two points are selected.

j. Look at the last row of Tables 2 and 3. Write the equation that represents the relationship. (For Table 2, $y = 0x + 8$, and for Table 3, $y = 12x - 24$.) What do students notice about the equations and the rate of change? (The rate of change is the coefficient of x.)

k. What relationship do students notice between the size of the coefficient of x and the steepness of the graph?

TASK 8.8: COVERED WITH PAINT

 Available to download at **resources.corwin.com/classroomreadymath/algebra**

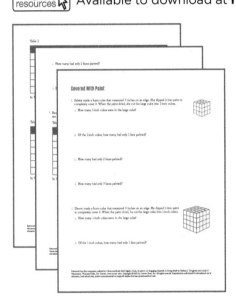

POST-TASK NOTES: REFLECTIONS AND NEXT STEPS

• Is students' spatial sense well developed, or is this an opportunity for learning?

• Can this task be used in later lessons to connect linear functions with polynomial functions?

• Did the task provide enough support for students to recognize that the slope of a line is the same no matter which two points are chosen?

• Could this task be extended by using a different three-dimensional shape?

Mathematics Content Standard(s)

- A-CED.2: Create equations in two or more variables to represent relationships between quantities; graph equations on coordinate axes with labels and scales.

- 8.SP.4: Understand that patterns of association can also be seen in bivariate categorical data by displaying frequencies and relative frequencies in a two-way table. Construct and interpret a two-way table summarizing data on two categorical variables collected from the same subjects. Use relative frequencies calculated for rows or columns to describe possible association between the two variables.

Mathematical Practice(s)

- Reason abstractly and quantitatively.
- Construct viable arguments and critique the reasoning of others.
- Model with mathematics.
- Use appropriate tools strategically.
- Attend to precision.

Task 8.9
If the Shoe Fits

TASK

If the Shoe Fits

1. In your group, measure each person's height *in inches*. Record the height and shoe size (also in inches) in the table.

Group Member Initials	Height (x)	Shoe Length, in Inches (y)

2. Share your data with other groups or the whole class so that you have data on at least 10 people.

3. Graph the data from each table on a *separate* Cartesian coordinate system.

4. a. For each set of data points you graphed, draw the line of best fit.

   b. Explain how your group decided where to draw the line of best fit.

   c. Find an equation of each line you drew.

5. If Sam is 5 feet 1 inch tall, what would you estimate their shoe size to be? Explain how you got your estimate.

6. If Brae is 6 feet 3 inches tall, what would you estimate their shoe size to be? Explain.

7. The police found a deep footprint for a 10-inch-long shoe shaped like this:

Source: Pabletex/iStock.com

What conjectures might they make?

TASK PREPARATION CONSIDERATIONS

- What prior experiences have students had with measuring and producing real-world data?

- How familiar are students with using a measuring tape or yardstick to measure lengths?

- How much support will students need in determining an appropriate scale for their graphs?

- What process will I use for groups to get additional data from other groups for graphing?

- Should I collect all the data from the groups and then use a graphing application to graph the full-class data? How will that change the task?

SCAFFOLDING OR DIFFERENTIATING THE TASK

- Review how to read a measuring tape and yardstick when the measurement is between whole numbers.

- Provide support for creating the scaling on the axes.

WATCH-FORS!

- Students may use a scaling on the axes that increments by only 1 unit.

- Students may think that the scales on the *x*- and *y*-axes have to be the same.

- Look for and express regularity in repeated reasoning.

Vocabulary

- rate of change
- conjecture

Materials

- 1 If the Shoe Fits task per student
- Grid or graph paper per student
- Tape measure or yard stick per group of 4 students

Task Type

	Conceptual
X	Procedural
X	Problem-Solving Application
	Problem-Solving Critical Thinking

	Reversibility
	Flexibility
X	Generalization

EXTEND THE TASK

- Have students measure the length of their foot and record their shoe size. Graph the ordered pairs and determine a line of best fit.

LAUNCH

1. Arrange students in groups of 3 or 4.

2. Ask students if they think there is a relationship between their height and shoe size. Tell them they are going to investigate that relationship.

3. Distribute the If the Shoe Fits task to each student and a tape measure or yardstick to each group.

4. Review the directions for the task.

5. Provide guidance on how students can measure their heights such as placing a piece of tape on a wall and measuring the height.

6. Encourage students to double-check the measurements for their heights.

7. Describe the process you will use for collecting more data for graphing.

8. Allow 30 minutes for students to complete the task.

FACILITATE

1. When students have completed the task, combine the data into one class set. Discuss conjectures that could be made based on similarities and differences that students notice in their tables and graphs.

2. Use a graphing software or application for students to input their data and compare their graphs.

3. Ask students to analyze the data by discussing what could be expected findings and unexpected findings.

EXPECTED SOLUTION

Answers will vary and should be justified by findings from the class data.

CLOSE AND GENERALIZATIONS

1. Discuss the graphs. Are the graphs the same? Why or why not?

2. Discuss the rate of change. Is it the same for all sets of data? The shape of the graphs should approximate a linear relationship.

3. Ask students what affects the slope.

TASK 8.9: IF THE SHOE FITS

Available to download at **resources.corwin.com/classroomreadymath/algebra**

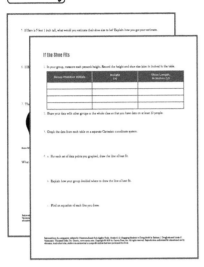

POST-TASK NOTES: REFLECTIONS AND NEXT STEPS

• How did students' measurements affect their ability to detect patterns?

• What modifications do I need to make for the task when I use it again?

Systems of Equations Tasks

The tasks in Chapter 9 are focused on systems of equations and their conceptual and procedural aspects. Often, strategies to solve systems of equations are taught in an algorithmic fashion, and students do not develop the flexibility that would deepen their understanding. These tasks will provide opportunities for them to consider the meaning of a solution to a system of equation, analyze worked examples, and compare structures of systems of equations that lead to a relationship using particular solution strategies.

Shantelle's Special Number incorporates ideas about prime factorization as students use ideas based on the Quotient Remainder Theorem to solve the problem. This leads to Baskets of Mangoes where students are given information about sums of two quantities and asked to determine each individual quantity. Both of these tasks build flexibility in students' thinking about systems of equations.

Sets of Systems provides opportunities for students to analyze the structure of a system in order to apply an efficient and appropriate solution strategy. The equations in the systems are presented in different formats, such as $y = 3x + 1$ or $3x + 2y = -7$, so that students can see how the structure of the equations is related to a solution approach.

Broken Plates includes a mixture of problems. The first problem is contextual, and the other two are worked examples where students analyze the solution process. Exploring Systems of Equations also includes worked examples but additionally provides problems that are reversed. That is, students are given information about the solution and use that information to determine the system of equations.

Mathematics Focus

- Students use the Quotient Remainder Theorem.

Mathematics Content Standard(s)

- A-APR.2: Know and apply the Remainder Theorem: for a polynomial $p(x)$ and a number a, the remainder on division by $x - a$ is $p(a)$, so $p(a) = 0$ if and only if $(x - a)$ is a factor of $p(x)$.

- A-CED.3: Represent constraints by equations or inequalities, and by systems of equations and/or inequalities, and interpret solutions as viable or nonviable options in a modeling context.

Mathematical Practice(s)

- Make sense of problems and persevere in solving them.

- Reason abstractly and quantitatively.

- Model with mathematics.

- Attend to precision.

- Look for and make use of structure.

Task 9.1
Shantelle's Special Number

TASK

Shantelle's Special Number

Shantelle said, "Ben, I have a number challenge for you."

"I'm up for it!" said Ben. "What is the challenge?"

"Well," said Shantelle, "I have a special number. I'll give you some clues, and let's see if you can figure out what it is. I will tell you that it is less than 3,000.

1. Divided by 10, the remainder is 9.

2. Divided by 9, the remainder is 8.

3. Divided by 8, the remainder is 7.

4. The pattern continues down to a remainder of 1 when it is divided by 2."

What is Shantelle's special number?

Describe your solution process.

TASK PREPARATION CONSIDERATIONS

- How do students interpret quotients and remainders?

- What solution approaches will students use if they do not recognize this as a problem that can be solved using the Quotient Remainder Theorem?

SCAFFOLDING OR DIFFERENTIATING THE TASK

- Suggest students try a guess-and-test approach and organize their guesses and results.

- Have students investigate relationships between two numbers such as 9 and 8 with remainders as a simpler problem.

WATCH-FORS!

- Students may consider only the quotient and not take into account the remainder.

- Students may try to use a system of equations to solve the problem.

EXTEND THE TASK

- Change the task so that there is a remainder of 2 if divided by 10, 9, 8, 7, 6, 5, 4, and 3. Other similar changes are possible.

LAUNCH

1. Place students in pairs.

2. Review the directions for the task and include any additional discussion on quotients and remainders as necessary for your students to access the task.

3. Allow about 20 minutes for students to work.

FACILITATE

1. Monitor the pairs as they work.

2. Have pairs share their solutions.

3. Ask if pairs solved it in a different way.

EXPECTED SOLUTION

Shantelle's special number is 2,519.

CLOSE AND GENERALIZATIONS

1. If students used a guess-and-test approach, discuss an alternate solution process using least common multiples (LCM).

   $(10 - 1), (9 - 1), (8 - 1), \ldots (2 - 1)$

   LCM (9, 8, 7, 6, 5, 4, 3, 2)

   Find the prime factorization: $9 = 3^2$, $8 = 2^3$, $7 = 7$, $6 = 2 \times 3$, $5 = 5$, $4 = 2^2$, $3 = 3$, $2 = 2$

   $3^2 \times 2^3 \times 7 \times 5 = 2,520$; $2,520 - 1 = 2,519$

Vocabulary

- remainder
- least common multiple
- prime factors

Materials

- 1 Shantelle's Special Number task per student
- 1 calculator or calculator application per student or pair of students

Task Type

X	Conceptual
	Procedural
	Problem-Solving Application
X	Problem-Solving Critical Thinking

X	Reversibility
X	Flexibility
X	Generalization

TASK 9.1: SHANTELLE'S SPECIAL NUMBER

 Available to download at **resources.corwin.com/classroomreadymath/algebra**

Shantelle's Special Number

Shantelle said, "Ben, I have a number challenge for you."

"I'm up for it!" said Ben. "What is the challenge?"

"Well," said Shantelle, "I have a special number. I'll give you some clues, and let's see if you can figure out what it is. I will tell you that it is less than 3,000.

1. Divided by 10, the remainder is 9.
2. Divided by 9, the remainder is 8.
3. Divided by 8, the remainder is 7.
4. The pattern continues down to a remainder of 1 when it is divided by 2."

What is Shantelle's special number?

Describe your solution process.

POST-TASK NOTES: REFLECTIONS AND NEXT STEPS

- What spontaneous strategies did students use?

- What evidence did I see of students' number sense?

- How did students' understanding of remainders affect the strategies they used?

Task 9.2
Baskets of Mangoes

TASK

Baskets of Mangoes

Five baskets of mangoes have been collected to make mango smoothies for the farmers market. The farmer does not need all five baskets at the start of the market and needs to decide which baskets to take first. The first and second baskets together have a total of 52 mangoes. The second and third baskets have 43 mangoes. The third and fourth baskets have 34 mangoes. The fourth and fifth baskets have 30 mangoes. And the first and fifth baskets have 47 mangoes.

How many mangoes are in each basket? Describe your solution process.

TASK PREPARATION CONSIDERATIONS

- How familiar are students with the problem's context?

- Have students had experience with a system of equations with more than two equations?

- What nonroutine problem-solving strategies do students use?

SCAFFOLDING OR DIFFERENTIATING THE TASK

- Suggest students try a guess-and-test approach and organize their guesses and results to develop some parameters about the solution.

- Have students identify a variable to represent the quantity in each basket and write equations that represent the relationships between two baskets as given in the problem.

- Ask if students can find the total number in all of the baskets and write an equation that represents that amount.

- Provide two-color counters for students to model the problem.

Mathematics Focus

- Students create a system of equations to solve a contextual problem.

Mathematics Content Standard(s)

- 8.EE.8: Analyze and solve pairs of simultaneous linear equations.

- A-CED.2: Create equations in two or more variables to represent relationships between quantities; graph equations on coordinate axes with labels and scales.

- A-REI.6: Solve systems of linear equations exactly and approximately, focusing on pairs of linear equations in two variables.

Mathematical Practice(s)

- Make sense of problems and persevere in solving them.
- Reason abstractly and quantitatively.
- Model with mathematics.
- Attend to precision.
- Look for and make use of structure.

Vocabulary

- system of equations

Materials

- 1 Baskets of Mangoes task per student
- 1 calculator or calculator application per student or pair of students

Task Type

X	Conceptual
	Procedural
	Problem-Solving Application
X	Problem-Solving Critical Thinking

X	Reversibility
X	Flexibility
	Generalization

WATCH-FORS!

- Students may attempt to use a system of equations using the equations for only two of the baskets at a time to solve the problem.

- Students may focus on a straightforward approach to solving a system of equations and not consider a more novel way to think about the relationships.

EXTEND THE TASK

- Present a similar problem. Baskets 1 and 2 have a total of 59 mangoes. Baskets 2 and 3 have a total of 81 mangoes. Baskets 3 and 4 have a total of 87 mangoes. Baskets 4 and 5 have a total of 37 mangoes. Baskets 1 and 5 have a total of 56 mangoes. There are 160 mangoes altogether. Have students solve using their chosen method.

LAUNCH

1. Place students in pairs.

2. Review the directions for the task.

3. Allow about 20 minutes for students to work.

FACILITATE

1. Monitor the pairs as they work.

2. Have pairs share their solutions.

3. Ask if pairs solved it in a different way.

   a. Have different solution strategies presented.

   b. Ask, "How are the solution strategies alike? How are they different?"

EXPECTED SOLUTION

Basket 1: 30 mangoes

Basket 2: 22 mangoes

Basket 3: 21 mangoes

Basket 4: 13 mangoes

Basket 5: 17 mangoes

Solution approaches may include guess-and-test.

Let a = number of mangoes in Basket 1

Let b = number of mangoes in Basket 2

Let c = number of mangoes in Basket 3

Let d = number of mangoes in Basket 4

Let e = number of mangoes in Basket 5

One possible solution method: Equations: $a + b = 52$; $b + c = 43$; $c + d = 34$;

$d + e = 30$; $a + e = 47$

$2a + 2b + 2c + 2d + 2e = 206$	Divide by 2
$a + b + c + d + e = 103$	Substitute 52 for $a + b$ and 34 for $c + d$
$52 + 34 + e = 103$	Combine like terms
$86 + e = 103$	Subtract 86 from both sides
$e = 17$	

Substitute 17 into the appropriate equations and solve for the quantities in the other baskets.

CLOSE AND GENERALIZATIONS

1. Ask, "Why can we add equations together to create another equation that will have the same solution?"

TASK 9.2: BASKETS OF MANGOES

 Available to download at **resources.corwin.com/classroomreadymath/algebra**

Baskets of Mangoes

Five baskets of mangoes have been collected to make mango smoothies for the farmers market. The farmer does not need all five baskets at the start of the market and needs to decide which baskets to take first. The second and third baskets have 43 mangoes. The third and fourth baskets have 34 mangoes. The fourth and fifth baskets have 30 mangoes. And the first and fifth baskets have 47 mangoes.

How many mangoes are in each basket? Describe your solution process.

POST-TASK NOTES: REFLECTIONS AND NEXT STEPS

- What solution strategies did students use that surprised me? What solution strategies did I expect?

- Is students' concept of equality well developed so they understand why you can add equations to create another equivalent equation?

Task 9.3
Sets of Systems

Mathematics Focus

- Students match three representations of systems, including equations, graphs, and solutions.

TASK

Sets of Systems

Find the cards that show the equation, graph, and solution for a system of equations. Tape or glue the cards in the appropriate cells.

Set	Equation	Graph	Solution
1			
2			
3			
4			
5			

Mathematics Content Standard(s)

- A-REI.6: Solve systems of linear equations exactly and approximately (e.g., with graphs), focusing on pairs of linear equations in two variables.
- A-REI.10: Understand that the graph of an equation in two variables is the set of all its solutions plotted in the coordinate plane, often forming a curve (which could be a line).

TASK PREPARATION CONSIDERATIONS

- Are students comfortable solving systems of equations?
- Have students solved systems of equations by graphing?

SCAFFOLDING OR DIFFERENTIATING THE TASK

- Suggest students use the solutions to the system of equations to see if they form true equations.
- Use graphing software to graph the system and compare it to the given graphs.

WATCH-FORS!

- Students may not recognize why parallel lines and their associated system of equations do not have a solution.

EXTEND THE TASK

- Have students create their own set of up to three cards to trade with others in class.

Mathematical Practice(s)

- Reason abstractly and quantitatively.
- Model with mathematics.
- Look for and make use of structure.

Vocabulary

- system of equations

Materials

- 1 Sets of Systems task per student
- 1 set of Sets of Systems cards per pair of students
- Glue or tape per pair of students

Task Type

	Conceptual
X	Procedural
	Problem-Solving Application
	Problem-Solving Critical Thinking

X	Reversibility
X	Flexibility
	Generalization

LAUNCH

1. Place students in pairs.

2. Distribute the Sets of Systems task and cards.

3. Tell students that they will be given three representations of a system of equations: the equations, the graph, and the solution.

4. Tell students they will match the three representations and glue or paste the cards that form a set in a row.

5. Allow about 20 minutes for students to work.

FACILITATE

1. Monitor the pairs as they work.

2. Have pairs share their solutions.

3. Ask pairs to share how they determined which cards formed a set.

EXPECTED SOLUTIONS

Copy a set of cards for each pair of students. Cut apart, shuffle, and place each set in a baggie (or attach them with a paper clip) before you distribute them to students. Each row in the table is the solution for each set.

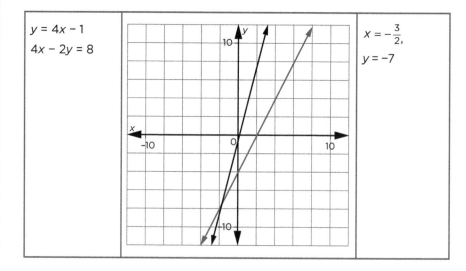

$y = 4x - 1$
$4x - 2y = 8$

$x = -\dfrac{3}{2},$
$y = -7$

$2x - 2y = -7$ $x - 2y = -4$	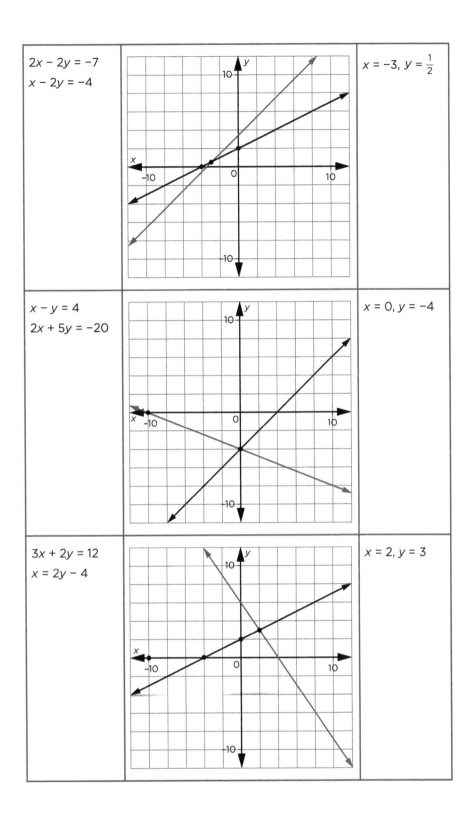	$x = -3,\ y = \frac{1}{2}$
$x - y = 4$ $2x + 5y = -20$		$x = 0,\ y = -4$
$3x + 2y = 12$ $x = 2y - 4$		$x = 2,\ y = 3$

| $x = 3y - 8$ $2x - 6y = 12$ | 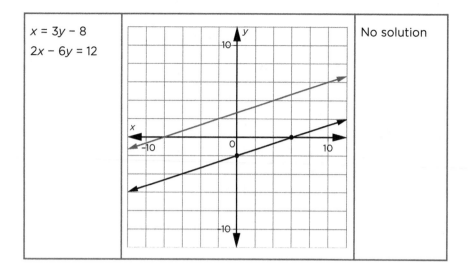 | No solution |

CLOSE AND GENERALIZATIONS

1. Discuss the solution approaches used by students.

2. Show each system of equations. Ask students to decide which solution process (substitution, elimination, graphing, or inspection) is most appropriate based on the structure of the equations in the system. For example, students may notice that if the equation/graph of a system indicates the same slope, there will not be a solution to the system.

3. Summarize that the systems of equations in this task had one solution or no solution. Ask students if it is possible for a system of equations to have an infinite number of solutions. Why or why not?

TASK 9.3: SETS OF SYSTEMS

online resources Available to download at **resources.corwin.com/classroomreadymath/algebra**

POST-TASK NOTES: REFLECTIONS AND NEXT STEPS

- In other lessons and tasks that I use for systems of equations, do I push students to identify structural aspects of systems of equations that lend themselves to solving the system in certain way, or do I specify which solution process they should use?

- Are the connections among the graphical representations, table, and equation well developed so that students can predict the number and type of solution before solving?

Mathematics Focus

- Students solve a contextual problem with a system of equations.

Mathematics Content Standard(s)

- 8.EE.8: Analyze and solve pairs of simultaneous linear equations.

- A-CED.2: Create equations in two or more variables to represent relationships between quantities; graph equations on coordinate axes with labels and scales.

- A-REI.6: Solve systems of linear equations exactly and approximately (e.g., with graphs), focusing on pairs of linear equations in two variables.

Mathematical Practice(s)

- Make sense of problems and persevere in solving them.

- Reason abstractly and quantitatively.

- Model with mathematics.

- Attend to precision.

- Look for and make use of structure.

Task 9.4
Broken Plates

TASK

Broken Plates

1. Jess worked at Plates-R-Us packing plates to be shipped to customers. He received 15 cents for each plate he packed successfully and was fined 23 cents for each plate he broke. He handled 387 plates. He was paid $32.97.

   How many plates did Jess break? Describe your thinking or solution process.

2. Kayla solved a system of equations. This is her solution.

$$3x + 8y = 40 \longrightarrow 3x + 8y = 40$$
$$x - 2y = 4 \longrightarrow 3x - 6y = 12$$
$$\text{Multiply by 3} \quad \overline{}$$
$$2y = 28$$
$$y = 14$$

   The solution is (32, 14).

   Do you agree with Kayla's solution method and answer? If yes, explain why. If no, solve the problem.

3. Micah solved a system of equations and got the solution (−2, −4). Write a system of equations that Micah could have solved.

TASK PREPARATION CONSIDERATIONS

- Are students comfortable solving systems of equations?

- Which methods for solving systems of equations have students used?

- Should students have access to graphing applications or calculators to solve the problems?

SCAFFOLDING OR DIFFERENTIATING THE TASK

- Suggest estimating the solution and testing it using a guess-and-test approach for problem 1.

- Have students solve the system in problem 2 and compare their process to Kayla's solution.

WATCH-FORS!

- Students may write one equation rather than writing a system of equations for problem 1.

- Students may write a linear equation in the form $x + y = z$ for problem 3.

EXTEND THE TASK

- Have students give two numbers. Use those as a solution to a system of equations. Ask them to find the system of equations that has these two numbers as its solution. For example, if students say −3 and 8, the solution to the system is (−3, 8).

LAUNCH

1. Place students in pairs.

2. Tell students that they will be working in pairs to solve problems related to systems of equations.

3. Distribute the Broken Plates task to each student.

4. Remind them to describe their thinking related to the solution process they used.

5. Allow about 20 minutes for students to work.

FACILITATE

1. Monitor the pairs as they work.

2. Have pairs share their solutions and solution approaches for problems 1 and 2.

EXPECTED SOLUTIONS

1. 66 plates were broken.

2. Students should disagree because Kayla subtracted incorrectly. The solution is (8, 2).

3. Accept any system that has (−2, −4) as a solution. For example, $x + y = −6$ and $3x + 5y = −26$.

CLOSE AND GENERALIZATIONS

1. Have students share their systems of equations for problem 3.

   a. Record their systems of equations to refer to.

2. Ask, "How are the systems of equations alike? Do they all have the same solution?"

3. Discuss student responses.

Vocabulary

- system of equations
- solution to a system of equations

Materials

- 1 Broken Plates task per student

Task Type

	Conceptual
X	Procedural
X	Problem-Solving Application
X	Problem-Solving Critical Thinking

X	Reversibility
X	Flexibility
X	Generalization

TASK 9.4: BROKEN PLATES

Broken Plates

1. Joao worked at Worcalad's making plates to be shipped to customers. He received 15 cents for each plate he packed successfully and was fined 25 cents for each plate he broke. He handled 987 plates. He was paid $32.07. How many plates did Joao break? Describe your thinking or solution process.

2. Kayla solved a system of equations. This is her solution.

$$3x + 8y = 40 \qquad \longrightarrow \qquad 3x + 8y = 40$$
$$x - 2y = 4 \qquad \qquad 3x - 6y = 12$$
$$\text{Multiply by 3} \qquad \qquad \overline{2y = 28}$$
$$y = 14$$

The solution is (32, 14).

Do you agree with Kayla's solution method and answer? If yes, explain why. If no, solve the problem.

3. Micah solved a system of equations and got the solution (−2, −4). Write a system of equations that Micah could have solved.

POST-TASK NOTES: REFLECTIONS AND NEXT STEPS

- Which of the problems were most accessible to students? Why was that?

- Using problem 2 as a model, how can I include more worked examples in my teaching?

Task 9.5
Exploring Systems of Equations

TASK

Exploring Systems of Equations

1. The solution of a system of equations is (–2, –1). If one of the equations is $y = 2x + 3$, what might the other equation be?

2. The solution of each of the following systems is (–2, 3). Find the values for $\square$.

   a. $x + \square y = -8$

   $\square x + 4y = 6$

   b. $\square x + 5y = 3$

   $3x + \square y = 12$

3. Korey and Emma solved systems of equations. If the method is correct, finish solving the problem. If the method is not correct, tell what is wrong with it.

   a. $y = 2x - 2$

   $y = 3x - 1$

   Korey substituted $2x - 2$ for y in the second equation, getting $2x - 2 = 3x - 1$.

   b. $x = -3y$

   $y - 2x = 175$

   Emma substituted $-3y$ for x in the second equation, getting $y - 6y = 175$.

TASK PREPARATION CONSIDERATIONS

- What solution methods have students used to solve systems of equations problems?

SCAFFOLDING OR DIFFERENTIATING THE TASK

- Revise the missing values in problem 1.

- Have students think about a similar or simpler problem.

- Encourage students to work backward on some of the problems.

Mathematics Focus

- Students apply their understandings of systems of equations to solve problems.

Mathematics Content Standard(s)

- 8.EE.8: Analyze and solve pairs of simultaneous linear equations.

- A-REI.6: Solve systems of linear equations exactly and approximately, focusing on pairs of linear equations in two variables.

Mathematical Practice(s)

- Make sense of problems and persevere in solving them.

- Reason abstractly and quantitatively.

- Construct viable arguments and critique the reasoning of others.

- Model with mathematics.

- Attend to precision.

- Look for and make use of structure.

- Look for and express regularity in repeated reasoning.

Vocabulary

- system of equations
- solution of a system of equations

Materials

- 1 Exploring Systems of Equations task per student
- Calculator or graphing/ calculator application (optional)

Task Type

X	Conceptual
X	Procedural
X	Problem-Solving Application
X	Problem-Solving Critical Thinking

X	Reversibility
X	Flexibility
X	Generalization

WATCH-FORS!

- Students may think that a system of equations always has one solution.

- Students may not consider the substitution method as one of the solution strategies.

- Students may not be sure how to use the solution of a system of equations to work backward.

EXTEND THE TASK

- Change the problems with different solutions.

LAUNCH

1. Place students in pairs.

2. Distribute the Exploring Systems of Equations task.

3. Tell students to work in a pair to find solutions to the problems and remind them to think in a reverse order.

4. Allow about 20 minutes for students to work.

FACILITATE

1. Monitor the pairs as they work.

2. Have pairs share their solutions with the class.

3. Ask, "How did you find the second equation for problem 1? Is the answer unique?" Students should recognize that there are an infinite number of equations that could be the second equation. Any equivalent equation will work.

EXPECTED SOLUTION

1. Answers will vary. For example, any equivalent equation to $x + y = -3$.

2. a. $x +$ **(−2)**$y = -8$ **3**$\underline{x} + 4y = 6$

   b. **6**$x + 5y = 3$ $3x +$ **6**$y = 12$

3. a. Korey's method is correct. The solution is $(-1, -4)$.

   b. Emma's method is incorrect. When she multiplied, she should have gotten $-6y$ instead of $6y$. The solution is $(-75, 25)$.

CLOSE AND GENERALIZATIONS

1. Summarize the similarities and differences between solution approaches.

2. Ask students which solution approach they would use if they were to do a similar problem.

TASK 9.5: EXPLORING SYSTEMS OF EQUATIONS

 Available to download at **resources.corwin.com/classroomreadymath/algebra**

POST-TASK NOTES: REFLECTIONS AND NEXT STEPS

- Do students understand what the solution to a system of equations means? How did their solutions and solution approaches to these problems indicate their understanding?

- How do "working backward" problems impact student learning?

CHAPTER

10

Polynomial and Rational Expressions and Equations Tasks

The tasks in Chapter 10 provide unique situations for students to explore more complex algebraic expressions and equations. The first three tasks build student understanding by using visual representations. The last three tasks require students to use that foundation to solve the tasks.

Square Up provides a foundation for students to conceptually understand the difference of two squares and trinomial squares. Students substitute values into two factors that are binomials and their products. The information is organized in a table so that students can detect patterns and make generalizations.

Completing the square is a method for solving quadratic equations, and Sew, Sew introduces that idea through a contextual problem. Students use area to consider this solution method.

As with other algebraic topics, Diagonals Galore uses a geometric context to identify a generalization about the number of diagonals in a polygon as related to the sides. It provides a visual representation that will help students see the relationship. Additionally, it incorporates multiple representations with tables, graphs, geometric shapes, and algebraic expressions or equations.

Sticks and Marshmallows continues development with a geometric context as well. Students should see a connection with previous tasks that used a growing pattern, such as The Symmetric Staircase (Chapter 4) or Sticks and Squares (Chapter 6).

When students first read Paying the Bill, they may not realize the implications of the task. The task presents a context that is plausible and interesting as it relates to rational equations while it engages students in practicing skills from previous years.

Ivone's Problem gives students an opportunity to find solutions to two rational equations. They may find that using a guess-and-test approach is a way to initiate a solution strategy.

Mathematics Focus

- Students compare quadratic expressions with a focus on the sum of two squares and difference of two squares.

Mathematics Content Standard(s)

- A-SSE.2: Use the structure of an expression to identify ways to rewrite it.

Mathematical Practice(s)

- Reason abstractly and quantitatively.
- Model with mathematics.
- Look for and make use of structure.
- Look for and express regularity in repeated reasoning.

Vocabulary

- square
- binomial
- distributive property of multiplication over addition
- distributive property of multiplication over subtraction
- product
- factor

Task 10.1
Square Up

TASK

Square Up

1. a. Complete the table.

x	y	$(x + y)^2$	$x^2 + y^2$	$x^2 + 2xy + y^2$
4	3	49		
5	-4			1
-6	0			
1.5	2.5		8.5	16

   b. What do you notice?

2. a. Complete the table.

x	y	$x + y$	$x - y$	$(x + y)$ $(x - y)$	$x^2 + y^2$	$x^2 - y^2$
10	7					51
-3	-9				90	
$4a$	1	$4a + 1$				
3	$-5w$				$9 + 25w^2$	

   b. What do you notice?

TASK PREPARATION CONSIDERATIONS

- Can students evaluate an algebraic expression given a value for the variables?

SCAFFOLDING OR DIFFERENTIATING THE TASK

- Give students a calculator if the values in their table are not accurate.

- Ask students which of the columns in the table produce the same results.

WATCH-FORS!

- Students may think that $(x + y)^2$ means to square each term separately, resulting in $x^2 + y^2$.

- Students may use FOIL (first, outer, inner, last) without realizing that they are using the distributive property of multiplication over addition or multiplication over subtraction.

EXTEND THE TASK

- Present students with $(x + y)^3$ and discuss the relationship of the product to $(x + y)^2$.

- If students have not factored quadratic expressions yet, reverse the task and give them the product $x^2 + 8x + 16$ or $x^2 - 16$ and ask them what factors could have produced that product. To further extend, give the product $x^2 - 12x + 36$.

LAUNCH

1. Distribute the Square Up task.

2. Tell students they are to complete the tables with the values given for the variables.

3. Then, they will analyze the table and look for patterns.

4. Allow about 15 minutes for students to work.

FACILITATE

1. Monitor the students as they work.

   a. Watch for students who say "plug in" instead of "substitute." Restate using "substitute."

2. Place students in pairs and have them compare the values in the table and the patterns they noticed.

3. Have pairs share their patterns.

EXPECTED SOLUTIONS

1. a.

x	y	$(x + y)^2$	$x^2 + y^2$	$x^2 + 2xy + y^2$
4	3	49	25	49
5	-4	1	41	1
-6	0	36	36	36
1.5	2.5	16	8.5	16

   b. Students should notice that $(x + y)^2 = x^2 + 2xy + y^2$ OR $(x + y)^2 \neq x^2 + y^2$.

Materials

- 1 Square Up task per student

Task Type

X	Conceptual
X	Procedural
	Problem-Solving Application
X	Problem-Solving Critical Thinking

X	Reversibility
	Flexibility
X	Generalization

2. a.

x	y	$x + y$	$x - y$	$(x + y)(x - y)$	$x^2 + y^2$	$x^2 - y^2$
10	7	17	3	51	149	51
−3	−9	−12	6	−72	90	−72
$4a$	1	$4a + 1$	$4a - 1$	$16a^2 - 1$	$16a^2 + 1$	$16a^2 - 1$
3	$-5w$	$3 - 5w$	$3 + 5w$	$9 - 25w^2$	$9 + 25w^2$	$9 - 25w^2$

b. Students should notice that $(x + y)(x - y) = x^2 - y^2$ OR $(x + y)(x - y) \neq x^2 + y^2$.

CLOSE AND GENERALIZATIONS

1. Introduce trinomial square and difference of two squares.

2. Discuss the distributive property of multiplication over addition and the distributive property of multiplication over subtraction, and avoid the use of FOIL (Dougherty et al., 2021).

3. Ask students if there are any values for x and y for which $(x + y)^2$ would equal $x^2 + y^2$ (e.g., if $x = 1$ and $y = 0$).

TASK 10.1: SQUARE UP

online resources  Available to download at **resources.corwin.com/classroomreadymath/algebra**

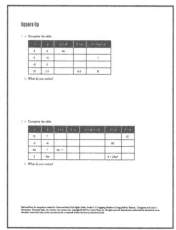

POST-TASK NOTES: REFLECTIONS AND NEXT STEPS

- Did students spontaneously use FOIL or say "plug in"? If so, how can I change their mathematical language to be more accurate and precise? Do I use accurate and precise language when I'm talking about substitution and the distributive property?

- How did using a table to organize the information help students make generalizations?

Mathematics Focus

- Students complete the square to solve a quadratic equation in an introductory task.

Mathematics Content Standard(s)

- A-SSE.2: Use the structure of an expression to identify ways to rewrite it.
- A-SSE.3.a: Factor a quadratic expression to reveal the zeros of the function it defines.
- A-SSE.3.b: Complete the square in a quadratic expression to reveal the maximum and minimum value of the function it defines.
- A-CED.1: Create equations and inequalities in one variable and use them to solve problems.
- A-CED.4: Solve quadratic equations in one variable.

Mathematical Practice(s)

- Make sense of problems and persevere in solving them.
- Reason abstractly and quantitatively.
- Model with mathematics.
- Use appropriate tools strategically.
- Look for and make use of structure.

Task 10.2
Sew, Sew

TASK

Sew, Sew

1. Tyrone has pieces of fabric he is sewing into a square blanket for his sister's bed. The diagram shows three pieces that he has laid out with their measurements in inches. (The model is not drawn to scale.)

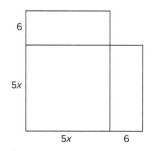

a. What is the area of each piece he has laid out?

b. What is the area of the piece he needs to complete his square blanket?

c. The total area of the completed blanket is 4,356 square inches. What is the value of x?

d. If the total area of the three pieces Tyrone started out with was 2,565 square inches, what would be the value of x?

2. The following diagram shows part of a square blanket that Caylee is designing. The area of each panel is indicated in square feet.

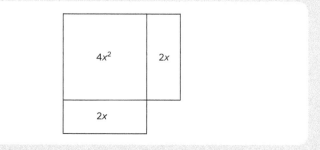

a. What is the area of the small piece that would complete Caylee's square blanket? Explain how you got your answer.

b. Caylee wants her completed square blanket to have a total area of 49 square feet so that it will fit her bed. What should the value of x be?

TASK PREPARATION CONSIDERATIONS

- What methods have students used to reason about or solve quadratic equations?

- Have students used algebra tiles (or other physical materials) to create area models of quadratic relationships? Will I have to adapt the task for the physical materials I will use?

- Have students had experience with square roots?

SCAFFOLDING OR DIFFERENTIATING THE TASK

- Have students use a guess-and-test approach to establish parameters for the numerical solutions.

- Remind students that they can use the square root of a quantity to find the original value that was squared.

WATCH-FORS!

- Students may think that any value that makes an equation true is a solution to a problem without considering the context of a problem.

EXTEND THE TASK

- Have students create a square-blanket problem similar to the one in the task for others to solve.

LAUNCH

1. Place students in pairs or small groups.

2. Distribute algebra tiles to pairs or small groups of students.

3. Use algebra tiles to create area models of polynomials with the class if they have not used them in this way prior to the lesson or if they need to activate their prior learning.

   a. Show the area model for $x^2 + 4x + 4$.

   b. Have students indicate the lengths of the sides of the square $(x + 2)$.

   c. Tell students to create an area model that is a square with side lengths of $(x + 3)$.

   d. Ask, "What is the area?" $(x^2 + 6x + 9)$.

4. Tell students they will be using area models in the task.

5. Distribute the Sew, Sew task.

6. Allow about 25 minutes for students to work.

Vocabulary

- quadratic
- completing the square
- square root

Materials

- 1 Sew, Sew task per student
- 1 set of algebra tiles per pair or small group of students

Task Type

X	Conceptual
	Procedural
	Problem-Solving Application
X	Problem-Solving Critical Thinking

X	Reversibility
X	Flexibility
X	Generalization

FACILITATE

1. Monitor the students as they work.

2. Assist students in creating the area models as appropriate.

3. Select pairs to share their responses.

EXPECTED SOLUTIONS

1. a.
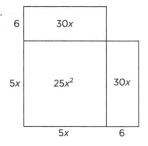

   b. 36 square inches

   c. $x = 12$ inches

   d. $x = 9$ inches

2. a. 1 square foot

   b. $x = 3$ feet

CLOSE AND GENERALIZATIONS

1. Focus students' attention on the algebra tile representation, noting that when they filled in the missing amount on problem 1, they were completing a square.

2. Discuss the "completing the square" method for quadratics.

TASK 10.2: SEW, SEW

online resources ⌐ Available to download at **resources.corwin.com/classroomreadymath/algebra**

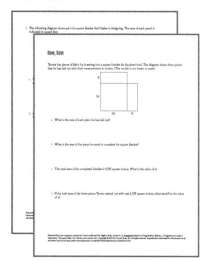

POST-TASK NOTES: REFLECTIONS AND NEXT STEPS

• How does this approach to introducing completing the square compare to the way I have done it in the past?

• How can I build on the student understanding developed through this task to introduce the algorithmic process for completing a square?

Task 10.3
Diagonals Galore

TASK

Diagonals Galore

Mason said, "I found some awesome patterns when I drew the diagonals in polygons."

1. Complete Mason's table.

Number of Sides (x)	Number of Diagonals (y)
3	
4	
5	
6	
7	
8	
9	
10	

2. Describe in words the patterns you notice.

3. Graph the ordered pairs from your table.

4. Write an equation whose graph would include the points given by the data in your table.

5. A polygon has 17 sides. How many diagonals does it have?

6. A polygon has 209 diagonals. How many sides does it have?

TASK PREPARATION CONSIDERATIONS

- Will students recognize a nonlinear pattern?

- Should students graph the ordered pairs by hand or use a graphing application?

- How can I make use of the graphs they create to look at the effect of scaling differences on the shape of the graph?

SCAFFOLDING OR DIFFERENTIATING THE TASK

- Suggest students look at the change in the number of diagonals as the number of sides increases by 1. Is the change consistent?

WATCH-FORS!

- Students may consider the relationship to be linear because the number of sides consistently increases by 1.

- Students may graph the equation in quadrants II, III, and IV, not realizing that those values are not realistic for the context.

EXTEND THE TASK

- Have students consider concave polygons. Does the same pattern hold? Why or why not?

LAUNCH

1. Place students in pairs.

2. Review diagonals of a polygon and discuss the names of polygons as needed.

3. Distribute the Diagonals Galore task.

4. Tell students to work in a pair to complete Mason's table and identify patterns.

5. Allow about 20 minutes for students to work.

FACILITATE

1. Monitor the pairs as they work.

2. Have a pair share the completed table and describe the patterns they noticed.

   a. Ask if other pairs found different patterns.

3. Select a pair to share their graph.

   a. Have other pairs compare their graphs to the shared one.

   b. Discuss any differences that they notice.

Mathematical Practice(s)

- Reason abstractly and quantitatively.
- Model with mathematics.
- Look for and express regularity in repeated reasoning.

Vocabulary

- polygon
- diagonal
- sides
- ordered pairs
- quadrant

Materials

- 1 Diagonals Galore task per student
- Graph paper or graphing application per student

Task Type

X	Conceptual
	Procedural
	Problem-Solving Application
X	Problem-Solving Critical Thinking

X	Reversibility
X	Flexibility
X	Generalization

c. Ask, "How does the scaling on the graphs compare? How does it affect the shape of the graph?"

d. If students graphed points in quadrants II, III, and IV, discuss the reasonableness of those points.

e. Ask, "Is the graph a continuous graph or a discrete graph?" Students should notice that it must be a discrete graph.

4. Discuss the equation in problem 4. How did pairs determine what the equation would be?

5. Discuss problems 5 and 6. Ask pairs to share their solution method and solutions.

EXPECTED SOLUTIONS

1. a.

Number of Sides (x)	Number of Diagonals (y)
3	0
4	2
5	5
6	9
7	14
8	20
9	27

2. Answers will vary.

3. Graphs will vary but should be a discrete graph with points only in quadrant I.

4. Let x = number of sides of a polygon

$$y = \frac{x(x-3)}{2}$$

5. 119 diagonals

6. 22 sides

CLOSE AND GENERALIZATIONS

1. Discuss why the graph should only be done in quadrant I and why it is discrete.

2. Ask students to create another scenario that would result in a quadratic relationship and should only be graphed in quadrant I.

TASK 10.3: DIAGONALS GALORE

 Available to download at **resources.corwin.com/classroomreadymath/algebra**

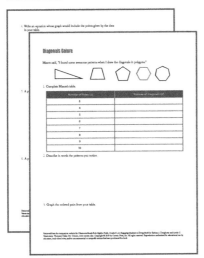

POST-TASK NOTES: REFLECTIONS AND NEXT STEPS

• Were semi-concrete representations sufficient for students, or should I have used concrete polygon materials in addition?

• How do geometric contexts support the development of algebraic thinking?

Mathematics Focus

- Students determine the quadratic generalization for a geometric pattern.

Mathematics Content Standard(s)

- A-SSE.1: Interpret expressions that represent a quantity in terms of its context.
- F-BF.1: Write a function that describes a relationship between two quantities.
- F-LE.1: Distinguish between situations that can be modeled with linear functions and with exponential functions.
- F-LE.2: Construct linear and exponential functions, including arithmetic and geometric sequences, given a graph, a description of a relationship, or two input-output pairs.

Mathematical Practice(s)

- Make sense of problems and persevere in solving them.
- Reason abstractly and quantitatively.
- Model with mathematics.
- Attend to precision.
- Look for and express regularity in repeated reasoning.

Task 10.4
Sticks and Marshmallows

TASK

Sticks and Marshmallows

1. Lennie created a structure with sticks and marshmallows. She made a pattern of squares. Here are Lennie's first four stick and marshmallow figures.

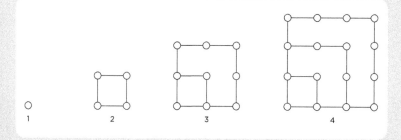

a. Sketch the fifth and sixth figures in Lennie's pattern of stick and marshmallow squares.

b. Record the number of sticks and marshmallows for each cell in the table.

No. in Pattern	1	2	3	4	5	6
No. of Sticks	0	4				
No. of Marshmallows	1	4				

c. What patterns do you notice? Describe.

d. Without building the squares, how many sticks and marshmallows will be in the tenth figure? Describe your process.

e. If *n* = number in the pattern, how could you generalize your patterns?

2. Sam was inspired by his sister, Lennie, and decided to make equilateral triangles with sticks and marshmallows. Here are Sam's first four figures in the triangle pattern.

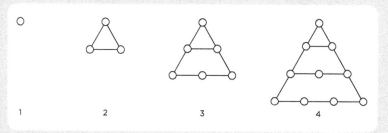

a. Sketch the fifth and sixth figures in Sam's pattern of stick and marshmallow equilateral triangles.

b. Record the number of sticks and marshmallows for each cell in the table.

No. in Pattern	1	2	3	4	5	6
No. of Sticks	0	3				
No. of Marshmallows	1	3				

c. What patterns do you notice? Describe.

d. Without building the triangles, how many sticks and marshmallows will be in the tenth figure? Describe your process for finding the number.

e. If n = number in the pattern, how could you generalize your patterns?

TASK PREPARATION CONSIDERATIONS

- Will students need concrete manipulatives (physical materials) to model the figures?

- How would graphing the relationships of the number of the figure as the x-value and the number of sticks or marshmallows as the y-value support students in identifying and generalizing the patterns?

SCAFFOLDING OR DIFFERENTIATING THE TASK

- Suggest that students use physical materials or draw on grid paper to model the squares and triangles.

- Have students focus on either the sticks or the marshmallows, one at a time.

- Ask students to describe from the previous square or triangle to the next one and use that as a way of generalizing the pattern.

WATCH-FORS!

- Students may consider the patterns as linear rather than quadratic representations.

- Students may describe the patterns by looking at the differences from one term to the next rather than identifying the relationship to square numbers.

Vocabulary

- equilateral triangle

Materials

- 1 Sticks and Marshmallows task per student
- Concrete materials, such as marshmallows and toothpicks or connector rods and spools (optional)
- Grid paper (optional)

Task Type

X	Conceptual
	Procedural
	Problem-Solving Application
X	Problem-Solving Critical Thinking

X	Reversibility
X	Flexibility
X	Generalization

EXTEND THE TASK

- Tell students that you have 150 sticks and 20 marshmallows. What is the largest square figure they can make in this pattern?

LAUNCH

1. Place students in pairs.

2. Show the first square figure.

   a. Have students give the number of sticks and the number of marshmallows. Record in the table. Continue with the second square figure in a similar fashion.

   b. Ask students to predict what the third square figure will look like.

   c. Show the third figure, count the sticks and marshmallows, and record the numbers in the table.

3. Distribute the Sticks and Marshmallows task.

4. Tell students they will describe the patterns they notice in the progression of figures.

5. Encourage students to work independently to analyze the pattern before they talk with their partner.

6. Allow about 25–30 minutes for students to work.

FACILITATE

1. Monitor the pairs as they work.

2. Select different pairs to share their responses to the problems' parts a, b, c, and d.

   a. As they share the patterns they noticed, have them link each one to the geometric pattern. How is the pattern represented in the figure?

   b. Ask if other pairs found other patterns.

EXPECTED SOLUTIONS

1. a.

5

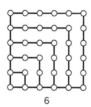
6

b.

No. in Pattern	1	2	3	4	5	6
No. of Sticks	0	4	9	16	25	36
No. of Marshmallows	1	4	10	18	28	40

c. Answers will vary.

d. For the tenth figure, there are 100 sticks and 108 marshmallows.

e. Sticks: n^2; marshmallows: $n^2 + (n - 2)$.

2. a.

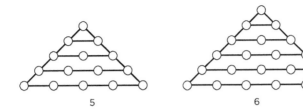

b.

No. in Pattern	1	2	3	4	5	6
No. of Sticks	0	3	7	12	18	25
No. of Marshmallows	1	3	6	10	15	21

c. Answers will vary.

d. For the tenth figure, there are 53 sticks and 45 marshmallows.

e. Sticks: $\dfrac{n(n+1)}{2} + (n - 2)$; marshmallows: $\dfrac{n(n+1)}{2}$.

CLOSE AND GENERALIZATIONS

1. Have students share the algebraic generalizations for part e in the problems.

2. Ask, "What do you notice about the two generalizations?"

   a. Discuss how the generalizations align with the geometric representations.

TASK 10.4: STICKS AND MARSHMALLOWS

online resources Available to download at **resources.corwin.com/classroomreadymath/algebra**

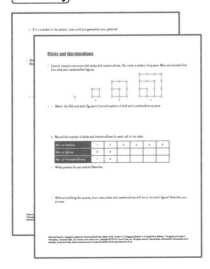

POST-TASK NOTES: REFLECTIONS AND NEXT STEPS

• Did I make sufficient connections to previous "growing patterns" problems?

• Did students use covariational thinking?

• Could I adapt the task to other shapes for future lessons?

Task 10.5
Paying the Bill

TASK

Paying the Bill

A group of friends went to a pizza restaurant. They all agreed they would split the bill evenly so each one paid an equal amount.

The waiter brought the bill of $120 to the table after two members of the group had slipped away. (See if they get invited again!) This meant that each of the rest of the group had to pay $5 more than they expected.

How many people were originally in the group?

TASK PREPARATION CONSIDERATIONS

- How many different strategies could be used to solve the problem?

- Should students work individually, in pairs, or in small groups?

SCAFFOLDING OR DIFFERENTIATING THE TASK

- Have students use a guess-and-test approach to establish parameters for the numerical solutions.

WATCH-FORS!

- Students may use only a guess-and-test approach because the relationships in the problem do not seem to lend themselves to other solution possibilities.

EXTEND THE TASK

- Change the bill to $180, with two people leaving and those remaining paying an extra $5.

LAUNCH

1. Place students in pairs.

2. Distribute the Paying the Bill task.

Mathematics Focus

- Students use a rational equation to solve a problem.

Mathematics Content Standard(s)

- A-APR.7: Understand that rational expressions form a system analogous to the rational numbers, closed under addition, subtraction, multiplication, and division by a nonzero rational expression; add, subtract, multiply, and divide rational expressions.

Mathematical Practice(s)

- Make sense of problems and persevere in solving them.
- Reason abstractly and quantitatively.
- Construct viable arguments and critique the reasoning of others.
- Model with mathematics.
- Attend to precision.

Vocabulary

- rational equation

Materials

- 1 Paying the Bill task per student

Task Type

	Conceptual
X	Procedural
X	Problem-Solving Application
	Problem-Solving Critical Thinking

	Reversibility
X	Flexibility
	Generalization

3. Tell students to work in a pair to find the number of people in the group.

   a. If they finish the problem before others, ask them to find another solution method.

4. Allow about 20 minutes for students to work.

FACILITATE

1. Monitor the pairs as they work.

2. Have pairs share the solution method or strategy they used.

   How are the solution methods alike? How are they different?

3. Select pairs to share their answers.

EXPECTED SOLUTION

Eight people were originally in the party.

CLOSE AND GENERALIZATIONS

1. Present the problem extension.

2. Ask students which approach they will use to solve it, based on the discussion of the original problem.

TASK 10.5: PAYING THE BILL

 Available to download at **resources.corwin.com/ classroomreadymath/algebra**

POST-TASK NOTES: REFLECTIONS AND NEXT STEPS

• What solution strategies were most often used?

• Did I or the students make explicit connections to a similar problem such as Shantelle's Special Number?

• Does the classroom environment support students' perseverance on problems like this?

• Did the scaffolding strategies support students who had difficulty engaging in the problem?

Mathematics Content Standard(s)

- A-APR.7: Understand that rational expressions form a system analogous to the rational numbers, closed under addition, subtraction, multiplication, and division by a nonzero rational expression; add, subtract, multiply, and divide rational expressions.

Mathematical Practice(s)

- Make sense of problems and persevere in solving them.
- Reason abstractly and quantitatively.
- Construct viable arguments and critique the reasoning of others.
- Look for and make use of structure.
- Look for and express regularity in repeated reasoning.

Task 10.6
Ivone's Problem

TASK

Ivone's Problem

Ivone said, "I have a challenge for you. I created two rational equations. To meet the challenge, you have to find values for w and y to make the equations true. And remember, the value for w and the value for y are the same in both equations."

"I accept your challenge, Ivone," said Jeff.

How could Jeff solve the problem?

$$\frac{w-y}{w+y} = 9$$

$$\frac{wy}{w+y} = -60$$

TASK PREPARATION CONSIDERATIONS

- How many different strategies could be used to solve the problem?
- Should students work individually, in pairs, or in small groups?
- Do students have fluent strategies to use with rational numbers?

SCAFFOLDING OR DIFFERENTIATING THE TASK

- Have students use a guess-and-test approach to establish parameters for the numerical solutions.

WATCH-FORS!

- Students may think that w and y have different values in each equation.

EXTEND THE TASK

- Use the expressions to graph ordered pairs (w, y). Discuss the shape of the graph and relationship to the equations given.

LAUNCH

1. Place students in pairs.

2. Distribute the Ivone's Problem task.

3. Tell students to work in a pair to find a solution for *w* and *y*.

    a. Remind students that the value of *w* in one equation must be the same value in the other; the same is true for the value of *y*.

    b. If they finish the problem before others, ask them to find another solution method.

4. Allow about 20 minutes for students to work.

FACILITATE

1. Monitor the pairs as they work.

2. Have pairs share the solution method or strategy they used.How are the solution methods alike? How are they different?

3. Select pairs to share their answers.

EXPECTED SOLUTION

$w = 15, y = -12$

CLOSE AND GENERALIZATIONS

1. Present the problem extension.

2. Have students predict the shape of the graph before they graph.

3. Graph the relationships and discuss the graphs.

4. Relate the graphs to the solution of the two equations.

Task Type

X	Conceptual
X	Procedural
	Problem-Solving Application
X	Problem-Solving Critical Thinking

	Reversibility
X	Flexibility
	Generalization

TASK 10.6: IVONE'S PROBLEM

POST-TASK NOTES: REFLECTIONS AND NEXT STEPS

- What solution methods did students use to solve the problem?

- How does graphing the two expressions help students visualize the solution?

Your Turn

Now that you have had the opportunity to use rich algebra tasks and implement instructional strategies to maximize classroom learning for all students, you may be thinking about how to continue fueling your professional learning journey and providing high-quality tasks for your students. Let's look first at your professional learning journey.

Professional Learning Journey

As teachers, we know that exchanging ideas with our colleagues can be incredibly motivating. Even though it may seem like an added step in your routine, we believe regular dialogues with colleagues about pedagogical topics are critical to elevating our profession. This has held true for each of us throughout every stage of our careers, and our learning continues! As you implement the tasks, the artifacts of your students' work and your own reflection on the implementation can be the basis of dialogue with your colleagues.

Here are some ways you can prompt that dialogue in your own context:

- Invite colleagues to observe your class and share your lesson plan for the task. Ask them for feedback that focuses on student learning and teacher moves that lead to productive learning behaviors.

- Plan with your colleagues to implement the same task. Following everyone's teaching experience, share your notes in a debriefing meeting and support each other in using effective teaching practices. Did you use the same debriefing and grouping strategies? What seemed to work well for that task? How will you revise the task the next time you use it?

- Collect and share student work, either their mathematics or reflections about their learning (i.e., the student interview with a partner to promote discourse; see Chapter 3 for the interview protocol). What tasks built conceptual understandings? What tasks connected prior learning to the new topics? Were the tasks accessible to students? How did your students' learning change as a result of using the tasks?

- Compare the tasks from your textbook or regular curriculum with the tasks from this book. What differences or trade-offs are you concerned about as you accommodate rich algebra tasks in your class? Who might you speak with to navigate your concerns?

- Co-plan a task and observe each other's classes. Make observation notes on student engagement, evidence of student learning, instructional techniques, or other areas that you and your partner identify. Did the two classes have different outcomes? What techniques could you adapt for your class?

- If you are ready for next steps, explore the idea of a book study, such as one from the 2020 Math Pact series from Corwin, to foster whole-school agreements and support dialogue across the grades or mathematics department at your school.

Providing High-Quality Tasks for Your Students

As you continue your professional learning journey, you will likely want to continue the use of rich algebra tasks for students. The tasks in this volume are not exhaustive of all the high-quality tasks available for algebra. They represent a starting point, one that you can build from by selecting tasks from other sources and adapting or creating tasks to span more topics within algebra.

Your curriculum is also a starting point. Although you, your school, or your district may have chosen a high-quality textbook, students' learning experiences can be enhanced with rich tasks. A first step, then, is to identify places where you feel your students will benefit from having a task that aligns well with the content in your textbook. If, for example, your textbook does not offer a conceptual basis for factoring polynomials, you may want to identify a task that supports the foundational aspects of that topic. Or, maybe your textbook doesn't include enough problem-solving critical thinking tasks. Knowing the type of task and the related content standards you want to include is a first step.

Once you have completed that step, you are ready to select a task and adapt and create a task. We offer some suggestions for how you can expand your library of these tasks.

SELECTING RICH ALGEBRA TASKS

How do you decide a task will address your learning goals? When you select a task from another resource, you may want to consider the criteria in Figure 11.1 to determine if the task is a rich algebra task. Consider using the template provided as a guide for your selection.

If you indicated that the task you selected has these characteristics, then you are well on your way to adding a richer task to your collection. If you found some of the characteristics missing but you think the task has potential, then you might want to consider ways to adapt the task as given in the next section.

ADAPTING TASKS

Some tasks may present an interesting perspective or provide an opportunity for students to gain new understandings, but there may be some aspects of the task that could be enhanced to make it more effective. This is your opportunity to adapt or revise it in a way that addresses the missing components.

One way to adapt or revise a task is to apply the reversibility, flexibility, and generalization (RFG) process framework. Take a few minutes to do the staircase task and think about the richness of the task in terms of the questions in Figure 11.1.

Figure 11.1 Guide for Selecting Rich Algebra Tasks

Criterion	Notes
Does the task connect to important mathematical practice at a level that is appropriate for my students?	
How does the task develop, build on, or connect to important mathematical understandings?	
Does the task promote reversibility, flexibility, or generalizability?	
Does the task include appropriate representations?	
Is the mathematical idea represented in more than one way?	
Does the task engage students in doing mathematics?	
Does the task require high-level thinking and reasoning?	
Does the task have multiple solution approaches or multiple solutions?	
Is the task accessible to *all* students?	
Does the task connect to additional mathematics topics (or other content areas), and if so, how?	

Source: Adapted from Kobett et al., *Classroom-Ready Rich Math Tasks, Grades 4–5: Engaging Students in Doing Math* (Corwin, 2021). Used with permission.

> Look at the staircase pattern. How many squares will be in the next staircase?
>

The task is accessible for all students, can incorporate multiple representations, can be solved in multiple ways, and connects well to patterns with triangular numbers. However, this version of the staircase task doesn't go far enough. It can be made more robust by asking students to create the staircase that would be the sixth figure in the pattern. Then, students can create a generalization for any staircase that would fit the pattern.

To develop your own insights for creating a robust adaptation of a task, you must first solve the task yourself and assess the level and type of thinking that was required by the task. This is a great opportunity for you to collaborate with your colleagues to brainstorm different solution strategies and approaches to the problem, and then collaborate on ways to enhance the task.

One of the easiest ways to adapt a task is to use the process of reversibility. You noticed in the staircase problem that students are merely asked to find the number of squares in a staircase. By reversing the task, you can ask students to find the largest staircase that can be made with 75 (or more!) squares.

Having your students study and expand a pattern allows them to practice flexible thinking. You might use a follow-up problem to the staircase pattern task so that students can apply their solution strategy to a new problem. For example, building on what they found as a generalization for the relationship between the number of tiles needed to build the figure and where the figure falls in the sequence, have students represent their finding graphically and describe their findings. This can also help bridge connections to the geometry of the task.

You can adapt a task in other ways as well. If a task involves a relatively straightforward problem, such as solving a linear or quadratic equation, you can ask students to solve the equation in more than one way. You can set the parameters of the solution process by telling students that one way must involve a semi-concrete or concrete representation. By doing this, you create an opportunity to make connections among concrete, semi-concrete, and abstract representations—CSA!

Some tasks lend themselves to multiple solutions. You can push students to explore more solutions by asking if the solution is unique. If students answer yes, then they need to justify how they know. If they respond no, then they need to find other solutions. When multiple solutions are possible, you can ask students to identify any patterns they see in the solutions or provide a rationale as to why there is more than one solution. For example, if you ask students to find a quadratic equation that has the solution $(-3, 7)$, there are an infinite number of answers. Some students may write the equation $(x + 3)(x - 7) = 0$, $x^2 - 4x - 21 = 0$, $2x^2 - 8x - 42 = 0$, or $4x^2 - 16x = 84$. They should notice that these equations are equivalent.

If the task focuses on procedural aspects of a topic, it can be enhanced by changing the task to a worked example where students have to analyze someone else's work. Worked examples are a great way to have students identify their understandings—and misunderstandings (Vendetti et al., 2015). For example, if students are asked to find the solution to the equation $x^2 - 4x = 21$, you can show two worked examples as in Figure 11.2.

Figure 11.2 Worked Examples

Micah and Jodi solved the equation $x^2 - 4x = 21$. Decide if you agree with their solution process and solution. If yes, explain your reasoning. If no, identify the error and complete the solution correctly.

Micah's solution	Jodi's solution
$x^2 - 4x = 21$	$x^2 - 4x = 21$
$x(x - 4) = 21$	$x = \frac{-4 \pm \sqrt{16+84}}{2}$
$x = 21$ or $x - 4 = 21$	$x = \frac{-4 \pm \sqrt{100}}{2}$
$x = 21$ or $x = 25$	$x = \frac{-4 \pm 10}{2}$
	$x = \frac{6}{2}$ or 3
	$x = \frac{-14}{2}$ or -7

In Figure 11.2, both Micah and Jodi have misinterpreted the problem with errors that we often see in students' work. As you have pairs solve the task, students confront their own misunderstandings, which leads to stronger learning.

CREATING A TASK

If you cannot find a rich algebra task that aligns with a learning outcome, you may want to create a new one to fit that particular topic or need of your class. This is an opportunity to collaborate with other colleagues to brainstorm ways to frame and design a task. Here are some starting points that you can use to begin this process:

1. Decide which standards and learning outcomes you want to target. Even though you will identify a standard that the task aligns with, this task will represent one instructional step in the progression toward a full understanding of the standard.

2. Determine the type of task you need. Are you targeting the introduction of a concept or procedure? Are you focusing on problem solving? Where does the task fit in the instructional sequence?

3. Address your students' strengths and opportunities to learn. What knowledge and skills can you build on? Where are opportunities for them to learn? What contexts will support their learning?

4. Identify vocabulary that will be addressed and materials needed. What language will you include or introduce through this task? What representations will you use? Do you have materials that will appropriately model the mathematical ideas?

5. Create the instructional strategy. How will students complete the task? What grouping strategies will you use? How will students share their solution strategies and solutions?

6. Determine your feedback approach. How will you convey your expectations to students? How will you give feedback to students?

7. Plan how you will reflect on the task after you implement it. What will determine the task's effectiveness in meeting your learning outcome? What questions will guide your reflection? Do you want another colleague to observe the task as you implement it?

8. Decide how you will archive tasks so you can reuse them and share with your colleagues. What shared platform will you use: Google Drive, Dropbox, or other? How will you indicate revisions to your original task?

Whatever method you choose, you can use the Template for the Rich Algebra Tasks found in this book's appendix, which is also downloadable. After you have planned your task, gather some colleagues to solve the task and give you feedback. This allows you to test the task before you implement it in your classroom. Your colleagues may have some ideas that will enhance the task and make it richer. Additionally, this creates a collaborative relationship with fellow teachers and builds a professional community.

Summing Up

In this chapter, we described ways you can extend your library of rich algebra tasks. At a time in which an abundance of algebra tasks can be quickly found online, we hope our book helps you to prioritize quality. By using materials that support students' development of their own mathematical practice and conceptual understanding, together with effective teaching practices, we believe you and your students will find your greatest success.

Professional Learning and Discussion Questions

Read and discuss the following questions with colleagues in your department.

- What resources have you found to be most useful?

- In what ways have you adapted a task?

- In what topics do you need rich tasks to better support students?

- What is challenging for you as you adapt or create tasks?

- What instructional practices have you found to be most effective for using rich algebra tasks?

- How can you support each other in developing your teaching practices?

- How might artifacts of student work support your discussions?

 Available to download at **resources.corwin.com/classroomreadymath/algebra**

Appendix

TEMPLATE FOR THE RICH ALGEBRA TASKS

Task Name	
Mathematics Focus	
Mathematics Content Standard(s)	
Mathematical Practice(s)	
Task	
Vocabulary	
Materials	

Task Type

	Conceptual
	Procedural
	Problem-Solving Application
	Problem-Solving Critical Thinking

	Reversibility
	Flexibility
	Generalization

Task Preparation Considerations
Scaffolding or Differentiating the Task
Watch-Fors!
Extend the Task
Launch
Facilitate **Expected Solutions**
Close and Generalizations
Post-Task Notes: Reflections and Next Steps

online resources ☞ Available to download at **resources.corwin.com/classroomreadymath/algebra**

References

Blanton, M., Stephens, A., Knuth, E., Gardiner, A. M., Isler, I., & Kim, J. (2015). The development of children's algebraic thinking: The impact of a comprehensive early algebra intervention in third grade. *Journal for Research in Mathematics Education, 46*(1), 39–87. http://www.jstor.org/stable/10.5951/jresematheduc.46.1.0039

Bush, S., Karp, K., & Dougherty, B. J. (2021). *The math pact, middle school: Achieving instructional coherence within and across grades*. Corwin.

CAST. (2018). *Universal Design for Learning guidelines version 2.2*. http://udlguidelines.cast.org

Devlin, K. (2009, January). Should children learn math by starting with counting? *Devlin's Angle*. Mathematical Association of America. https://www.maa.org/external_archive/devlin/devlin_01_09.html

Dougherty, B. J. (2008). Measure up: A quantitative view of early algebra. In J. J. Kaput, D. W. Carraher, & M. L. Blanton (Eds.), *Algebra in the early grades* (pp. 389–412). Erlbaum.

Dougherty, B., Bryant, D. P., Bryant, B. R., Darrough, R. L., & Pfannenstiel, K. H. (2015). Developing concepts and generalizations to build algebraic thinking: The reversibility, flexibility, and generalization approach. *Intervention in School and Clinic, 50*(5), 273–281.

Dougherty, B. J., Bryant, D. P., Bryant, B. R., & Shin, M. (2016). Helping students with mathematics difficulties understand ratios and proportions. *TEACHING Exceptional Children, 49*(2), 96–105.

Dougherty, B. J., Bush, S., & Karp, K. (2021). *The math pact, high school: Achieving instructional coherence within and across grades*. Corwin.

Hiebert, J. C., & Grouws, D. A. (2007). The effects of classroom mathematics teaching on students' learning. In F. K. Lester Jr. (Ed.), *Second handbook of research on mathematics teaching and learning* (Vol. 1, pp. 371–404). Information Age.

Karp, K., Bush, S., & Dougherty, B. (2015). Avoiding middle grades rules that expire. *Mathematics Teaching in the Middle School, 21*(4), 208–215.

Kaufman, J. H., Doan, S., & Fernandez, M.-P. (2021). *The rise of standards-aligned instructional materials for U.S. K–12 mathematics and English language arts instruction: Findings from the 2021 American Instructional Resources Survey* (RR-A134-11). RAND Corporation. https://doi.org/10.7249/RRA134-11

Kobett, B. M., Fennell, F., Karp, K. S., Andrews, D., & Mulroe, S. T. (2021). *Classroom-ready rich math tasks, grades 4–5: Engaging students in doing math*. Corwin.

Kobett, B. M., & Karp, K. S. (2020). *Strengths-based teaching and learning in mathematics: Five teaching turnarounds for grades K–6*. Corwin.

Krutetskii, V. A. (1976). *The psychology of mathematical abilities in school children* (J. Kilpatrick & I. Wirszup, Eds.). University of Chicago.

Liljedahl, P. (2014). The affordances of using visually random groups in a mathematics classroom. In Y. Li, E. Silver, & S. Li (Eds.), *Transforming mathematics instruction: Multiple approaches and practices*. Springer. https://doi.org/10.1007/978–3-319–04993-9_8

Liljedahl, P. (2020). *Building thinking classrooms in mathematics, grades K–12: 14 teaching practices for enhancing learning*. Corwin.

Liljedahl, P. (n.d.). *Good problems*. https://www.peterliljedahl.com/teachers/good-problem

Linchevski, L., & Herscovics, N. (1996). Crossing the cognitive gap between arithmetic and algebra: Operating on the unknown in the context of equations. *Educational Studies in Mathematics, 30*, 39–65.

Luria, S. R., Sriraman, B., & Kaufman, J. C. (2017). Enhancing equity in the classroom by teaching for mathematical creativity. *ZDM, 49*(7), 1033–1039.

Malkevitch, J. (2004, December). *Euler's polyhedral formula*. American Mathematical Society. http://www.ams.org/publicoutreach/feature-column/fcarc-eulers-formula

Meyer, D. (n.d.). *Three-act math*. https://blog.mrmeyer.com/

Moreno, R., Ozogul, G., & Reisslein, M. (2011). Teaching with concrete and abstract visual representations: Effects on students' problem solving, problem representations, and learning perceptions. *Journal of Educational Psychology, 103*(1), 32–47.

National Council of Teachers of Mathematics. (2000). *Principles and standards for school mathematics*. https://www.nctm.org/standards/

National Council of Teachers of Mathematics. (2014a). *Access and equity in mathematics education*. https://www.nctm.org/Standards-and-Positions/Position-Statements/Access-and-Equity-in-Mathematics-Education/

National Council of Teachers of Mathematics. (2014b). *Principles to actions: Ensuring mathematical success for all*. https://www.nctm.org/PtA/

National Governors Association Center for Best Practices & Council of Chief State School Officers. (2010). *Common Core State Standards for mathematics*. http://www.corestandards.org/Math/

National Research Council. (2001). *Adding it up: Helping children learn mathematics*. National Academies Press.

Nazari, K. B., & Ebersbach, M. (2019). Distributed practice in mathematics: Recommendable especially for students on a medium performance level? *Trends in Neuroscience and Education, 17*, 100122.

Okazaki, C., Zenigami, F., & Dougherty, B. J. (2006). Measure up: A different view of elementary mathematics. In S. Smith & S. Smith (Eds.), *Teachers engaged in research* (pp. 135–152). Information Age.

PBS Digital Studios. (2019, March 13). Music from the Golden Ratio and Fibonacci Sequence (Season 1, Episode 4) [Video]. In *Sound Field*. https://www.pbs.org/video/music-from-the-golden-ratio-and-fibonacci-sequence-afdd5k/

Richland, L. E., Stigler, J. W., & Holyoak, K. J. (2012). Teaching the conceptual structure of mathematics. *Educational Psychologist, 47*(3), 189–203.

Sellars, M. (2017). *Reflective practice for teachers*. SAGE.

Smith, M. S., & Stein, M. K. (2011). *5 practices for orchestrating productive mathematics discussions*. National Council of Teachers of Mathematics.

Smith, M. S., & Stein, M. K. (2012). Selecting and creating mathematical tasks: From research to practice. In G. Lappan, M. S. Smith, & E. Jones (Eds.), *Rich & engaging mathematical tasks: Grades 5–9* (pp. 4–120). National Council of Teachers of Mathematics.

Smith, M. S., & Stein, M. K. (2018). *5 practices for orchestrating productive mathematics discussions* (2nd ed.). National Council of Teachers of Mathematics.

Snow, C. E., & Uccelli, P. (2009). The challenge of academic language. In D. R. Olson & N. Torrance (Eds.), *The Cambridge handbook of literacy* (pp. 112–133). Cambridge University Press.

Sullivan, P., Clarke, D., & Clarke, B. (2012). *Teaching with tasks for effective mathematics learning* (Vol. 9). Springer Science & Business Media.

Vendetti, M. S., Matlen, B. J., Richland, L. E., & Bunge, S. A. (2015). Analogical reasoning in the classroom: Insights from cognitive science. *Mind, Brain, and Education, 9*(2), 100–106.

Index

**JENNIFER M. BAY-WILLIAMS,
JOHN J. SANGIOVANNI,
ROSALBA SERRANO,
SHERRI MARTINIE,
JENNIFER SUH, C. DAVID WALTERS**

Because fluency is so much more
than basic facts and algorithms.

Grades K–8

**ROBERT Q. BERRY III, BASIL M. CONWAY IV,
BRIAN R. LAWLER, JOHN W. STALEY,
COURTNEY KOESTLER, JENNIFER WARD,
MARIA DEL ROSARIO ZAVALA,
TONYA GAU BARTELL, CATHERY YEH,
MATHEW FELTON-KOESTLER,
LATEEFAH ID-DEEN,
MARY CANDACE RAYGOZA,
AMANDA RUIZ, EVA THANHEISER**

Learn to plan instruction that engages
students in mathematics explorations
through age-appropriate and culturally
relevant social justice topics.

**Early Elementary, Upper Elementary,
Middle School, High School**

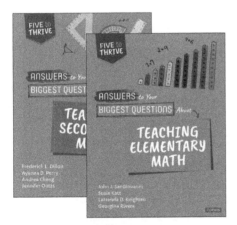

**JOHN J. SANGIOVANNI, SUSIE KATT,
LATRENDA D. KNIGHTEN,
GEORGINA RIVERA,
FREDERICK L. DILLON,
AYANNA D. PERRY,
ANDREA CHENG, JENNIFER OUTZS**

Actionable answers to your most
pressing questions about teaching
elementary and secondary math.

Elementary, Secondary

**SARA DELANO MOORE,
KIMBERLY RIMBEY**

A journey toward making
manipulatives meaningful.

Grades K–3, 4–8

CORWIN HAS ONE MISSION: to enhance education through intentional professional learning.

We build long-term relationships with our authors, educators, clients, and associations who partner with us to develop and continuously improve the best evidence-based practices that establish and support lifelong learning.